Shamrock Ranch

To Penny

SHAMR☘CK RANCH

Celebrating Life in
Colorado's Pikes Peak Country

David A. Wismer

with Gary T. Wright

Thank you for many years of conscientious advice and friendship.

Best wishes,

David Wismer

Ps. 121: 1-2

JOHNSON BOOKS
BOULDER

3/09

Published by Johnson Books, a Big Earth Publishing company.
1637 Pearl Street, Suite 201, Boulder, Colorado 80302.
1-800-258-5830
E-mail: books@bigearthpublishing.com
www.bigearthpublishing.com

Cover design by Jake Ryan
Text design by Rebecca Finkel

9   8   7   6   5   4   3   2   1

Library of Congress Cataloging-in-Publication Data
Wismer, David A., 1938–
Shamrock Ranch: celebrating life in Colorado's Pikes Peak country /
by David A. Wismer; with Gary T. Wright.
p.   cm
Includes bibliographical references and index.
978-1-55566-427-5
1. Shamrock Ranch (El Paso County, Colo.)—History.
2. Ranch life—Colorado—Pikes Peak Region. 3. Pikes Peak Region (Colo.)—
Social life and customs. 4. Ranchers—Colorado—Pikes Peak Region—Biography.
5. Pikes Peak Region (Colo.)—Biography. I. Wright, Gary T. (Gary Thorup). II. Title.

F784.S39W57 2008
978.8'56—dc22
2008029900

Printed in China

To Jeannette Billings

who loves the land and its Creator

as we do,

and who shows that love to us every day

in more ways than we can count.

David and Mary Anne Wismer

Contents

Introduction.. 1

Beginnings 25

The Original Patentees 39

The Colorado Pinery Trust Era......................... 45

The Husted Era 55

The Benjamin C. Allen Era............................. 69

The Maria McKean Allen Era 95

The Wharton Allen Era 115

Allen Ranch Employees and Tenants 125

The Hardesty/McCullough Era......................... 149

The McLaughlin Era 163

McLaughlin's Employees and Neighbors................. 189

The Pendleton Equestrian Era......................... 207

The Wismer Era... 239

Epilogue.. 277

Endnotes.. 281

Appendices... 286

Acknowledgments.. 292

References.. 294

Index... 298

LIKE THE LAND,

CHARACTER IS PRIZED

FOR THE BOUNTY OF ITS HARVEST

INTRODUCTION

Welcome to Shamrock Ranch, one of most picturesque and pristine expanses of land in Pikes Peak Country.

Located at the heart of the heavily forested region known as Colorado's Black Forest, the ranch's landscapes are stunning, regardless of the season.

As one of the largest contiguous tracts of undeveloped property
that remains in the Black Forest, 2,586-acre Shamrock Ranch
is a rare gem of beauty, grandeur, and tranquility.

Shamrock Ranch . . .

. . . is Colorado at its best!

Shamrock Ranch is also . . .

. . . Colorado ranching
at its best!

From a horse's
point of view,
Shamrock is
undoubtedly
a paradise . . .

. . . as it is for a thriving population of wildlife, including a herd of elk.

The owners are David A. Wismer and his wife Mary Anne (shown here with their dog, Muffy in 1996).

They live in the charming historic ranch house shown here.

If you're lucky enough to visit them, you'll probably stay in the guest house.

Jeannette Billings is the ranch manager (shown here with her dogs Heidi and Cricket in 2000).

She lives in the quaint ranch manager's house located in the clearing just east of the Wismers' house.

The ranch has some impressive facilities for raising cattle and horses. For over fifty years prize cattle bred on Shamrock Ranch were shown and sold at stock shows around the country. More recently, cattle are brought to the ranch only from May to October each year when the lush grasses are most nutritious.

At one time, champion American Saddlebred show horses were also bred and trained here. Currently the Wismer's quarter horses enjoy the Kentucky-style barn and indoor riding arena shown here.

Native grass hay is still raised on the ranch, just as it was
by the first homesteaders who lived here during the 1860s.

As can be seen from this satellite view, the Shamrock Ranch runs from State Highway 83 on the west to Black Forest Road on the east, and is almost surrounded by subdivisions. The city of Colorado Springs is literally at its doorstep. The ranch's vast domains of dense forest and lush prairie are impressive. A prominent ridge, called the Palmer Divide, runs through the heart of the ranch. At the southeastern corner of the ranch, this lofty ridge reaches its peak elevation of 7,633 feet. This is also the ranch's highpoint.

Satellite view of Shamrock Ranch showing surrounding features.

Located at the heart of the Black Forest, Shamrock Ranch helps transition the Great Plains to the rugged Rocky Mountains of Colorado and is not far from the state's center.

Boasting an average elevation of approximately 7,600 feet, the divide forces northward and southward moving weather systems to drop rain and snow in greater amounts as their moisture-laden clouds become caught between it and the Front Range of the Rocky Mountains. In this way, it acts as a "weather divide," stopping storms that come from the south before they reach Denver and preventing those that approach from the north from reaching Colorado Springs.

The Palmer Divide divides the waters of the South Platte River to the north from the waters of the Arkansas River to the south. Black Squirrel Creek originates near the northern border of the ranch and runs southwest to feed the Arkansas River. A branch of the East Cherry Creek once originated in the northeastern portion of the ranch and fed the South Platte River. The lowest point of the ranch, which has an elevation of 7,060 feet, is found at its southwestern corner.

Approximately 60 percent of Shamrock Ranch is forested with towering ponderosa pines. The rest of the ranch consists of beautiful open fields, such as the one on page 20. From the satellite photograph on the previous page, notice that the Palmer Divide marks the end of the forested area and the beginning of the open fields.

According to the National Park Service, conifer trees grow in the Black Forest rather than deciduous trees because of its higher altitude, cooler climate, and the additional moisture that falls there because of the Palmer Divide.

Antelope running across a plain on Shamrock Ranch (2008).

(left) Shamrock Ranch ponderosa pines (2008).

(below) Afternoon thunderstorm on the Shamrock Ranch.

Key to Map of Black Forest

Towns, Public Facilities — 0
B.C. — Brush Corral
D.E.S. — Divide Experiment Station
E.V. — Eastonville
Gr. — Granger
G.P. — Glider Port
G.V. — Gwillimville
H. — Husted
L.F. — La Foret Camp
N.C.M. — National Carver's Museum
S.V. — Spring Valley
T.R. — Table Rock
W.M. — Western Museum of Mining and Industry

Early Roads — • — • — • — • — •
C.S.B.B. — Colorado Springs and Bijou Basin Wagon Road
H.W.R. — Husted Wagon Road
J.C.T. — Jimmy Camp Trail
P.P.L.E. — Pikes Peak and Leavenworth Express Stage Road
W.C.S. — West Cherry Stage Route

Schools ⇑
B.S. — Bluff School
Bl. S. — Bleeker School
E.S. — Elton School
E.V.S. — Eastonville School
F.S. — Fairview School
F.V. — Forest View School
P.G. — Pine Grove School
S.S. — Stout School

Ranches, Sawmills — •
A.R. — Ayer Ranch
B.W. — Brentwood Country Club
B.X. — Bar X Ranch
D.L. — Dreamland Country Club
E.L.B. — Edgar Lumber and Box Company
G.R. — Grandview Ranch
I.D. — Indian Doctor's Place
J.P. — J.J. Pettigrew Ranch
J.R. — Johnson Ranch
K.K. — KK Ranch
L. — Latigo
P.M. — Pat Murphy Ranch
S.R. — Stout Ranch
W. — Weir Mill
W.R. — Wonderland Ranch

Cemeteries, Churches — †
E.C. — Eastonville Episcopal Church
E.V.C. — Eastonville Cemetery
G. — Three infant graves (moved when Woodn Road was built)
T.R.C. — Table Rock Cemetery
Sh. S. — Shadeland School
T.R. — Table Rock School
G.V.S. — Gwillimville School

The Black Forest lies in the northern part of El Paso County. This hand-drawn map and key of the region was published in the 1979 book *Thunder, Sun and Snow—the History of Colorado's Black Forest* by Judy von Ahlefeldt[1] and is reproduced courtesy of Judy. The region is bordered on the north by County Line Road (shown erroneously on the map as Hodgen Road); on the south by Falcon Road (now Woodmen Road); on the west by the Denver and Rio Grande Railroad; and on the east by the Colorado and Southern Railroad (the trackage of which was abandoned in 1935). The area shown covers roughly 200 square miles and played an important role in building Pikes Peak Country. Shamrock Ranch's center is marked with a green shamrock.

The exact origin of the name "Black Forest" is unknown, but most local historians attribute it to the similarity in appearance with Germany's Black Forest, or "Schwartzwald." The name Black Forest has been in common usage in Pikes Peak Country since the early part of the twentieth century. Before that, starting as early as the 1860s, the entire region was known as "the Divide Country," and the timbered portion was called "the Pinery." [2]

The portion of the Black Forest that contains Shamrock Ranch averaged 82 inches of snow annually from 1995 to 2005; its annual precipitation ranged from 20 to 22 inches. By comparison, Colorado Springs—whose center is only 15 miles from the ranch—averaged 45 inches of snow and 17 inches of precipitation.

The winters are colder and longer in the Black Forest than in either Colorado Springs or Denver, hence the growing season is about a month shorter—extending variably from June 10 to September 10. Shamrock Ranch is typically 5–10° F cooler than Colorado Springs. In 1968, Eastonville (some 10 miles east of Shamrock Ranch) was frost-free only from June 30 to August 24! [3]

In the last fourteen years, temperature extremes have ranged from 102° F to -17° F. However, temperatures seldom get above 90° F or below zero nowadays.

But the climate hasn't always been this mild.

During the first three decades of the twentieth century, temperatures ranged from -10° F to -20° F every night from the first of November to the first of February! The ground was covered with snow all winter long. It was so cold the nearby lakes froze over to a depth of more than 24 inches—thus enabling a thriving ice business in Monument only 10 miles to the northeast of Shamrock Ranch. But when the winters began to warm up in the early 1930s, the ice business had to close down.

In September of 1878, a reporter writing for Colorado Spring's *The Weekly Gazette* who signed his name "Tenderfoot" wrote an article titled "On the Divide." It describes his visit to the ranch of Calvin R. Husted, Esq., one of the first ranchers to homestead Shamrock Ranch land. (For a copy of this colorful article, see appendix A.)

Describing the weather on his journey, Tenderfoot wrote the following:

The afternoon was decidedly a cold one. One of Colorado's northern zephyrs pierced our very inmost anatomy, causing our teeth to rattle like a castanet and imparting to our nose, ears and hands a color bordering on sky blue. Of course we had left our gloves at home and were therefore entirely at the mercy of Old Boreas. [Note: a zephyr is a west wind and Boreas was the Greek god of the north wind.]

Muffy, the Wismers' dog, helps to illustrate how deep the snow can get on Shamrock Ranch (1996).

Many current residents of the Palmer Divide can relate to this description!

The Palmer Divide is notorious for fierce snow storms. The first on record occurred April 30, 1858, causing disaster for a Utah-bound military expedition led by Captain Randolph Marcy. The next big snow was on Halloween 1864. Blizzards swept across Shamrock Ranch in the winter of 1881–82 and again in 1889, when 3,000 sheep were lost on the southeast edge of the Palmer Divide. Author Judy von Ahlefeldt gives the following account of the next major storm:

The Great Snow of 1913 began the week of December 6 with sunny mornings and a foot of new snow each night for a week. Residents drove herds of cattle or horses ahead of them to open roads, shoveling the animals loose from the drifts. Deer walked on fifty foot drifts, eating pine needles from the tree tops. Dairy farmers stored milk in the family bathtub until the roads were opened to the towns. The following summer, the high water table made work in the fields nearly impossible, and logging rigs sank into sinkholes in the timber.[4]

Other major snows occurred in November 1946, April 1957, November 1966, October 1972, December 1973 and March 1977. Snowfall at Shamrock Ranch and surrounding areas during the winter of 1972–73 added up to 270 inches (22.5 feet)—quite different from the severe drought conditions of the early 2000s!

Heavy rains have also pounded Shamrock Ranch. The flood of 1935 was so severe it washed out all the bridges of the Colorado and Southern Railroad east of Shamrock Ranch and eventually contributed to the town of Eastonville being abandoned, along with the all of the railroad's trackage. Heavy rains in 1965 caused more flooding that washed out many roads and bridges in the area, including a bridge over Kettle Creek that has never been rebuilt.[5]

A common but uniquely beautiful winter scene at Shamrock Ranch (2007).

As extreme as some of these stories and numbers may seem, Colorado's Black Forest is a beautiful place to live with few hazards or dangers, although the vagaries of the weather make farming a chancy business. Today, the most serious potential hazards are lightning and fire.

At the heart of the charming Black Forest region, Shamrock Ranch has had a colorful history. With its many partial owners, it has produced a great deal of timber, cattle, show horses, sheep, hay, and crops over the years and has hosted numerous community events. Many celebrated people have visited the ranch and enjoyed its beauty—including mayors, governors, movie stars, and a United States president.

Present-day proprietors David and Mary Anne Wismer purchased all the parcels that comprise the present-day ranch. Their common interest in its history led to publication of this book.

Many wonderful people have lived and worked on Shamrock Ranch. This book, based on interviews and research covering the period from 1803 to 2008, tells their stories. For the most part, the stories are fascinating and uplifting, but more important is to look beyond the words and sense the character of these people. This came through again and again in the interviews and an attempt is made here to pass along these intangible qualities in a common theme: "Like the land, character is prized for the bounty of its harvest." Big or little, male or female, shy or boisterous, wealthy or not so wealthy, these people possessed an inner strength, moral fiber, and fortitude that seems to lessen with each passing generation. True, they loved the land, but they loved their fellow man more.

David and Mary Anne hope you enjoy reading this history as much as they enjoyed gathering the facts and publishing it.

BEGINNINGS

LONG AGO, before Christopher Columbus made his first voyage to the Western Hemisphere, Native Americans roamed the land known today as Shamrock Ranch. They found it ideal for hunting game, such as deer, elk, and antelope. Other predators, including cougar, bobcat, bear, coyote, fox, and wolves, shared the land with these nomadic hunters, who came from the Sioux, Arapaho and Cheyenne nations. Living in harmony with the land

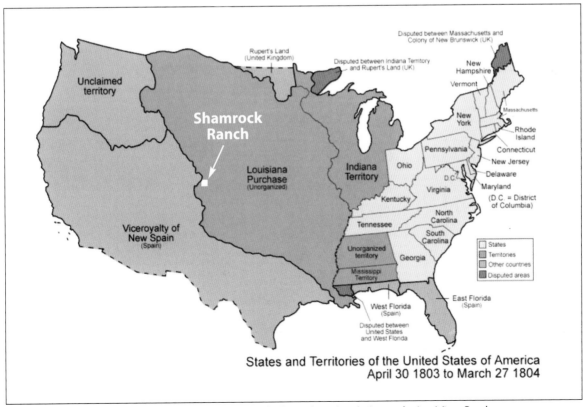

Present-day location of Shamrock Ranch, shown here in relation to the Louisiana Purchase.

and nature, they were the first human beings known to have viewed the beauty of the ranch and to have walked its venerable trails.

Then, in 1803, the beginnings of drastic change for these Native Americans were unleashed with the Louisiana Purchase, illustrated on the previous page.

Thomas Jefferson, third president of the United States, decided to purchase this territory because he was uneasy about the power of France and Spain to block American traders' access to the port of New Orleans.[1] The purchase price was approximately three cents an acre. Little did President Jefferson know at the time how strategic his purchase was!

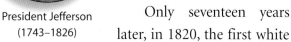

President Jefferson
(1743–1826)

Only seventeen years later, in 1820, the first white Americans known to have seen the land near the Shamrock Ranch entered what we now call Colorado's Black Forest under the leadership of Major Stephen H. Long.[2] They were a party of explorers sent by the United States government. One of Long's men, Captain John R. Bell, penned a description of the area that is the first on record.

Monday, July 10 . . . The hunters out in pursuit of buffalo, the first seen for several days—about 8 o'clock we bid adieu to the waters of the Platte, having crossed the last of the rivulets that issue from the mountains, which mingle with those running to the north and east and are tributaries to the Missouri—those to the south of us discharge into the Mississippi or Gulf of Mexico. At 9 o'clock we halted on a rivulet near to the base of the mountain—and is the head of a very considerable fork of the Arkansas River. As it courses along the vicinity of the mountains, it is increased by the number of small streams flowing from springs or the melting snows—I am inclined to think from springs.

The dividing place of the waters that discharge into the Platte and the Arkansas is a moderate hill or swell. On the top it is nearly level, where is a small pond of water which, when filled by heavy rains, discharges to the right and left—that is it flows in outlets to the Platte and Arkansas at the same time. . . . We are delighted with our first entrance into what we may now call the Arkansas country—cool water from the mountains, numberless beaver dams and lodges. Naturalists find new inhabitants, the botanist is at a loss which new plant he will first take in hand, the geologist grand subjects for speculation—the geographer and topographer all have subjects for observation.[3]

(Note: Black Squirrel Creek, with headwaters on the Shamrock Ranch, is likely one of the small streams described above. The "small pond of water" is thought to be Palmer Lake, located about 9 miles northwest of Shamrock Ranch. Also, Longs Peak, a fourteener just 94 miles north by northwest of the ranch, is named after Major Long.)

Fifteen years later, Colonel Henry Dodge and his First Regiment of Dragoons journeyed across the Black Forest, hoping to impress the Native Americans with the strength of the U.S. government.[4] The company traveled along the Front Range of the Rocky Mountains from the South Platte River to Bent's Old Fort. Although they were on a peace mission, the dragoons' militaristic display marked the first threat to the Native Americans' way of life on the lands of Shamrock Ranch. One of Dodge's captains was Nathan Boone, Daniel Boone's youngest son.[5]

In 1843, Major General John Charles Fremont, "The Great Pathfinder," journeyed up Kiowa Creek, traveling, perhaps, within 2 or 3 miles of Shamrock Ranch's eastern boundary. He reported that the area was occupied by Sioux, Arapaho, and Cheyenne Indians. On July 11, he recorded the following:

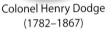

Colonel Henry Dodge
(1782–1867)

We followed the stream to its head in a broken ridge, which according to the barometer was about 7,500 feet above the sea. This is a piney elevation into which the prairies are gathered, and from which the waters flow in almost every direction to the Arkansas, Platte and Kansas Rivers . . . Although somewhat rocky and broken, and covered with pines, in comparison with the neighboring mountains it scarcely forms an interruption to the great prairie plains which sweep up to their bases.[6]

Fremont, who was a remarkable explorer, made five expeditions to the Great American West between 1842 and 1854. All of them went through Colorado. He saw more of the West than any other explorer of the time. With the help of his talented and devoted wife, Jessie Benton, he

John C. Fremont
"The Great Pathfinder"
(1813–1890)

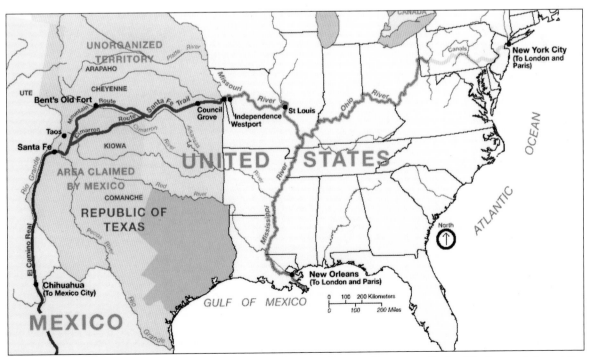

The Santa Fe Trail The Mountain Route, which diverged from the Cimarron Route near Garden City, Kansas, followed the Arkansas River upstream through southeastern Colorado to Bent's Old Fort, then turned down to Santa Fe.

wrote accurate and fascinating reports of his journeys that were published by the United States Congress and inspired many Americans to move west.[7]

Native and white American relationships in the Black Forest became interwoven soon after explorers and trappers began to penetrate the area. At first the contacts were friendly and casual. But by the end of the 1840s, whites were pouring into the region from the Santa Fe Trail on the south and the Oregon Trail to the north. These frontiersmen plunged the Black Forest into the mainstream of land disputes between the U.S. government and the Native American nations.

The Oregon and Santa Fe Trails both led over vast stretches of treeless plains and arid deserts, and crossed turbulent streams and wide, muddy rivers. By the late 1840s, travelers on these trails had to be constantly on guard against Indian attacks. But they were eager for new opportunities and were willing to risk their lives in order to reach their destinations. Many who set out on these westward trails died along the way, but few turned back.[9]

A family heading to Pikes Peak Country typically got on the trail in Independence, Missouri, and had to plan for a journey of at least two months. For most of the voyage, they

Bent's Old Fort A replica is shown here. Built by William Bent, the original fort was the largest and most popular trading post along the Santa Fe Trail. Kit Carson was its buffalo hunter until 1842, supplying meat for both residents and traders. In 1846, Bent's Old Fort became the headquarters of the Indian Agency and was used by the U.S. Army to station troops. According to some, Bent blew it up in 1849 when the U.S. government refused to pay the sale price he wanted for it.[8]

Replica of a prairie schooner.

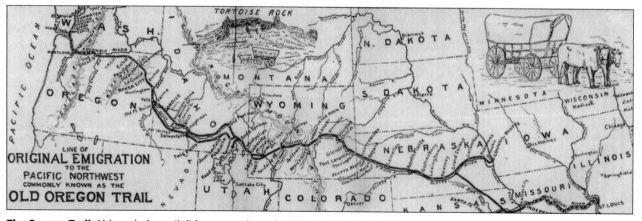

The Oregon Trail Although the trail did not pass through Colorado, it had a significant impact on Native Americans throughout the Great Plains, including the plains of Colorado.

lived in a canvas-covered wagon called a prairie schooner (from a distance, its white top looked like the sails of a ship). A prairie schooner was a half-sized version of the historic Conestoga wagon (named for the Pennsylvania valley where it was first built) that had been used extensively by earlier pioneers to reach the eastern frontiers of America, but was too heavy for crossing the Great Plains. Several teams of oxen or mules were used to pull a prairie schooner, which was typically 4 feet wide and 10–12 feet long.[10, 11]

Up to a hundred families would band together to form a caravan of prairie schooners, called a wagon train. Most men with families drove their own wagons. Single men rode on horseback and herded the group's livestock. Each wagon train was guided by a scout who knew the route and the best places to camp.[12]

One famous scout was Kit Carson. Leaving his Kentucky home at an early age, Kit headed for Independence, Missouri, where a wagon train brought him further west in return for herding horses, mules, and cattle. Arriving in Santa Fe, New Mexico, he teamed up with a trapper named Kincaid, who taught him how to read maps and speak Spanish, French, and some Native American languages.

From 1829 to 1841, Kit hunted and trapped with the mountain men of the Rocky Mountain Fur Company. By the time he was twenty-six years old, he had traveled throughout the Southwest with trappers, traders, and explorers. After meeting the Bent brothers (William and Charles), he became buffalo hunter for Bent's Old Fort in 1841. Then, in 1842, he met John C. Fremont, who hired him as a guide while exploring the Rocky Mountains. Kit was Fremont's guide for three different expeditions between 1842 and 1845. He also carried letters and reports about the West to Washington, D.C. The information they contained encouraged many Americans to come west. Kit Carson became famous for his scouting, explorations, courage, and skill, and many Indians respected him for his integrity and fairness.[13]

On the journey westward, pioneers always heeded an important rule—"Keep moving!" A wagon train would typically halt only at noon and nightfall, covering between 15 and 20 miles each day. If the oxen hauling the wagons became exhausted, they were replaced by animals being herded behind the wagons and then left to die. While this harsh treatment resulted in the death of many animals, it saved many human lives.[14]

Describing the migration of such pioneers during the 1840s, nineteenth-century author Octavius T. Howe wrote:[15]

. . . Those who crossed the plains, though they lived beyond the age allotted to man, never forgot the ungratified thirst, the intense heat and bitter cold, the craving hunger and utter physical exhaustion of the trail, and the rude crosses which marked the last resting places of loved companions. But there was another side. Neither would they ever forget the level prairie, covered with lush grass and dotted with larkspur, verbena, lupin, and geranium; the glorious sunrise in the mountains; the camp fire of buffalo chips at night, the last pipe before bedtime and the pure, sweet air of the desert. True they had suffered, but the satisfaction of deeds accomplished and difficulties overcome more than compensated and made the overland passage a thing never to be forgotten and a life-long pleasure in remembrance.

To defend against Native American attacks at night, prairie schooners in a wagon train would form a circle called a night ring. Travelers would sleep inside the ring with their guns ready, while animals were allowed to graze outside. Native Americans usually stayed away from night rings because they feared the barrage of gunfire that would immediately result if they attacked.[16]

However, Native American attacks on wagon trains were a persistent threat. In 1845, Colonel Stephen W. Kearney commanded an expedition intended to discourage of these attacks.[17] His mission, which crossed the Black Forest, undoubtedly fostered a good deal of hostility and resentment.

Then in 1851, Thomas Fitzpatrick, government agent to the Cheyenne and Arapaho nations, organized the largest council of Native Americans of the Plains ever assembled and negotiated the first Treaty of Fort Laramie. This historic treaty retained all the territory of Colorado, including the lands of Shamrock Ranch, for these Native Americans.

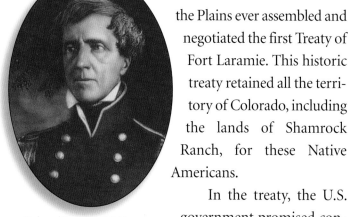

Colonel Stephen W. Kearney (1794–1848)

In the treaty, the U.S. government promised control of the Great Plains to the Native Americans for "as long as the river flows and the eagle flies,"[18] and guaranteed them an annuity in the amount of fifty thousand dollars annually for fifty years. In return, the natives guaranteed safe passage for travelers on the Oregon Trail and agreed to allow roads and forts to be built along it. Unfortunately, the United States Congress later cut appropriations for the treaty to ten years of annuities, and several tribes never received the commodities that they were promised as payments.

Just two years after this treaty was signed, Fitzpatrick wrote prophetically, "On the high table lands a . . . nutritious grass affords excellent grazing, and will cause this country to be someday much prized for pastoral purposes."[19]

Thomas Fitzpatrick was a trapper and trailblazer who became the head of the Rocky Mountain Fur Company. He was one of the most colorful of the mountain men, and was party to many of the most important events that opened the Great American West. For example, he was responsible for shepherding the first two wagon trains to Oregon, guiding John C. Fremont on his longest expedition, guiding Colonel Kearny and his dragoons along the westward trails on their mission to impress the Native Americans with their howitzers and swords, and, along with Jedediah Smith, leading the trapper band that discovered South Pass, Wyoming. South Pass was a strategic discovery because it provided a natural crossing point of the Rocky Mountains for three important historic trails—the Oregon Trail, the California Trail, and the Mormon Trail.[20]

In the early 1850s, upon their return from the California Gold Rush, some Cherokee gold seekers from Georgia told stories of gold they had found along Cherry Creek at the base of the Rocky Mountains. Not many whites took them seriously, but William Green Russell did.[21] A Forty-Niner himself, he got other men interested and they left early in the spring of 1858 to see if the stories were true. On their way to the Rockies, they were joined by a band of Cherokee in Kansas. This motley company consisted of thirty-three yoke of oxen, a couple of two-horse teams, twenty-four Cherokee, and sixty-four whites.

When they didn't find much of the coveted metal at Cherry Creek, most of the whites returned home dejected. But some stayed with Russell and eventually found two hundred dollars worth of flour gold on a sand bar in the South Platte River four miles north of the Cherry Creek junction. Then they found another four hundred dollars worth of gold in Little Dry Creek, three miles above its junction with the South Platte (now Englewood, Colorado).

A trader named Cantrell took some of the gold-bearing soil from Russell's camp and had it checked by an experienced miner. When this miner confirmed that it did indeed contain gold, the news spread like wildfire . . . and the Pikes Peak Gold Rush was on! Before it was over, a hundred thousand gold seekers would make a pilgrimage to Pikes Peak Country.

The flames of this raging wildfire were deliberately fanned with outlandish propaganda by entrepreneurs looking to capitalize on the fortuitous opportunity to outfit prospectors. The following verse, "A Call to the Mines," was published by the *Kansas Tribune* of Topeka on January 20, 1859: [22]

Hurra for Pike's Peak! Hurra for Pike's Peak!
A rich El Dorado has lately been found,
Far, far to the westward, and near Cherry
*   Creek;*
Where gold in abundance is scattered
*   around.*
Ah! Hurra for Pike's Peak!

Hurra for Pike's Peak! Hurra for Pike's Peak!
There's gold in the mountain, there's gold
*   in the vale,*
There's plenty for all who are willing to
*   seek—*

Believe me; believe me—'tis no idle tale
Come, Hurra for Pike's Peak.

The fact that the gold was not exactly in the shadow of Pikes Peak had little significance to an adventurous man in eastern Kansas Territory who had his face set eagerly to the west. Most mid–nineteenth-century Americans thought Pikes Peak represented all the Rocky Mountains. The goldfields of Cherry Creek and those directly west became known as the Pikes Peak goldfields, even though the peak was 70 miles to the south! [23] Many prairie schooners on their way to the goldfields proudly displayed the slogan *"Pikes Peak or Bust."*

Gold seekers in eastern Kansas who wanted to get to the Pikes Peak fields as quickly as possible were faced with a problem. There were already two established routes to the mountains, but both took travelers far out of their way.

One followed the Leavenworth and Pikes Peak (L&PP) Express Road that ran from Leavenworth, Kansas, to Denver. This trail followed the mail route of the Oregon Trail to Station No. 18 on the Republican River, near present-day Benkleman in Dundy County, Nebraska. From there it turned southwest to Station No. 24 on the Big Sandy Creek in Lincoln County, Colorado. Turning northwest again, it eventually converged with Cherry Creek and ended at Station No. 27 in Denver City. [24]

The aggravating thing about this route was that it was over a hundred miles out of the way—taking the traveler far to the north before bringing him back. But it also provided a relatively safe journey because of easy access to water and firewood. [25]

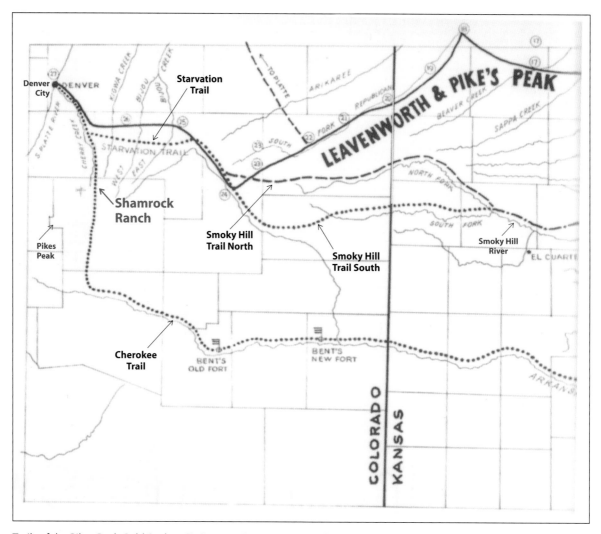

Trails of the Pikes Peak Gold Seekers.[26] *Courtesy Caxton Printers Ltd.*

The other established route was the Cherokee Trail, sometimes called the "Trappers' Trail." This route was originally used by trappers to reach the Rocky Mountains. It was also used in 1850 by a large wagon train headed to the goldfields of California. Among this expedition party was the group of Cherokees who convinced William Green Russell to go west in search of Rocky Mountain gold.[27] Ironically, it was this group of Cherokees that ultimately brought about the Pikes Peak Gold Rush of 1859 and the exploitation of gold in Colorado—which in turn hastened the end of Native American control of the Great American West.

The Cherokee Trail ran from the Arkansas River near the Arkansas/Oklahoma line[28] to the Santa Fe Trail east of the Little Arkansas River. From there it followed the Santa Fe Trail Mountain Route, turning northwest at Bent's Old Fort and finally heading north along the base of the Front Range of the Rockies into the valley of the South Platte River. Like the L&PP stagecoach route to the north, it also took the traveler over a hundred miles out of his way, but provided ready access to water and firewood.

Shamrock Ranch was at the very heart of Colorado's explosive growth during the mid-nineteenth century. The Cherokee Trail ran

Pikes Peak Gold Seekers The Pikes Peak Gold Rush lasted from July 1858 until the creation of the Colorado Territory on February 28, 1861. Pikes Peak gold-seekers were called Fifty-Niners.

along the ranch's western side. Although not as well known as the Santa Fe Trail, it was traveled just as much by pioneers of the Great American West.[29] The notorious Cherry Creek, which played such an important role in launching the Pikes Peak Gold Rush of 1859 and brought a hundred thousand people to Colorado, has its origin on the eastern side of the Shamrock Ranch (see map this page).[30]

Since the Leavenworth and Pikes Peak Express Road and the Cherokee Trail both took gold seekers more than a hundred miles farther than they wanted to go, many prospectors set out on a more direct path that followed the Smoky Hill River. Their path became known as the Smoky Hill Trail (see map on previous page).

The Smoky Hill Trail ascended the Smoky Hill River across Kansas to the fork of its headwaters near the western state line. From this point, the Smoky Hill Trail North followed the north fork of the river into eastern Colorado,

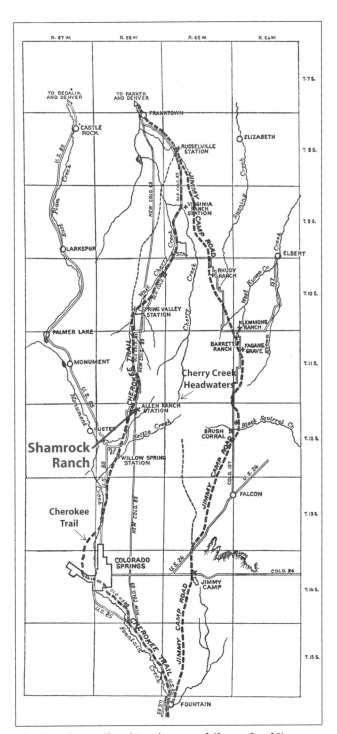

The Cherokee Trail and Headwaters of Cherry Creek[31]
Cherry Creek was synonymous with Rocky Mountain gold to the Fifty-Niners. As shown here, its origin was located on the Palmer Divide near the southeast corner of Section 36 of present-day Shamrock Ranch. The west side of the ranch was bounded by the Cherokee Trail—an important travel route for gold seekers as well as homesteaders and other frontiersmen in the mid 1800s. (Note: Shamrock Ranch was called the Allen Ranch at the time this map was made [circa 1943].)

and the Smoky Hill Trail South followed the river's south fork. Both trails converged at Big Sandy Creek a few miles north of Station No. 24 on the L&PP Express Road. From there, the Smoky Hill Trail continued northwest along the L&PP until it reached Starvation Trail, which turned directly west until it intersected the Cherokee Trail about 30 miles southeast of Denver.

The last leg of the Smoky Hill Trail—Starvation Trail—was so named because of the extreme hunger and thirst—sometimes leading to cannibalism—that many of its travelers endured due to the persistent desert conditions. Although it was the shortest route to the gold diggings in the Rockies, it was also the most difficult.[32] More people traveling the Smoky Hill Trail died from hunger and thirst than from Indian attacks. A *Rocky Mountain News* article[33] even called the trail "Smoky Hell." The following quotation from that article explains how Starvation Trail got its name: "Two footmen have just arrived via the Smoky route. They appear to have suffered severely from hunger and thirst. They report having passed some ten or fifteen dead bodies unburied, and many graves. These men say they lived for nine days on prickly pears and hawk."

Gold seekers came via the Smoky Hill Trail in covered wagons and on foot, even with handcarts and wheelbarrows. Poorly equipped and scantily fed, they faced the chilling winds, snow, and mud of early spring armed with an eagerness to reach their goal and little else. Like the Oregon Trail, the Smoky became lined with abandoned property, broken wagons, dead horses and oxen, and myriad unmarked graves.[34]

Many rivers and trails have received more publicity than the Smoky Hill River and the Trail that ran along its blood-soaked banks, but few were more important in settling the plains between the Missouri River and the Rocky Mountains.[35]

Adding to the danger of the journey, no place was more hotly contested by Native Americans than the Smoky Hill River Valley. It was a favorite pasture of buffalo—all fifty-eight thousand square miles of it—so it was also the main source of food for many tribes of the Plains Indians. These tribes made regular trips to this hunting paradise, which hosted buffalo herds as large as thirty miles across. According to Lee and Raynesford in their book, *Trails of the Smoky Hill,* "Although each tribe claimed the valley as its own, none could enforce its claim. Many fierce Native American battles were fought there—long before and well after the white man appeared." [36]

American bison (buffalo).

From mid-1854 to early 1861, the lands of Shamrock Ranch and the Black Forest were actually part of the organized Territory of Kansas. This territory extended from the Missouri River west to the summit of the Rocky Mountains, and from the 37th parallel north to the 40th parallel. Much of the eastern region of what is now the State of Colorado was part of the Kansas Territory, as shown on the next page.

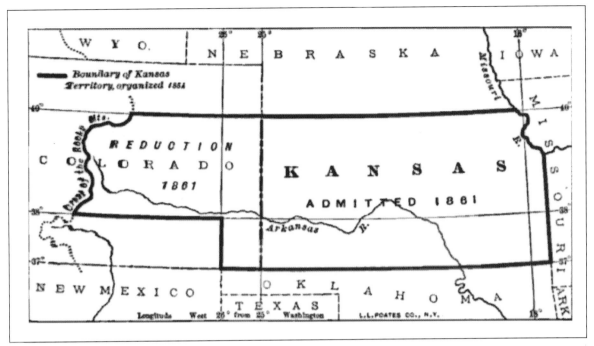

The Territory of Kansas.

This territory was created by the Kansas-Nebraska Act of May 30, 1854. It included all of the Smoky Hill River Valley (including that part which is in eastern Colorado), the desert-like country west of it, the Black Forest, Denver City, and the goldfields of the Pikes Peak Gold Rush.

Anxious Kansas Territory settlers met and drew up four different proposed state constitutions during the territorial period. Except for one that was created in 1859 in Wyandotte (now a county bordering on the Missouri River and hosting Kansas City, Kansas), they all specified the boundaries of the future state as the existing borders of the new territory—putting the western boundary at the crest of the Rocky Mountains.

The Wyandotte Constitution, however, put this boundary at the 25th longitude, which was considerably east of the mountains. This recommendation resulted from anticipation that the "State of Jefferson," which was being discussed in the gold region, would have its western boundary along the summit of the Rockies and therefore would need considerable land to the east in order to become a new state.

On January 29, 1861, the State of Kansas was admitted to the Union. Its borders were defined by the Wyandotte Constitution—rejecting all the former territorial land west of the 25th longitude.

Thus the vast portion of the Kansas Territory that lies in Colorado today, including Shamrock Ranch, Denver, and the Pikes Peak goldfields, was suddenly rendered an unofficial territory of the United States. Anticipating

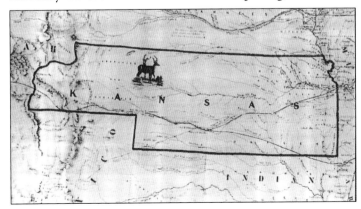

Proposed Boundaries for the State of Kansas.

that this would happen, settlers organized the Territory of Jefferson in October of 1859 and elected a provisional government for the new territory, which contained portions of the official Territories of Kansas, Nebraska, New Mexico and Utah. However, this democratically elected government was never recognized by the United States government, even though it governed the territory with free rein for sixteen months!

Then on February 28, 1861, outgoing president James Buchanan signed an act of Congress organizing the Territory of Colorado. The boundaries of this new territory were the same as the State of Colorado today and nullified the Territory of Jefferson. El Paso was one of the original seventeen counties created. For the first time, Shamrock Ranch was associated with the name Colorado.

President James Buchanan
(1791–1868)

Colorado was chosen as the territory's name because it was commonly believed at the time that the Colorado River (originally named Rio Colorado by early Spanish explorers because of the reddish-brown silt it carried from the mountains) originated in the territory. Interestingly, the headwaters of today's Colorado River (running from Rocky Mountain National Park to its confluence with the Green River in Utah) were originally called the Grand River. It wasn't until 1921 that the United States Congress changed the name of the Grand River to the Colorado River. [37]

Thomas Fitzpatrick's prediction that Colorado's plains would one day become prized for pastoral purposes began to come true when President Abraham Lincoln signed into law the Homestead Act on May 20, 1862.

This act gave homesteaders freehold title to a quarter section (160 acres) of undeveloped land. The acreage of Shamrock Ranch was included in the "unappropriated public lands" addressed by this important act. A person to whom title was granted had to be at least 21 years of age, must have lived for five years on the land in a house that was at least 12 x 14 feet in size, must have dug a well, and must have broken (plowed) at least 10 acres. Title could also be acquired after a 6-month residency with only trivial improvements, provided the claimant paid the government $1.25 per acre. After the Civil War, Union soldiers could deduct the time they had served from the residency requirements. [38, 39]

President Lincoln's signing of the Homestead Act marked the beginning of a new era in the American West that would have a tremendous impact on the use of Shamrock Ranch's fields and forests.

President Abraham Lincoln
(1809–1865)

It would also wield a devastating blow to the Native Americans whose ancestors had depended on the land for sustenance for centuries.

As settlers and fortune seekers continued to invade the Territory of Colorado, tensions between them and the Native Americans began to escalate. And when the first transcontinental railroad was completed at Promontory Summit, Utah, in 1869, the fever of western expansion elevated dramatically— putting even more pressure on the natives.

Earlier, in 1860, the United States Commissioner of Indian Affairs had attempted to

Ceremony for driving the golden spike at Promontory Summit, Utah, on May 10, 1869, to complete the first transcontinental railroad.

broker a peace by consulting with some tribal chiefs at Fort Wise, a historic meeting place 97 miles southeast of Shamrock Ranch. This fort was built by William Bent in 1853—after he had blown up his first fort (Bent's Old Fort). The U.S. Army took over Bent's New Fort in 1860 and named it Fort Wise. By then, William Bent had become an Indian agent. The Cheyenne, who respected him, nick-named him "Small White Man."[40]

Unfortunately, many of the northern chiefs did not attend the meeting at Fort Wise. It produced, in February of 1861, the Treaty of Fort Wise, which "purchased" most of eastern Colorado from the Cheyenne and Arapaho tribes. The treaty was doomed to fail. The northern tribes refused to sign it and other tribes were never even consulted.[41, 42]

Not only did this treaty break promises established in the 1851 Treaty of Fort Laramie,

it also removed the Cheyenne and Arapaho from the Colorado Front Range altogether. They were confined to reservations in south-eastern Colorado where the land was poor, and promised annuities for fifteen years as com-pensation. Consequently, the Native American tribes who had depended on the Shamrock Ranch area for hunting and shelter for hun-dreds of years were suddenly relegated to a des-olate tract along Sand Creek near Fort Wise.[43]

Sadly, the U.S. Government failed to pay the specified annuities during the Civil War. Receiving none of their promised goods while living on lands that could not support them, the Cheyenne and Arapaho clashed with whites in their struggle to avoid starvation.

Angered at the loss of their best lands and way of life, the young chiefs prepared to fight. In the summer of 1863, Cheyenne and Ara-paho warriors began attacking wagon trains along the Smoky Hill Trail, which ran just twenty-five miles north of the land that would become Shamrock Ranch.

By the following summer, these Native Americans had become desperate. In mid-June, they killed the Hungate family near Running Creek, about 15 miles north of Shamrock Ranch. The mutilated bodies were displayed in Denver, arousing intense hostility against the Indians. Throughout the Black Forest, various bands of Cheyenne and Arapaho harassed isolated settlers as they cared for their crops and livestock.

To protect themselves against these angry Native Americans, some residents of the Black Forest built small stone forts. One day, while the Jacob Guire family and their friends were "forted up," an Indian with tomahawk in hand rushed over the hill at Jacob's son, who was playing in the yard. Mrs. Isabella Trigg seized the boy and pulled him into the fort only a moment before the tomahawk imbedded itself in the heavy door![44]

But despite these Native American hostilities, settlers continued to arrive in the Black Forest throughout the 1860s. Many of them came to escape the ravages and devastation of the Civil War. They planted hay, oats, potatoes, barley, wheat, and rye. Some were also cattle ranchers and lumberjacks. These stout pioneers called the region the Divide Country and named the timbered portion the Pinery.

In 1861, township corners and range lines were established throughout the Divide Country. By 1866, the sections had all been surveyed, paving the way for the initial land patents to be issued by the U.S. government under the Homestead Act.

Thus, individual ownership of the Divide Country began, as the way of life the Native Americans had enjoyed in the area for centuries came to a violent and disconcerting end. The lands of Shamrock Ranch were part of this new beginning and inevitable ending. Clearly, Native Americans were a poignant part of Shamrock Ranch's early history.

THE ORIGINAL PATENTEES

WHEN THE U.S. GOVERNMENT first set out to survey the land it had acquired with the Louisiana Purchase (including Colorado's Black Forest), it adopted a rectangular surveying system that was originally proposed by Thomas Jefferson.[1] Called the Public Land Survey System (PLSS), it divided public lands into vertical strips (running north and south) called *ranges*, and subdivided these strips into 6-mile-square areas called *townships*. Townships were further divided into *sections*, which are each one square mile.

A township comprises thirty-six sections numbered 1 to 36 in a 6x6 grid, and a range is 36 townships also laid out in a 6x6 grid. Today, all the states use the PLSS, with the exception of Texas and most of the eastern states.[2]

The *section quarter-quarters*, or portions thereof, that make

up 2,586.24-acre Shamrock Ranch today are shown below as the smallest green squares.

The first legal owners of the land that makes up present-day Shamrock Ranch were known as *patentees*. They included homesteaders who farmed and/or ranched, business people who wanted to acquire the land for its

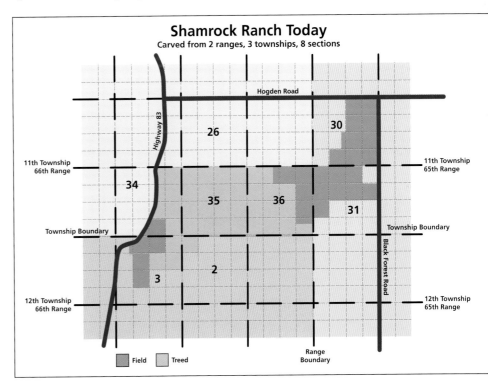

timber or grazing fields, and the State of Colorado. With the exception of the State of Colorado, these patentees filed petitions with the United States Government and were eventually granted *patents* for the land.

Patent petitions were normally made in increments of section quarter-quarters, which are each 40 acres in size. The colloquial term "the back 40" came from the definition of a section quarter-quarter.

The original patentees of Shamrock Ranch are listed below. Note that the first six patents were granted while Colorado was still a territory.

The first recorded patents were granted to George H. Bend, Abilgle W. Taylor, and Calvin R. Husted on July 1, 1870. Within three months, another patent was recorded for C.B. Lamborn. The western part of his land boasted the Divide Country's first stagecoach

route. The Leavenworth and Pikes Peak Express built it when they secured a mail contract to service Colorado City (now the southwest portion of Colorado Springs). On May 1, 1859, at the infancy of the Pikes Peak

A stagecoach like those used on the L&PP route bordering the west side of Shamrock Ranch (circa late 1800s). *Courtesy Tutt Library Special Collections, Colorado College.*

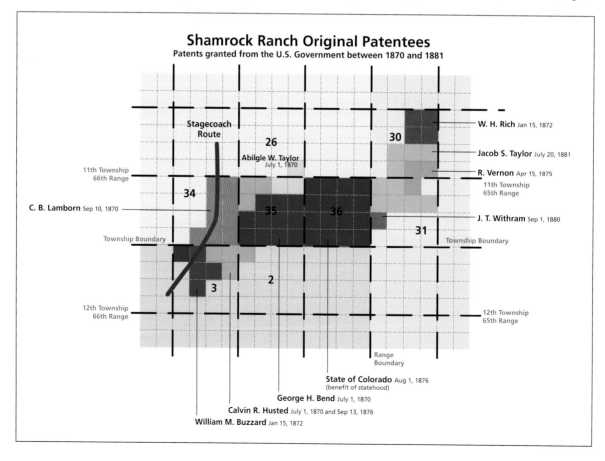

Shamrock Ranch Original Patentees
Patents granted from the U.S. Government between 1870 and 1881

Gold Rush, the first coaches to use this thoroughfare began their runs. Within a few years, the West Cherry Stage was also using it. The stagecoach road branched from the L&PP north of the ranch and followed the Cherokee Trail along its western extent (see maps, pages 21, 32, 33). Today, Colorado State Highway 83 (the westernmost boundary of Shamrock Ranch) follows nearly the same route.

A stagecoach station was located on Shamrock Ranch, a bit south of its current entrance. This station provided a barn where drivers changed their team of horses before making the final dash to Colorado City.

Shamrock Ranch entrance, 2007.

L&PP stagecoach barn.

Early in 1872, William M. Buzzard was granted a patent for four section quarter-quarters that now constitute the southwest corner of Shamrock Ranch. His land hosted the stagecoach station and a tavern.

Buzzard's tavern became known as "Buzzard's Roost." By the early 1870s, it was famous because it was the only place between Colorado City and Russellville where liquor could be obtained.[3] No doubt Buzzard's Roost was a favorite place for weary travelers to stop and seek refreshment!

The Weekly Gazette reporter Tenderfoot wrote the following about Buzzard's Roost in his September 21, 1878, article "On the Divide" (shown in its entirety in appendix A): "It was the rendezvous of all the 'characters' of the country, and has been the scene of many a pugilistic [boxing] encounter."

In her 1947 book *The Smoky Hill Trail*, Margaret Long provides an automobile log[4] that she kept while traveling along the Cherokee Trail in the 1940s, starting at Parker (see map, page 33). Her log includes the following entry regarding Buzzard's stagecoach station and tavern:

29.6 miles—ALLEN RANCH. Gate on the east side of the highway. A stage station and tavern were less than a mile southeast of the gate, on the north bank of Squirrel or Black Squirrel Creek. The stage buildings were falling down and were removed a few years ago. There is nothing left but a hole in the ground to mark the station site. Traces of the old stage road can be seen approaching the station from the north.

[Note: At the time that Long wrote this passage, Shamrock Ranch was called the Allen Ranch.]

It wasn't until over three years later that the first patent was recorded for ownership on the east side of Shamrock Ranch. It went to R. Vernon, who acquired three section quarter-quarters on April 15, 1875.

On August 1, 1876, only twenty-eight days after the United States Centennial celebration, United States President Ulysses S. Grant signed a proclamation admitting the State of Colorado to the Union. Soon after, a central section of today's Shamrock Ranch property was awarded to the State of Colorado as part of a generous land grant program designed to help the new state finance public schools.

In accordance with this program, the United States awarded Colorado every section within its boundaries that was numbered either 16 or 36. Section 36 of the 11th Township South in the 65th Range West of the 6th Principal Meridian is located at what is now the heart of Shamrock Ranch. The Palmer Divide runs diagonally through it at an elevation just over 7,600 feet, marking the highpoint of the Shamrock Ranch property. When the state owned this land during the late 1800s, they may have leased it out for logging, farming, and/or ranching, but no record is available to confirm this.

President Ulysses S. Grant
(1822–1885)

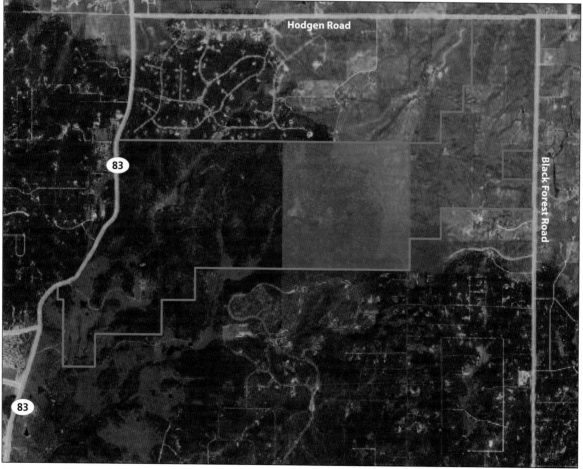

Section 36 of Shamrock Ranch was originally patented to the state of Colorado to finance education. It eventually became known as the "school section."

The final three patents that make up present-day Shamrock Ranch were recorded over the next five years. W. H. Rich recorded a patent for a quarter section on the property's eastern edge in 1876, however, evidence suggests that he deeded his land to Edmond Nicholson in 1875. Nicholson retained ownership of the land until the end of the century.

In 1881 when Jacob S. Taylor received the patent on 10 sections of land in Sections 30 and 31, he had known William Henry McBroom since 1876, when they became surveyors together in New Mexico Territory under Surveyor General Henry M. Atkinson. The two had purchased a house together in Santa Fe, New Mexico. Sometime earlier, while on a survey trip to Cheyenne, Wyoming, Henry stopped in the Divide Country at a stagecoach station near Table Rock, just a few miles from Shamrock Ranch's eastern border. Thinking it was the most beautiful country he had ever seen, he stated, "Someday I'm coming back and buying some of this land."

Originally from eastern Nebraska, William met and fell in love with Mary J. Peters when they were students together in a rural one-room schoolhouse. After attending the University of Nebraska for two years to study surveying, he took employment with Atkinson in Santa Fe. But he continued to court and correspond with Mary, who was then a school teacher in Nebraska. In one particular letter dated 1879, he surprised her with a deed in her name for the "Colorado Land," most likely in Township 12 of Range 65, just southeast of the Shamrock Ranch's eastern border.

He went back for Mary and they were married in Nebraska on February 5, 1881.

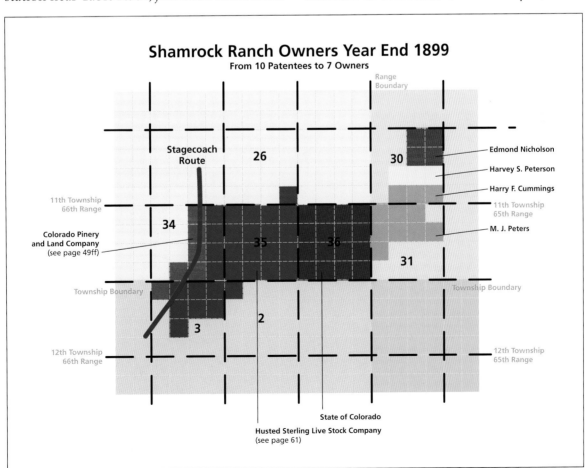

Shamrock Ranch Owners Year End 1899
From 10 Patentees to 7 Owners

They then moved into the house William owned with Jacob Taylor in Santa Fe and eventually to McBroom's large cattle ranch in eastern New Mexico. They finally moved to Colorado Springs in 1892, living in town, but continuing to acquire pasture land adjacent to the Shamrock Ranch. By the end of 1899, Mary was the owner of eight quarter-quarters in sections 30 and 31, seven of which were acquired from Jacob S. Taylor and one of which was acquired from J. T. Withram.

Mr. Taylor's other three quarter-quarters in Section 30 changed hands six times before being purchased by Harvey S. Peterson, and R. Vernon's three quarter-quarters changed hands a few times before being deeded to Harry F. Cummings in 1895.

Eventually, Mary and William did build a house north of the Divide on their land in the Black Forest. They raised three children there, Clieve, Paul, and Mary. William died in 1909 and Mary continued to live there until her death in 1915.

In 1873, Buzzard's land, including Buzzard's Roost, was acquired by Edward H. Talbert. The 1878 *The Weekly Gazette* article "On the Divide" said regarding Talbert's ranch, ". . . a more respectable or well conducted ranch cannot be found on the Divide." At the time the article was written, Mr. Talbert had 15 acres of wheat, 15 acres of oats, 30 head of cattle, 14 milk cows, and a horse. He was expecting to harvest 40 bushels of wheat per acre that fall.

By the end of the 1800s, ownership of the Shamrock Ranch property had consolidated from ten patentees to seven major land owners.

THE COLORADO PINERY TRUST ERA

William Jackson Palmer
(1836–1909)
*Courtesy the Colorado Springs
Pioneers Museum.*

WILLIAM JACKSON PAL-MER was born to a Quaker family on a farm in Leipsic, Delaware. When he was five years old, his family moved to the Borough of Germantown near Philadelphia, Pennsylvania. As a young boy, his fascination with steam locomotives spurred him on to learn all he could about railroads.

In 1853, at age seventeen, he was employed by a railroad construction company and worked on a line to Pittsburgh. From there he went to England and France, using money he had borrowed from his uncle, to study railroad engineering and mining.[1]

Upon his return to the United States in 1856, he went to work for the Pennsylvania Railroad, where he rose to the position of private secretary to the company's president, John Edgar Thomson. Here Palmer was exposed to the inner workings of the railroad empire and learned firsthand about state-of-the art railroading.

From his studies in England, young Palmer shared with Thomson that coal could replace wood as the railroad's fuel source. At the time, the Pennsylvania Railroad was creating an ecological crisis—burning 60,000 cords of wood each year and rapidly exhausting its access to trees. Upon Palmer's advice, the Pennsylvania Railroad became the first American railroad to convert to coal.[2]

Over the next four years, Palmer focused on the problems of combustion efficiency for steam generation. Among his collaborators were the Pennsylvania Railroad Vice President, Thomas A. Scott, and Scott's assistant, Andrew Carnegie—an immigrant from Scotland one year older than Palmer who later founded Carnegie Steel Company (which subsequently became U.S. Steel).[3]

Then the Civil War began. Although his Quaker upbringing had taught him to loath violence, Palmer's passion to see the slaves set free drove him to enter the conflict anyway. He accepted a commission as a colonel in the Union Army where he was an expert scout and an effective military recruiter for the Union cause, helping with the formation of the 15th Pennsylvania Volunteer Cavalry.

Palmer during the Civil War (1861–1865) *Courtesy the Colorado Springs Pioneers Museum.*

In 1862, he was captured while scouting prior to the Battle of Antietam. He was well within Confederate lines when he was apprehended, dressed as a civilian and gathering information for General George McClellan. Upon questioning, Palmer gave his name as "W. J. Peters" and claimed to be a mine owner on an inspection trip.

While the Confederates didn't know he was a spy, his circumstances were suspicious, so he was detained and sent to Richmond where he was incarcerated at the notorious Castle Thunder Prison. He was eventually set free in a prisoner exchange and rejoined his regiment in February of 1863.[4]

Later, Palmer was active in pursuing Confederate General John B. Hood following

Civil War Medal of Honor

the Battle of Nashville. After the war, he was awarded the Medal of Honor for his gallantry and retired with the rank of Brevet Brigadier General.[5]

Palmer then resumed the railroad career he had started previous to the war. In 1867, he headed west

and became the construction manager for the Kansas Pacific Railroad, an enterprise of the Pennsylvania Railroad. Under General Palmer's direction, the Kansas Pacific was extended from Kansas City to Denver, reaching the Mile-High City in August of 1870. Upon completion of that line, Palmer founded his own railroad—the north-south running Denver and Rio Grande Western Railroad. Its first line went from Denver to Pikes Peak Country.

William met Mary Lincoln Mellen while she and her father were on a train going to see the West. The happy couple married on November 8, 1870, in Flushing, New York, where the Mellen family lived. Mary was only twenty years old. William called her "Queen" and loved her dearly. She bore him three daughters—Elsie, Dorothy, and Marjory—who he also adored. Queen Palmer founded Colorado Springs' first public school in 1871 when she was only twenty-one years old.[6, 7]

On their honeymoon to the British Isles, Palmer saw narrow gauge railroads in operation. He readily grasped the advantages of narrow gauge for his own line that was soon to be built. The narrow, three-foot distance between rails would provide substantial savings in manpower and materi-

Queen Palmer (1850–1894) *Courtesy the Colorado Springs Pioneers Museum.*

als. Narrow gauge was also better suited for mountainous terrain because of its ability to handle sharper curves and steeper grades. Upon his return, Palmer instructed that the Denver and Rio Grande Western Railroad be built in narrow gauge.[8]

As Colorado's railroad lines expanded, so did the demand for steel. Recognizing this need as a new business opportunity, Palmer began building the Colorado Coal and Iron Company's steel mill south of Pueblo in 1879. In 1892, CC&I merged with the Colorado Fuel Company to form Colorado Fuel and Iron. This company rapidly became the state's largest employer and dominated its railroad industry for decades.[9]

Palmer was fascinated with Pikes Peak Country. In 1871, he acquired 10,000 acres east of the former Colorado territorial capital—Colorado City—and founded a new community, calling it Colorado Springs. He envisioned an elegant city as culturally advanced as London, which helped earn it the nickname of "Little London."

Saloons and gambling houses were not allowed in Palmer's new city, so its residents had to travel to Colorado City or Manitou Springs in order to obtain liquor. The production and sale of alcohol were illegal in Colorado Springs until 1933, when Prohibition was lifted nationally.[10]

Palmer built his and Queen's dream estate, which he called Glen Eyrie (meaning Eagle's Nest), in the beautiful foothills just north of the Garden of the Gods. After constructing a large carriage house there, where the family lived for a time, he built a twenty-two-room frame house. In 1881, they remodeled the frame house to resemble a stone castle reminiscent of those native to England, adding a tower and additional rooms.[11]

In 1880, Queen suffered a mild heart attack and was advised to move to a lower altitude. She and the girls went to the East Coast and then on to England, where William visited them as often as he could.[12]

Queen died in England on December 28, 1894, at the age of forty-four. She had been

Garden of the Gods. *Courtesy of the Experience Colorado Springs at Pikes Peak Convention & Visitors Bureau, photo by Amy H. Long.*

married to William Jackson Palmer for twenty-four years. In sorrow, General Palmer brought his daughters back to Colorado Springs after the funeral so he could be with and care for them.[13, 14]

After a Supreme Court decision in 1901 denied him right-of-ways to extend the Denver and Rio Grande Western Railroad to Mexico, General Palmer sold the railroad and spent his last years enjoying his fame while acting as a benefactor to Colorado Springs. Among other things, he donated to his city four beautiful parks, Prospect Lake, and the land for Colorado College—which, for a time, became known as "the Harvard of the West." Other land grants donated by Palmer resulted in the Colorado School for the Deaf and Blind, the International Typographical Union's Printers Home, and a tuberculosis sanatorium that eventually became the University of Colorado at Colorado Springs. Palmer also built the Antlers Hotel, as well as golf courses and polo fields.[15, 16]

Statue of General Palmer, Colorado Springs.

While riding in the Garden of the Gods one day in 1906, Palmer was thrown from his favorite horse and broke his neck.[17] The tragic accident confined him to a wheelchair for the last three years of his life.

He died in 1909 at age seventy-two and is revered today for sharing the bounties of his life's harvest so generously and wisely. The Palmer Divide, which runs through Shamrock Ranch, was named after him.

IN THE LATE 1860s, General Palmer was acting as construction director of the Kansas Pacific Railroad. While working on a segment that cut across the prairie northeast of the Divide Country, he toured Pikes Peak Country with a survey team and became interested in the Pinery—the timbered portion of today's Black Forest. After completing the Kansas Pacific Railroad project in September of 1870, he formed the Colorado Pinery Trust with financial backing from George H. Bend and Francis H. Jackson (both of New York City), Thomas J. Wood (Dayton, Ohio), and Dr. William A. Bell (Ireland).

His motive for forming this trust was to provide timber and income for the Denver and Rio Grande Western Railroad he was planning to build. In order to form the trust, the four financiers mentioned above raised $102,000 in capital and purchased over 43,000 acres of land in El Paso and Elbert Counties, which hosted nearly all the marketable timber in Pikes Peak Country. The purchase included much of the Pinery.[18]

In anticipation of the Colorado Pinery Trust, George Bend sought and achieved patents for twelve section quarter-quarters of modern-day Shamrock Ranch (see map, page 49). But even before these patents were recorded, he had acquired a warranty deed for the Shamrock Ranch land in section 34 that was patented to C.B. Lamborn and recorded on September 10, 1870. On October 12, 1870—only twenty-five days after the Trust was formed—Bend obtained the two quarter-quarters of section 35 and the single quarter-

quarter of section 26 that had been patented to Abilgle Taylor. Evidently, Charles B. Lamborn and Abilgle W. Taylor were agents Mr. Bend used to increase the Colorado Pinery Trust's holdings as rapidly as possible.

Before this land was harvested for timber, it most likely had a greater diversity of pine and fir trees than it has now. It also had many ponderosa pines with diameters of 3 feet or more. Today, a ponderosa pine in the Black Forest with a diameter of 2 feet is a large tree.

Logging in the Pinery occurred in three phases. The first occurred during the 1870s, when the Colorado Pinery Trust was created and General Palmer's Denver and Rio Grande Western Railroad was being built into Colorado Springs. During this time, there was great demand for lumber from the Pinery to

Born in Chester County, Pennsylvania, **Charles B. Lamborn** was one of the first to offer his services to the U.S. government when the Civil War broke out. He became a lieutenant colonel while serving under William J. Palmer in the 15th Pennsylvania Volunteer Cavalry. Like Palmer, he worked for the Pennsylvania Railroad after the war. In 1866, he became secretary of the Kansas Pacific Railway Company and worked closely with Palmer, its construction manager. When General Palmer was President of the Colorado Coal and Iron Company, he asked Colonel Lamborn to serve as Vice President. Lamborn was also vice president of the National Land and Improvement Company and the Colorado Springs Company—affiliated organizations involved in the founding of Colorado Springs.[19, 20]

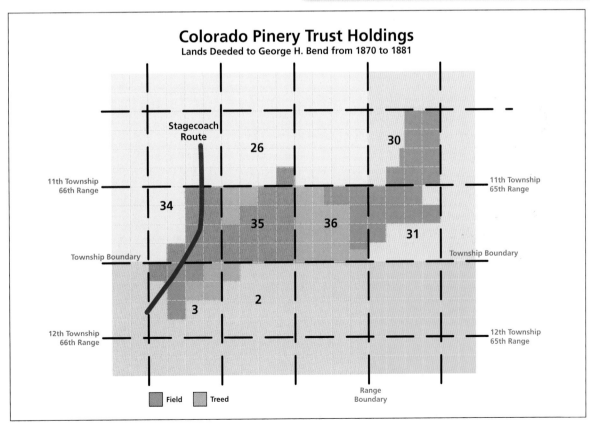

Colorado Pinery Trust Holdings
Lands Deeded to George H. Bend from 1870 to 1881

Shown in purple is the portion of Shamrock Ranch that was under control of the Colorado Pinery Trust from 1870 to 1881. Notice that most of the treed area outside of section 36 (which belonged to the State of Colorado and therefore was not for sale) was purchased by Mr. Bend for the Trust.

Grandma (left) and Grandpa (right) trees on Shamrock Ranch (2007).

build the railroad and the new town. Trees from the Shamrock Ranch land undoubtedly supported this building boom, for there is not an abundance of ponderosa pines with diameters over two feet remaining on the ranch today.

Two ponderosa pines that did survive this initial logging phase can still be seen on Shamrock Ranch. David Wismer refers to them as the Grandma and Grandpa trees. Grandma tree stands 75 feet tall and has a circumference of 11 feet 3 inches—making its diameter nearly 4 feet (43 inches). Grandpa tree has a girth just 2 inches less than Grandma, but stands quite a bit taller, towering approximately 88 feet into the air.

For some reason, the Colorado Pinery Trust decided to preserve some trees on a piece of property called "The Twenty Acres," located about a mile below Shamrock Ranch and west of Bridle Bit Ranch, near Shoup Road. Perhaps because this piece of ground has a spectacular view of Pikes Peak, the trees that populated it were saved from logging. Several huge trees remain to this day. One large tree, which died naturally in 2000, measured 9 feet 9 inches around its girth and was nearly 75 feet high. Counting the rings from a slice of its trunk showed it to be 271 years old—which places the birth of this venerable tree in 1729.

Assuming a linear relationship between trunk diameter and tree age, we can estimate that the Grandma and Grandpa trees on Shamrock Ranch are 313 years old, which means they sprouted in the year 1695—only 75 years after the Pilgrims reached Plymouth Harbor!

During the 1870s, the Colorado Pinery Trust sold hay and leased land for farming to generate income. In some areas, charcoal was made by slowly charring logs underground. It is probable that one or more of these activities took place on Shamrock Ranch.

In 1870, General Palmer hired Samuel C. Stout to manage the Colorado Pinery Trust. He was a bright young man who had served with Palmer during the Civil War. For fifteen years, the Trust operated successfully under Stout's leadership.

In 1873, a U.S. Geological Survey report prepared by A. C. Peale said the following, giving a good indication of the thriving lumber industry operating at Shamrock Ranch at the time: "The Colorado Divide, or Pinery, is a ridge with a mesa-like top extending eastward from the mountains. . . . The Divide is well timbered and is already the seat of an extensive lumber trade. The shrill whistle of the steam sawmills echoes and re-echoes among the hills, while the valleys are all being rapidly settled and capabilities of the land for agriculture pursuits are being demonstrated."[21]

Samuel C. Stout photograph taken in 1863 during the Civil War, when he served in the 15th Pennsylvania Volunteer Cavalry. *Courtesy Judy von Ahlefeldt.*

Lumberjacks used broad axes and crosscut saws to fell the trees, which were then loaded onto wagons. Oxen or mules hauled the timber to sawmills located throughout the Pinery. These early mills were steam powered and used a wood-fired boiler to turn their blades. A constant supply of water was required, so the mills were located on larger, spring-fed creeks.

The 1873 *Annual Report of the Pinery Trust*, which accounted for the timber cut during the first year of operation, cited that the

Mayflower in Plymouth Harbor (1620).

Trust's Sloan Mill had produced 2,862,646 board feet of manufactured lumber; 58,946 railroad ties; 1271 cords of wood; 2407 telegraph poles; and 809,616 shingles. The Weir Mill produced 619,616 board feet of lumber and an unknown amount of other products. In 1880, a *Gazette Telegraph* newspaper article reported that the Divide annually produced 8,479,536 board feet of lumber; 1,250,000 board feet of lathe; 100,000 railroad ties; and 3,500,000 shingles![22]

Before the railroad was built, the finished lumber was hauled to Colorado City or Colorado Springs by a freighter. It was a long, slow-going haul. Sometimes oxen were used; at other times horses. Usually a team of six animals was hitched to the main wagon, then a trailer was attached. The driver would take along a tent and pass a night on the way into the city, since a good haul would cover no more than 15 miles a day.[23]

According to Sam Stout's son, at least sixteen sawmills operated under the auspices of the Colorado Pinery Trust.[24] Most were portable, moving as the timber was cut. No doubt some of them were located on Shamrock Ranch since Black Squirrel Creek was an excellent source of spring water for steam power.

Sam Stout built his own ranch very close to the entrance of Shamrock Ranch—it was located at the current intersection of Highway 83 and Old Northgate Road, not far from "The Twenty Acres," and only a 0.5 mile southwest of Shamrock Ranch's entrance.

On November 15, 1885, the Colorado Pinery Trust became a public corporation under Colorado law and called itself the Colorado Pinery and Land Company. A deed was issued on December 21, 1885 that assigned ownership of 40,730 acres to this new corporation, which is approximately 3,000 acres less than the Colorado Pinery Trust had held

Gutshall's Logging Outfit in the Pinery (1880s). *Courtesy Judy von Ahlefeldt.*

Sam Stout Ranch (circa 1880). Notice the stark lack of trees in the background after a decade of logging. *Courtesy Judy von Ahlefeldt.*

A much finer Sam Stout house (circa 1900). *Courtesy Judy von Ahlefeldt.*

earlier. The charter for the new company was valid for twenty years.

Not all of the Shamrock Ranch land which the Colorado Pinery Trust held was transferred to the Colorado Pinery and Land Company—in fact, very little of it was. On March 12, 1881, George Bend deeded most of this land to Calvin R. Husted, perhaps because so much of the marketable timber had already been cut. With that transaction, the Colorado Pinery Trust era in the history of Shamrock Ranch came to a close.

Samuel Stout in his later years. *Courtesy the Colorado Springs Pioneers Museum.*

THE HUSTED ERA

CALVIN R. HUSTED, one of the original "Fifty-Niners," came to Pikes Peak Country in 1859, the same year that Colorado City, the oldest established city in Pikes Peak Country, was founded.[1,2] Twenty-six-year-old Calvin arrived in Denver in a covered wagon.

Born December 30, 1832, Calvin grew up working in his father's sawmill in Salem, New Jersey. He acquired a limited education from the public schools there. After spending two years at sea, he settled in Illinois for a couple of years and worked at various sawmills there.

When Calvin heard about the Pikes Peak Gold Rush, he developed gold fever, heading out across the plains in the spring of 1859. However, once he reached Colorado he heard discouraging reports about the area from the hundreds of people he met there. His growing apprehension turned to disappointment when he failed to locate any of the elusive yellow metal, so that fall he joined a human stampede leaving Colorado and spent the winter in Eastern Kansas.[3]

Prairie schooners like this replica were used to cross the Great Plains during the 1800s.

Life must not have been any better there, because he returned to the Rockies in May of 1860. This time he didn't search for gold. Instead, he leveraged his experience with sawmills and took charge of a mill owned by the T. J. Bayaud Company.[4] It was located at the Bentley Pinery on Cherry Creek, near Franktown (26 miles north of present-day Shamrock Ranch).

Calvin ran this sawmill for three years, then returned to his home in New Jersey for a winter. But something drew him back the following summer. It might have been the Rocky Mountains, it may have been the chance to run Bayaud's sawmill again, or it may have been a certain young lady named Miss Amanda Talbert.

Along with her mother, Amanda (the older sister of Edward H. Talbert, see previous chapter) operated a boardinghouse for employees of the Bayaud sawmill. Calvin quite

possibly took a liking to her while running the mill. In the fall of 1865, Calvin married Amanda Talbert.[5]

Amanda and Calvin spent that winter in Council Bluffs, Iowa, Amanda's home state. They returned to the Rockies the following spring and began to homestead on the Divide. Three quarter-quarters of section 35 (see map, page 40) were patented to Calvin in 1870 after his required five years of homesteading were up.

In 1873, Amanda's brother Edward Talbert bought Buzzard's Roost and the land around it. He later sold this land to Calvin Husted. By then Calvin had received additional patents for the northeast corner of section 3 and the northwest corner of section 2 (see map, page 40). In 1881, He acquired some Colorado Pinery Trust parcels. After that transaction, Calvin owned nearly all of the Shamrock Ranch land west of section 36. He later acquired all of

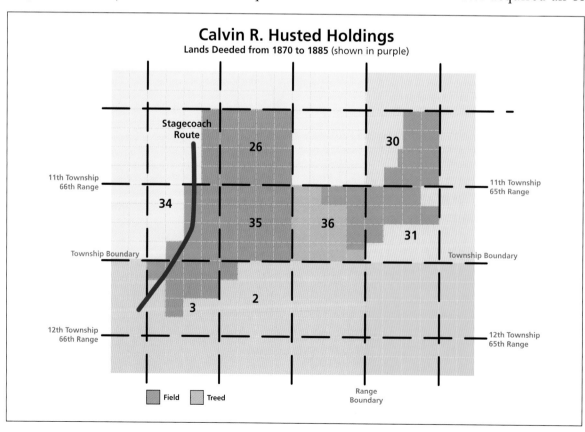

section 26. Calvin raised both cattle and horses on this fine ranch, which he called the Evergreen Ranch.[6] At this time, the Colorado Pinery and Land Company owned only the land to the west of Husted's ranch, which hosted the stagecoach route.

While homesteading, Calvin bought his own sawmill on Monument Creek about 4 miles west of his growing ranch. Then he formed a partnership with Charles Ruter and engaged in the lumber business. After three years, he bought Ruter's interest and continued the business by himself.[7]

His sawmill became one of the chief mills in the Pinery, employing a large force of men. A great deal of lumber was hauled from the Husted Mill to Colorado City and Colorado Springs to help build these cities, even though the mill's position in the Native American-inhabited region was a dangerous one.

The 1878 *Weekly Gazette* article "On the Divide" provides some colorful detail about Calvin (for the complete article, see appendix A). The article describes him as "one of the oldest and leading lumber men" in the county. Besides growing hay, oats, potatoes, and other vegetables, he had 110 head of cattle (including 20 milk cows) and 12 horses. Additionally, Calvin served two terms as an El Paso County Commissioner, starting in 1875.[8]

Calvin R. Husted
(1832–1908).
*Courtesy Ila Randall,
granddaughter of
Calvin Husted.*

During his career, Calvin maintained connections with mining interests in the southwestern part of Colorado. He was also a purchasing agent for the Denver and Rio Grande Western Railroad and furnished much of the cut lumber that was used to build its trackage.[9] At one point, he became a division superintendent of the railroad, which had its headquarters in Alamosa. He likely knew General William Jackson Palmer personally.

Known throughout Pikes Peak Country as "Cal Husted," he was especially influential in the Divide Country.[10] A station on the Denver and Rio Grande Railroad 6 miles south of Monument and about 4 miles west of Shamrock Ranch (near his sawmill) was named after him. The town of Husted grew up around this railroad station and eventually became a bustling center for ranchers and lumbermen—boasting a hotel, post office, general store, and saloon.

A road that ran from the town to Buzzard's Roost and the stagecoach stop near Husted's ranch was called the Husted Wagon Road. Later, when the United States Air Force Academy came to Colorado Springs, the Husted Wagon Road was paved and renamed North Gate Road, since it leads into the north entrance of the Academy. Today it is known as Old Northgate Road.

Calvin's wife, Amanda Husted, first came to Colorado in 1860 with her parents in a prairie schooner pulled by oxen. They traveled from eastern Iowa as part of a lengthy wagon train of pioneers. Though Colorado City had been founded only a year earlier, the family did not speak of it or Denver much as they journeyed westward. "It was just Pikes Peak," Amanda remembered in a 1930 *Colorado Springs Sunday Gazette and Telegraph* article. "We were on our way to Pikes Peak." They arrived at the foot of Pikes Peak on June 13, 1860.[11]

Amanda's father, Joseph Talbert, was evidently a gold seeker, for his destination was Tarryall—a mining camp 37 miles west of present-day Shamrock Ranch. Tarryall got its name from a group of Fifty-Niners who, after discovering placer gold in a nearby creek in 1859, identified it as "a place to tarry awhile." After all, they were finding lots of gold nuggets there—many the size of peas. Gold seekers arriving later were angered by the greedy possessiveness of this original group and nicknamed the area Graball. These late arrivers moved on to settle in Fairplay—named to suggest a more reasonable place than Tarryall.[12]

On the way to Tarryall, Talbert made a stop near Colorado City so that Amanda and her two brothers, Edward and Joseph, could see the mineral springs there. The place they visited is now Manitou Springs. When Amanda and her family visited, there were no houses near the springs. In fact, at the time there were only about 150 buildings in nearby Colorado City. Most were log houses with dirt floors and stone fireplaces—typical of small Colorado towns in those days.[13]

When the family eventually arrived at their destination, they stayed in a cabin near Tarryall Creek. Amanda greatly enjoyed life in the camp and found it very interesting. She was a young woman then (age fifteen), without any cares, and had never experienced anything quite like mining camp life before—she was especially impressed when miners took nuggets as large as the end of her finger from the stream!

Then tragedy struck. Only a few weeks after arriving in the camp, Mr. Talbert fell ill with pneumonia and died, leaving his young wife, Joanna Talbert, and their children far from home in a camp composed largely of men.

According to Amanda, the miners were very good to them, aiding Joanna in every way possible at the funeral and afterwards. The family returned to Iowa in September, finding passage across the plains with an ox team wagon train.[14]

On May 4, 1863, Joanna and her family started back for Colorado—her sons were dreaming of the wealth they might gain through mining. The family arrived in Denver on July 4.

Since Amanda already knew the ways of the West, she had an advantage over most other women in the wagon train, who were on their first trip west. She had learned to weigh gold dust to pay for things, and had become so proficient at it that she could weigh out twenty-five cents worth of the precious dust.

When they reached the South Park Basin (where Tarryall and Fairplay are located), they stayed with Joanna's brother, Robert Stubbs, who owned a hotel there. Amanda suddenly had a cousin about her own age with whom she could share her adventures—some of which were quite daring.

One such adventure involved two brothers, 28-year-old Peter Shook and 25-year-old Denton Shook, who traveled from Iowa with the Talbert family, driving a herd of 50 cattle all the way to Tarryall. One day, a large party of Plains Indians approached the Shook's camp, which they had set up near the hotel where Amanda and her family were staying. The chief spied a ham hanging in plain view and helped himself to it. Denton saw him take it and seized an ax to threaten the bold chief. In response, the chief's warriors began to shoot all the pigs, chickens, and other livestock in sight with their arrows and guns.

Amanda and her cousin heard the commotion and stuck their heads out of an open window on the upper floor of the hotel to see what happening. The Native Americans immediately shot arrows around the window. They could have shot the two young ladies, of course, but only wanted to scare them—which they succeeded in doing only mildly, as Amanda recalled later.

Since almost all the men were working at the Tarryall camp 4 miles away, Robert sent a boy for help and urged the Shook brothers to take refuge inside his hotel. Denton ran upstairs and covered himself with bedding so that the Native Americans wouldn't find him. Peter sat down near him with a revolver in hand.

The women inside the hotel hurriedly locked the doors, but the warriors came through the windows to search for Denton. They told the women they were going to take him outside and kill him, but would not harm anyone else. When they went upstairs, they mistook Peter for Denton. Seizing him, they dragged him downstairs. Appallingly, Denton remained in hiding and never emerged from the bedding piled on him until the incident was over.

When the Native Americans came down the stairs with Peter, Robert told the women to grab onto the captured young man. Amanda joined the others in pulling on him, but the warriors got him out the door anyway. Peter was able to break away and run back inside the hotel. The women all clustered around him once again, holding him tightly. One of the Native Americans put a pistol to Joanna's breast and told her he would shoot if she didn't let go. But Amanda's brave mother refused to do so. What happened next is best described in Amanda's own words:

We all held on and they could not get Peter Shook thru the door. At length they got very mad. They are ugly-looking creatures when they are mad. I never want to see one again. They took to beating the man we held to on the head with their bows, reaching over our heads to strike him, and at length he swooned and fell in our midst.

We still kept close around him and succeeded in shoving him over on the floor under a bed. The Indians were becoming very mad. I don't know what might have happened if at that time about twenty-five miners from the camp had not been seen approaching. They were all armed, and the Indians scattered before them.

Some of them told my uncle that if he had shot one of the Indians the others would have run. I do not think so. I believe that had he done so we would all have been murdered. Before leaving they stole almost everything in the house.[15]

Amanda (Talbert) Husted. *Courtesy Ila Randall, granddaughter of Calvin Husted.*

This experience frightened the Shook brothers so badly they returned to Iowa, disposing of their cattle in Colorado City. The miners named a stream "Shooks Run" after them.

Later on, Joanna and her family returned to Denver, where she obtained employment on a ranch. This work undoubtedly prepared her and Amanda to operate the boarding house near Bayaud's sawmill.

Calvin and Amanda's son Walter was born on the Husted's Evergreen Ranch in 1871—the year that Colorado Springs was founded.[16] The Husted's already had four other children—three daughters and a son

Walter E. Husted

named Bert, who worked for the Denver and Rio Grande Western Railroad.[17]

In March of 1949, Walter was interviewed by the *Gazette Telegraph* and related the following experience, which his parents had shared with him:

The plains Indians raided homes in the Black Forest area and even at the edge of Colorado City for stock. One day, I think it was in 1864, a man whose name I do not recall rode to the sawmill saying that the Indians had a group of white settlers surrounded on Sand creek, to the east. He had got away and had ridden in for help. No time was wasted. The men of the region began to collect at the Buzzard ranch, three and one-half miles east of where Husted station now is. The Buzzard ranch was then a stagecoach station.

When the party was ready to ride to the relief of the surrounded men it was found that there were two more men than horses. So lots were drawn to see who would be left behind. My Uncle Talbert and a man named Young were the unfortunate ones who were to stay behind. It was while they were walking back to the sawmill that Indians surprised them and killed them. My mother was at the sawmill at the time her brother was killed.

An unknown boy who was herding cattle at the time came to the top of a hill on foot and witnessed these murders. He had no horse with him because the men in the relief party had taken all the available steeds on their rescue mission. Assuming that the Native Americans had seen him on the hilltop, this brave boy turned to some imaginary followers behind him and shouted, while waving his arms frantically, "Here they are—the Indians. Let's get 'em. Follow me!"

Continuing to wave to these nonexistent followers, he ran unarmed down the hill right at the mounted Native Americans. Amazingly, his daring and clever scheme worked—the Native Americans fled, sparing all the women at the sawmill (including Amanda Talbert).[18]

There was no possibility of taking the bodies of Joseph Talbert and his murdered companion to Colorado City to be buried, or even going there for a coffin, so the men at the mill sawed up some boards and made crude coffins. Both corpses were buried in a single grave. Neither Amanda nor her mother were allowed to go to the grave after the funeral for fear of the Naïve Americans.[19]

Amanda's 1930 account of this incident identifies the other murdered man as Edward Davis, rather than "a man named Young" per Walter's 1949 statement. Also, she recounts that neither man had a gun and speculates that Hank Jackson, a white outlaw who became a renegade Native American leader, was involved. Talbert and Davis were each shot several times and neither was scalped. Jackson was later hanged, wearing Native American dress.

While Cal Husted was a county commissioner, he was actively involved in the early development of both Colorado Springs and El Paso County. In 1872, an election was held to determine the county seat. Calvin was in favor of Colorado Springs, but Colorado City won out—maintaining its existing status as the county seat.

But the very next fall, a great deal of excitement about moving the county seat arose once again. Calvin worked proactively with ranchers and lumbermen on the Divide to promote Colorado Springs. When voters chose Colorado Springs that year, he was given credit for bringing about the change, which remains in effect to this day.[20]

In 1885, Calvin joined forces with W. H. Sterling. They formed a company called the Husted Sterling Live Stock Company, deeding Calvin's land (shown in purple on the map on page 56) to each other and their company. They also bought other parcels that year, including 771 acres located less than 2 miles north of Evergreen Ranch. Eventually their ranch grew to more than 2,500 acres. The map below shows the known extent of this company's land holdings in the Divide Country.

In addition to continuing to log timber, Husted and Sterling raised livestock on the Evergreen Ranch. They considered the land they purchased an investment in the property itself as well, speculating that its value would increase.

They were not to be disappointed. In 1890, Robert "Crazy Bob" Womack discovered gold in a cow pasture along a small stream that drained the southwestern slope of Pikes Peak. The stream was Cripple Creek (supposedly so named when a calf slipped in it and broke its leg).[21] At its lofty elevation of 9,494 feet—just below the timberline—Cripple Creek Valley had been considered no more important than a cattle pasture for many years. Prospectors avoided the area after the 1884 Mount Pisgah hoax—a mini gold rush that had resulted from salting (adding gold to worthless rock)

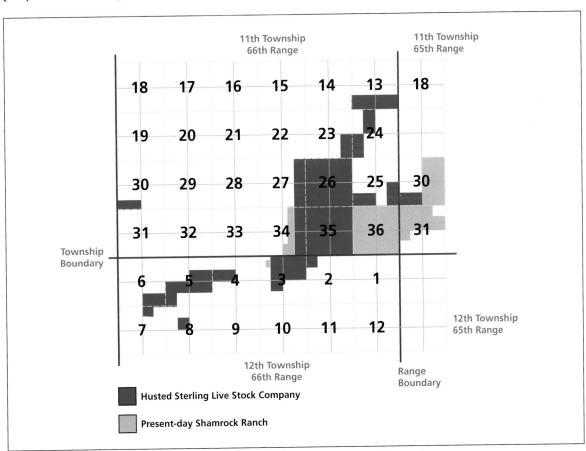

Known land holdings of the Husted Sterling Live Stock Company (shown in dark green).

during a notorious mining swindle by "Chicken Bill" of Leadville.

Bob Womack's discovery sparked "the last great gold rush" in Colorado.[22, 23] Thousands of miners, prospectors, gamblers, and fortune seekers flocked to the region. They set up tents, cabins, and lean-tos along the main street of the town of Cripple Creek in anticipation of becoming millionaires.

Robert "Crazy Bob" Womack[24] (circa 1890)

Before long, Winfield Scott Stratton (a friend of Bob's) discovered the Independence Lode, one of the richest gold strikes ever located on earth. He became the town's first millionaire in 1894.[25] Cripple Creek Valley created twenty-seven more millionaires in the next few years.

In 1890, less than 500 hundred people were living in Cripple Creek. But by 1893, there were 10,000 residents and people were streaming in at the rate of 500 per month.[26] According to the *Encyclopedia Britannica,* "Before the spring of 1892, the hills swarmed with prospectors. Yellow-pine shelters, saloons, dance halls and gaming houses sprang up. Violence and primitive emotions ruled. The gold output increased each year until 1900 when the peak was reached at $18,199,736."

Winfield Scott Stratton (1848–1902)

Of course, all this growth provided an enormous, profitable market for Husted's lumber enterprise.

The Colorado Silver Boom contributed significantly, though indirectly, to this rush of prospectors to the Pikes Peak area. In 1879, a silver lode worth $82 million was discovered in Leadville. A year earlier, responding to pressure from powerful interests to address the overproduction of silver from western mines, the U.S. Congress had passed the Bland-Allison Act authorizing coinage of silver, which resulted in large-scale purchases of it by the US government.[27] Once considered too unprofitable to mine, the shiny metal quickly became highly sought. The Silver Boom stretched on through the 1880s, resulting in a stunning increase in both the population and wealth of Colorado, especially in the mountain valleys. New prospectors flocked to many of the same mountain gullies that had previously been the site of the 1859 Gold Rush.

Government purchases of silver nearly doubled with the 1890 Sherman Silver Purchase Act, which required the government to purchase an additional 4.5 million ounces of silver bullion every month. As the boom extended into the early 1890s, Georgetown eclipsed nearby Golden and temporarily became the third most populous city in Colorado. The resulting opulence was most lavish in Leadville itself, where local citizens briefly entertained the notion of moving the state capital there from Denver.

The Sherman Act had a disastrous flaw. It required the U.S. Treasury to buy the silver with notes that could be redeemed for either silver or gold. Consequently, the law backfired as people (mostly investors) turned in their silver Treasury notes for gold dollars, using up the Government's gold reserves. The result was the Panic of 1893—at the time, the worst economic crisis to have ever hit the nation.[28]

As the Panic of 1893 set in, President Grover Cleveland oversaw the repeal of the Sherman Silver Purchase Act to prevent total depletion of the country's gold reserves.[29] When the Sherman Act was repealed, the price of silver immediately crashed. Gold prices, however, remained high—for gold was desperately needed to replenish federal reserves. As a result, the Colorado Silver Boom came to a cataclysmic end and silver miners from towns like Leadville, Aspen, Georgetown, and Idaho Springs flocked to the new Cripple Creek district gold mines to find work.

President
Grover Cleveland
(1837–1908)

By 1900, Cripple Creek and its sister city, Victor, had grown to be substantial communities. Their combined population topped 50,000. In contrast, the silver mining camps were ghost towns. Many of Colorado's silver mines closed and a large number never re-opened, and a significant number of narrow gauge railroads, which had been built to service the silver mines, went out

A Midland Railroad train (circa 1890s).[30]

of business. Even the Denver and Rio Grande Western Railroad stopped its ambitious plan, then under way, to convert from narrow gauge to standard gauge.

Calvin Husted's financial prospects rocketed as miners flooded the Pikes Peak area. Anticipating the influx of gold seekers and new residents that would inevitably result, he built a new lumber yard in Colorado City and profited handsomely from his foresight. In 1894, his was only one of two lumber companies located in Colorado City—which was known by then as the "Westside" of Colorado Springs. The Westside eventually became home to five gold ore reduction mills, and was at the very heart of the Cripple Creek Gold Rush frenzy.[31]

Between 1894 and 1901, three railroad lines began service to Cripple Creek from the Colorado Springs area—the Gold Belt Line, the Midland Terminal Railroad, and the Colorado Springs and Cripple Creek District Railway. Each carried passengers as well as gold ore. Once again, Calvin had a new, huge market for his lumber—supplying the railroad ties!

These new railroad lines and the Cripple Creek Gold Rush fueled the second phase of lumbering in the Divide Country. Calvin Husted and the Husted Sterling Live Stock Company were at the center of it.

One of Colorado's few remaining narrow-gauge steam locomotives (circa 2008).

Sometime prior to 1878, Calvin built a house on present-day Shamrock Ranch, not far to the northeast of Buzzard's Roost. This fine home, shown below, is the first residence known to have been constructed on Shamrock Ranch land. Because of its elaborate trim and the fact that its address was "Husted," it is possible—perhaps even probable—that Calvin and Amanda lived in it. Note also the smaller cement block house and shed behind the main house. Further support for this theory is found in the September 1878 *Weekly Gazette* article "On the Divide" (for the complete article, see appendix A), which says "Leaving the mill we returned to Mr. Husted's residence, which we have not yet described. It is situated on the old Denver and Santa Fe stage road, some sixteen miles north of Colorado Springs, and includes 700 acres of land, 500 of which are enclosed. The house is one of the finest on the divide and is furnished in a most comfortable manner." (Note: The "Denver and Santa Fe stage road" mentioned here ran along the Cherokee Trail next to present-day Shamrock Ranch.[32])

Walter E. Husted "was born on the old Husted homestead, about five miles east of Husted station" in 1871.[33] This birthplace could very well have been the house shown below.

Calvin eventually established a lumber yard in Cotopaxi (a town south of Pueblo) and another in Colorado Springs on Bijou Street between Tejon and Nevada.[34] Then, on September 1, 1891, he bought a beautiful Victorian Gothic mansion[35] at 3001 West Kiowa Street in Colorado City, so he could be closer to his businesses and the center of Cripple Creek Gold Rush activity. This residence, which cost $6,000 when it was built in 1884, was one of the finest houses to be found in the former county seat of El Paso County. Still standing today (shown on the next page), it is a testament to the prosperity Calvin enjoyed in 1891.

The first residence known to have been built on Shamrock Ranch (constructed by Calvin R. Husted) (circa the late 1800s). *Courtesy Allen Steppler and Susan (Steppler) Koch—hereafter referred to as the Steppler family.*

Husted House in Old Colorado City (2005).

Husted House parlor (2005).

Rear of Husted House (2005).

WILLIAM CLARK BROWN was the first ranch manager known for certain to have worked and lived on the Evergreen Ranch. In 1888, William and his wife, Adaline Straight, packed up their belongings in Bonaparte, Iowa (including their farm equipment), loaded everything onto a train, and came with their four children to Husted Station. From there they went to the Table Rock community (about 6 miles north by northeast of Husted station) and rented the Hodgen place (John Hodgen was the original homesteader, and Hodgen Road, the road that makes up the northernmost boundary of Shamrock Ranch today, is named after him). Two other Browns were living in the Divide Country at the time (one was also named William), but none were related.

William Clark Brown.
Courtesy the Steppler family.

Six years later, in 1894, William obtained employment with the Husted Sterling Live Stock Company and moved his family into the house shown on page 64. This was only 3 years after Calvin and his family moved to Colorado City to occupy their mansion there. Evidently, he wanted William to take over the Evergreen Ranch.

The next year, 1895, Adaline gave birth to Beulah Rae, the first person known for certain to have been born on the ranch. William and Adaline Brown's other

Adaline (Straight) Brown at age 18 (circa 1867).
Courtesy the Steppler family.

four children, Martha Jane (who went by Jennie), Sarah Fannie, Allie, and William Lester (who went by Billie), were born in Iowa.

The land that William managed for the Husted Sterling Live Stock Company was used for harvesting both lumber and livestock. After felling trees, the timber workers would transport them to Husted's sawmill by wagon. The finished lumber was then shipped by rail to Calvin's lumberyards in Colorado Springs, Colorado City, and Cotopaxi.

According to Allen Steppler, a great-grandson of William, Calvin employed a number of tie hacks—men who hand-cut railroad ties. These men lived temporarily on Calvin's Evergreen Ranch in "dugouts,"

Beulah Rae Brown.
Courtesy the Steppler family.

i.e., shallow caves cut into dirt banks. Before the Browns moved to the Evergreen Ranch, they often sent their daughter Jennie, who was a teenager at the time, to sell produce such as eggs, milk, and cream to the tie hacks and their families. Jennie reported that these families had beautiful tapestries hanging inside their dugouts to cover up the dirt walls. They also had tapestries on the floor. A small wooden dresser was used to store valuables and other items. Apparently, the dugouts weren't very large, but they were big enough for a small family.

IT SEEMED LIKE nothing could go wrong for Calvin Husted. He was the most successful lumberman in the State of Colorado, owned thousands of acres in the Divide Country, had a fortune estimated between $65,000 and

$75,000, and resided in a lavish mansion in Colorado City.[36]

But things did go wrong for him.

First his fortune began to dwindle through unwise speculation. Then he began to drink heavily. In 1898, he deeded his mansion to his wife. Finally, she left him, relocating to Salt Lake City. Calvin was only in his early sixties. By February 1904, things had gotten so desperate he sold his ranch in the Divide Country to Benjamin C. Allen.

And things got worse from there.

He lost everything. His wife and children would have nothing to do with him. His health deteriorated. He spent the last few years of his life as a laborer in the county poor farm—the same institution over which he had presided for four years as a County Commissioner while associating with other notable El Paso County history makers.[37]

He died at that poor farm on October 5, 1908, estranged from his wife and apart from his children. Sadly, he had squandered the bounty of his life's harvest. A February 19, 1956 *Colorado Springs Gazette Telegraph* article said the following about Calvin R. Husted: "In the early days he operated a sawmill in the Black Forest. Many Colorado Springs buildings were constructed from the lumber hauled from the Husted sawmill, hauled with oxen from the Black Forest. He was a generous man. He'd give anyone a grubstake. He fed and clothed passing tramps. And he died in a Colorado Springs poorhouse."

And so, a chapter of Shamrock Ranch's history closed on a tragic note as another one opened.

The Benjamin C. Allen Era

Benjamin Curtis Allen
(1903)

Benjamin Curtis Allen was exceptionally handsome, urbane and sophisticated. He was born in 1869 to Elizabeth J. Curtis and George Nelson Allen. His father was part owner of an earthenware store on Market Street that sold china and pottery imported from England, Europe and the Orient. A 1923 *New York Times* article about Benjamin said he was "a member of an old and wealthy family of Philadelphia." Not much is known about his youth, but he evidently had significant social status since he married a wealthy woman from one of Philadelphia's most prominent families at the age of twenty-five.

Benjamin Allen wedded Maria (mə-rī-ə) Wharton McKean (mə-kān) on June 2, 1894. Born on April 18, 1871, Maria was the great-great-granddaughter of Thomas McKean—an influential patriot and signer of the Declaration of Independence. It is also worthwhile to note Maria's legacy on her mother's side of the family. Elizabeth Wharton, mother of Maria, was the daughter of George Mifflin Wharton, a distinguished member of the Philadelphia Bar and a District Attorney of the United States serving under President James Buchanan.

The following article[1] was written in the Philadelphia *Public Press* upon the death of George Mifflin Wharton:

It is with profound regret that we record the death, on the 5th inst., of George Mifflin Wharton, Esq., one of our ablest lawyers and most distinguished citizens. In the decease of this gentleman the Philadelphia bar has lost one of its acknowledged leaders and the community one of its best and most useful members. . . .

As a lawyer he stood deservedly in the front ranks of the profession . . . his loss will be deeply deplored by his professional brethren, who looked up to him as a model of excellence.

Maria Wharton McKean
(circa 1918)

He took a deep interest in public schools, and was for many years one of the most active and useful members of the Board of Directors, and for some time was President of the Board on Control.

After the disruption of the old-time Whig party, his judgment upon national issues induced him to attach himself to the Democratic party, to which he adhered to the time of his death.

He served his fellow-citizens for several years as a member of the Select Council and President of that body, and held the post of District Attorney of the United States for this district during a part of the administration of Mr. Buchanan.

In private life Mr. Wharton was distinguished by sterling integrity and an amiability which endeared him to all who knew him. He was a man of eminent virtue, and what is still better, a devout and unostentatious Christian. . . . It is impossible in this notice to do justice to the character and services of Mr. Wharton. They require a larger space than we are able to give on this occasion, but we cannot let it pass without paying this faint and very imperfect tribute to his memory.

On June 04, 1835 George married Maria Markoe. Maria was born December 18, 1812 in Philadelphia. The descendant of yet another distinguished Philadelphia

family, the Markoes. The couple had eight children.

A LAWYER BY EDUCATION, Thomas McKean participated in the Stamp Act Congress of 1765, representing Delaware. At this congress he proposed a voting procedure that set the precedent for state equality in voting used today by the United States Senate. He also became the effective leader of American independence in Delaware and was a key voice in persuad-ing others to vote for the Declaration of Independence.[2]

BRITISH STAMP.

Prior to commanding the Fourth Battalion of the Pennsylvania Associators, a militia unit created by Benjamin Franklin that was part of Washington's defense of New York City, McKean was one of Delaware's delegates to the First Continental Congress. After the fighting, he returned to the Continental Congress and helped draft the Articles of Confederation.[3]

In 1781, McKean served as president of the United States congress, a single legislative body established under the Articles of Confederation and the highest political office in the United States at the time. While in this position, he was the first person to whom the title "President of the United States" was applied in an official document. However, this was not an executive position in any way comparable to the Presidency as configured in the later U.S. Constitution in 1787. During his term, a British army commanded by General Lord Cornwallis surrendered at Yorktown Battlefield, effectively ending the Revolutionary War.[4]

When he learned that he had been elected to a special convention tasked with drafting a new state constitution for Delaware, McKean made the long ride from Philadelphia to Dover in a single day. Upon his arrival, he took a room at an inn and spent the night writing his proposal for the constitution. It was adopted on September 20, 1776 and was the first state constitution to be produced after the Declaration of Independence. After being elected to Delaware's first House of Assembly, he served briefly as the president of Delaware (in the autumn of 1777).[5]

(Note: The Delaware State Constitution of 1776 that McKean authored called the chief executive a "president" rather than a "governor" because he was to preside rather than govern.[6])

Next, McKean had a long tenure as Chief Justice of Pennsylvania, his birth state. In this important role, he played a large part in developing Pennsylvania's rules of justice. According to biographer John Coleman, "Only the historiographical difficulty of reviewing court records and other scattered documents prevents recognition that McKean, rather than John Marshall, did more than anyone else to establish an independent judiciary in the United States."[7]

As Pennsylvania Chief Justice, McKean followed the practice of striking down legislation he deemed unconstitutional. Ten years later, the United States Supreme Court established this concept as the doctrine of judicial review.[8]

Thomas McKean was also a member of the Pennsylvania convention that ratified the Constitution of the United States. After being elected Governor of Pennsylvania, he served for three terms. John Adams described him as "one of the three men in the Continental Congress who appeared to me to see more clearly to the end of the business than any others in the body."[9]

During his impressive political career, Thomas McKean accumulated considerable wealth through investments in U.S. bonds, foreign shipping (including trade with China) and real estate.[10] He retired to Philadelphia and spent the remainder of his life writing, discussing political affairs, and enjoying his wealth. In his last will and testament, he left his posterity over ten thousand acres of land, a mansion, a smaller house, nine lots, two plantations, and more than $46,000.[11]

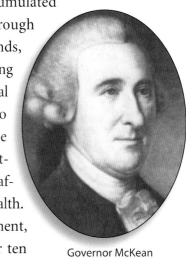

Governor McKean
(1733–1817)

To commemorate Thomas McKean's life and his contributions to Pennsylvania, McKean County, Pennsylvania is named after him, as is McKean Street in Philadelphia, which was originally called McKean Parkway.[12]

LIKE MARIA Wharton McKean's forebears, Benjamin C. Allen's ancestors can be traced back to the American Revolution. An early ancestor, Samuel Allen, was a carpenter by trade who fought in the Continental Army of the United States. Unfortunately, exposure to cold and fatigue brought on by the war ended his life in 1777. His son George Allan, born in January 1775, married Mary Ridg on March 20, 1794, and had ten children with her, including William B. (Benjamin Allan's grandfather). George Allen had a leather shop at Second and Vine in Philadelphia during the first term of George Washington's presidency. Later, he moved his leather business to Burlington, New

Jersey, where he lost everything due to inflation, an unscrupulous customer, and failed credit caused by the War of 1812. Following the Treaty of Ghent, which ended the war, George Allen worked on various jobs.

He served as postmaster of the City of Burlington for a time, then later became a preacher at the Burlington Baptist Church, where he served without a fixed salary for more than six years. Next, he worked as a lockmaster at the Delaware and Raritan Canal (which had been built in the 1830s to connect the Delaware and Raritan Rivers) for $50 a month. Then, in the spring of 1838, he invested with his son-in-law, Peter Simonson, in a mulberry tree business that resulted in great losses. His wife Mary and another son-in-law named Samuel Rogers died of cholera sometime after 1849 on their farm in Mount Holly, New Jersey.

Shortly before he died in 1956, George Allen wrote the following closing words to his autobiography:

It becomes my solemn duty to record that six of my children are numbered among the dead, together with their beloved mother and several grandchildren. Oh, that I could pray from the heart in the words of the Psalmist David: 'Lord, make me to know mine end, and the measure of my days, what it is; that I may know how frail I am. Behold, thou hast made my day as an handbreadth; and mine age is as nothing before thee: verily every man at his best state is altogether vanity.' (Psalm 39:4-5)

Born January 18, 1798, William B. Allen—Benjamin Allen's grandfather—was twice elected Mayor of Burlington, New Jersey. A portrait of him hangs in the Free Library of that city. He married Mary Ellis, daughter of Charles Ellis, and together they produced eleven children, including George Nelson Allen. William B. Allen died in 1878.

George Nelson Allen moved to Philadelphia as a young man, where he managed and was part owner of his father-in-law's earthenware store until he died. During the latter part of the nineteenth century, trade with China for vitreous porcelain wares (i.e., china dishes, vases, and ornaments) was at its peak in the United States, and Philadelphia was one of its three principal East Coast ports of entry. Because George's social status was such that it led to Benjamin Allen's marriage to Maria Wharton McKean, one may conclude that his earthenware import business was profitable.

While this is not a complete genealogy of the Allen family, it does contrast the paths of the McKean and Allen families commencing with the Revolutionary War.

The contrast in wealth between the families is readily apparent. However, let it be remembered that wealth by itself is no measure of character—in fact, wealth may become a stumbling block to character! The legacy of George Allen is one of struggle, perseverance, integrity, Christian service, and eventual personal triumph. With no legacy of material wealth, George's posterity undoubtedly had to work harder and depend more on their own skills for sustenance than the McKean posterity—but their characters may have been just as notable in terms of the bounty of their lives' spiritual harvests. Character is developed only through humility, service and self-discipline—it is not inherited.

Much has been written about the ancestors of Maria Wharton McKean, many of whom lived opulent lifestyles from inherited wealth—stemming largely from Thomas McKean. During his time and throughout the 1800s, wealth in America was not depleted by income and death taxes, so many families, such as the McKean family, were able to amass great fortunes and pass them on from generation to generation.

But all this changed in America during the early 1900s. First, the Sixteenth Amendment of the United States Constitution, ratified in 1913, gave the U.S. Congress broad power to tax incomes. Then, in 1916, Congress enacted the federal estate or death tax that remains in force today at much higher rates than when first enacted (originally the estate tax had a maximum rate of 10 percent for estates worth more than $5 million[13]).

Benjamin and Maria Allen were the first generation of the McKean posterity to encounter these significant tax changes. Their effects have made it much more difficult to pass on legacies of material wealth.

Benjamin and Maria Allen made their home in Germantown—the same community where William Jackson Palmer had been raised. By then, the borough of Germantown had been consolidated into the City and County of Philadelphia through the 1854 Act of Consolidation, so Germantown was a neighborhood in Northwest Philadelphia.

The Benjamin C. Allen Family (1903). From left to right the children are McKean, George, Curtis, Hope, and Wharton. *Courtesy Chapel of Our Saviour.*

Colorado Springs
A Tuberculosis Treatment Mecca

Because of the pioneering work of Dr. Gerald Webb and others, such as Dr. Edwin Solly, Colorado Springs became a mecca of tuberculosis treatment during the late 1800s. A highly infectious disease, tuberculosis was the leading cause of death in the United States during the nineteenth and early twentieth centuries. Colorado Springs was attractive as a treatment locale because of its altitude, dry climate, and clean air. The city became known as the "City of Sunshine." The real source of its treatment success was altitude—since tuberculosis bacteria require oxygen, they don't grow as well when altitude reduces the air's oxygen content.

One of sixteen tuberculosis sanatoriums in the Pikes Peak region, Cragmoor Sanatorium became the city's premier tuberculosis treatment facility. Today, the University of Colorado at Colorado Springs is located where it once stood. In 1890, the Glockner Tuberculosis Sanatorium opened and eventually became Penrose Hospital.

Another prominent treatment facility, and one of the largest, was the Modern Woodmen Tuberculosis Sanatorium, shown here, which provided free treatment for more than twelve thousand of its members and claimed a remarkable 60 percent recovery rate.[14] It was located on the city's northwest side (Woodmen Valley). Today Woodmen Road in Colorado Springs is named for it.

The only recognized treatment of the time included isolated living conditions to arrest the spread of the contagious disease, rest, wholesome food (including six raw eggs and ten glasses of milk per day), pure air, exercise, and the right mental attitude.

Modern Woodmen Tuberculosis Sanatorium (circa 1915). *Courtesy Modern Woodmen of America Archives.*

At the Modern Woodmen Tuberculosis Sanatorium, patients lived in individual octagonal-shaped cottages (shown here) that were open at the top to ensure a constant supply of fresh air. Attended by nurses, they spent the days sitting outside, no matter how cold the weather. Not all TB sufferers were treated in sanatoriums, but there is no doubt that the Pikes Peak Region's reputation as a place for curative treatment of tuberculosis drew many new residents.

Drugs to treat tuberculosis were finally developed in the late 1940s. So when tuberculosis dropped from being the number one killer in America to the eighth, the Woodmen facility closed—after nearly forty years of benevolent service.

Modern Woodmen Tuberculosis Sanatorium (circa 1915). *Courtesy Modern Woodmen of America Archives.*

While living in Germantown, the Allen's bore three children—identical twin boys named Wharton and Curtis (they were given the middle names of their parents), and a daughter named Hope. The twins were born April 2, 1895 and Hope's birthday was February 13, 1898.

Unfortunately, Benjamin contracted tuberculosis while living in Germantown. About the time of Hope's birth, he learned of a British doctor in Colorado Springs named Gerald Webb who had successfully treated the disease. Thanks to Dr. Webb, Benjamin and his family were soon to discover Pikes Peak Country.

Hoping for improved health from Dr. Webb's care, Benjamin and his young family moved to Colorado Springs in the latter part of 1898—along with many other wealthy Eastern families and British immigrants who also suffered from tuberculosis. As it turned out, Benjamin had poor health the remainder of his life, most likely from the effects of tuberculosis. His daughter Hope also suffered from tuberculosis when she was a young girl.

Upon their arrival in Colorado Springs, the Allen family moved into a large shingle house on the corner of Uintah Street and Cascade Avenue in the city's downtown. Mari gave birth to two more children there. Thomas McKean Allen, named after Maria's father, great-grandfather, and great-great-grandfather, was born November 12, 1900. He went by his middle name—McKean. George Nelson Allen, born July 29, 1902, was named after Benjamin's father.

Although Maria Allen's family had practiced the Quaker religion in Philadelphia, she attended Colorado Spring's Grace Episcopal Church with her husband (who was an Episcopalian). All their children were raised as Episcopalians, and their sons were sent to a private high school in Southborough, Massachusetts, that is affiliated with the Episcopal Church. Called St. Mark's School, it is still one of America's leading college-preparatory schools today. Wharton graduated with the class of 1913, but for some unknown reason Curtis did not graduate until a year later. McKean finished in 1918 and George was part of the class of 1919. During these years, St. Mark's was a school for boys only. Today it is coeducational and enrolls 359 students.

Maria and Benjamin Allen quickly became socialites in Colorado Springs. In January of 1901, they gave an extravagant colonial costume party dubbed *Bal Poudre* (Powder Ball). Eminent guests of the city wore powdered hair, knee breeches, frocked coats, and lace shirtwaists to this fancy affair.

One of their guests was George Bonbright, a member of the exclusive El Paso Club—the first private town club west of Chicago. To reach the ball, Bonbright drove up Cascade Avenue in his Stanley Steamer—one of the first horseless carriages in Pikes Peak Country and the first Stanley Steamer in Colorado Springs.[15]

George Bonbright's Stanley Steamer (circa 1901). *Courtesy the El Paso Club.*

Benjamin Allen was also a member of the prestigious El Paso Club—Records show him as a resident member in the years 1906, 1910, 1916, and 1925. The fact that he was a member of this club speaks of his wealth, which largely came from Maria's family. Between 1890 and 1900, the golden era of nearby gold mining community Cripple Creek, the El Paso Club was the preferred meeting place of newly made millionaires who spent money lavishly and entertained in a manner similar to that of London's high society. Social functions like the gala Benjamin and Maria hosted were one of the factors that contributed to Colorado Springs' nickname of "Little London."

Despite the conservative rules of the El Paso Club then (no gambling, no games played on Sunday, no gratuities, ladies admitted only on Thursdays, etc.), Benjamin became notorious for "the great billiard ball fight in 1910 between Ben Allen and Sam Shober."[16] It is interesting to note that Dr. Gerald Webb, Benjamin's tuberculosis doctor, was a member of the El Paso Club in 1901.[17]

Allen also joined the exclusive Cheyenne Mountain Country Club, which featured golf and lawn tennis among other sports and events. He is in the second row, third from the right in the picture below. The event that led to this photograph was the 1913 New Year's Day stag luncheon.[18] Notice the trendy raccoon coats that were popular that year!

Benjamin was active as an officer of this elite country club, which boasted "The Griz-

1913 New Year's Day Stag Luncheon at the Cheyenne Mountain Country Club. *Courtesy the Cheyenne Mountain Country Club.*

zlies" as its mascot. A letter typed on New Year's eve 1912 on his personal stationery that summarizes club officers' comments on rag dancing at annual balls is shown here.[19] Rag dancing is dancing to ragtime music—the first true American genre of music, which predates jazz and was popular between 1899 and 1918.

Rag dancing was a type of dancing that introduced a swing.

Benjamin Allen acted as president of the Cheyenne Mountain Country Club from 1916 to 1917. Today his photograph hangs on a wall of the club, along with pictures of most of the

BENJAMIN C. ALLEN.
CHEYENNE COURT
BROADMOOR

COLORADO SPRINGS December 31, 191 2

Mr. E. P. Shove, Pres.,
The Cheyenne Mountain Country Club,
Colorado Springs, Colorado.

Dear Sir:-
At an informal meeting held this morning of the following gentlemen:- Messrs. J. A. Connell, Godfrey Kissell, D. F. Carpenter, Joseph Harrison, E. J. Ulrich, E. P. Shove, C. A. Baldwin, Percy Hagerman, E. A. Swenson and B. C. Allen the question of "Rag dancing" at the coming Annual balls of The El Paso and The Cheyenne Mountain Country Clubs was earnestly discussed. and I was instructed by the above named gentlemen, with the single exception of Mr. E. A. Swenson, to write you and say that it was the opinion of those present that this kind of dancing should be discouraged at the forthcoming Annual balls.

Respectfully yours,

There was a friendly rivalry between the Grizzlies and the El Paso Club, even though certain members, like Benjamin Allen, belonged to both clubs. The photograph above (circa 1913) was taken at a shooting contest between the two clubs. Benjamin is seated in the first row, third from the right. Notice the unusual length of the rifle held by the man on the far right. *Courtesy the Cheyenne Mountain Country Club.*

Photograph of Benjamin C. Allen that hangs in the Cheyenne Mountain Country Club (circa 1916). *Courtesy the Cheyenne Mountain Country Club.*

presidents since the club's founding in 1891. Note Benjamin's initials on the side of his automobile.

In March of 1911, Benjamin's Cheyenne Mountain Country Club bill was as follows:

Dues	*15.00*
Locker	*$3.00*
Annual Dinner	*$2.85*
Bar locker	*$3.00*
Food and drink account	*$20.75*

An engraved silver cup on display at the club attests that Edith Farnsworth and Benjamin's son Wharton Allen won the mixed doubles lawn tennis tournament on July 18, 1914.

THE FOUNDER OF THE Cheyenne Mountain Country Club was Count James Pourtales, a fascinating character from Prussia. Although he could have lived sumptuously off the rent from his estates in Glumbowitz (now in Poland), this enterprising young Count came to America in 1884 seeking romance, fortune, and to enrich his experience beyond that of his aristocratic German forbearers. The principles that guided his life were, ". . . do not overestimate yourself; listen for you can learn something from everyone; do not steal; be polite, generous, but not weak; be an aristocrat by breeding and not false pride." [20]

Count James Pourtales (1853–1908). *Courtesy the Cheyenne Mountain Country Club.*

Arriving in Pikes Peak Country in 1885, Count Pourtales encountered a picturesque, fifteen-hundred-acre dairy on a mesa at the foot of Cheyenne Mountain. The property belonged to William J. Willcox—a Philadelphian who, like Benjamin Allen, had come to Colorado Springs for tuberculosis treatment. The two men became instant friends and Pourtales soon became a partner in Willcox's Broadmoor Dairy. Under Count Pourtales' guidance, the partnership purchased additional land with water rights and became one of the finest dairies in Pikes Peak Country, selling high quality products as far away as Denver and Leadville. [21]

Pourtales realized that a dairy could never meet his financial aspirations, so he came up with a strategy to develop the dairy's acreage into an upper-class suburb of Colorado Springs that he called "Broadmoor City." [22] This was a visionary move on his part.

His plans for Broadmoor City included a lake, a casino, a hotel, a power plant, and large lots (each half a city block in size) where the wealthiest people of Pikes Peak Country would want to build mansions. After forming the Cheyenne Lake, Land, and Improvement Company, he built Cheyenne Lake at an ultimate cost of $25,000. [23] This lake exists today

Cheyenne Mountain, 2008—the Broadmoor mesa is on the right side.

The Cheyenne Mountain Country Club near Cheyenne Lake, 2008.

on the property of the famed Broadmoor Hotel and is Pourtales' most enduring legacy.

In order to attract the unusually high number of young, well-to-do men in Colorado Springs to his Broadmoor mesa, Count Pourtales conceived the idea of the Cheyenne Mountain Country Club, which, when built, was only the second country club to be established in the United States![24]

Besides providing an appealing place where Colorado Springs' young bloods could play sports, associate, and negotiate, it also offered them (most importantly!) a place to drink.[25] Since General William Palmer's charter for Colorado Springs did not permit the sale of alcohol, there was nowhere within Colorado Springs city limits where a man could legally buy himself or his friends an alcoholic beverage.

Not surprisingly, the Cheyenne Mountain Country Club was an immediate success, and attracted many to the Broadmoor mesa.[26] Shown here, it is still a very successful club and is located at its original address of 9 Lake Avenue in Broadmoor.

Pourtales went on to build the Broadmoor Casino on the east side of Cheyenne Lake, and it was also a huge success. Then, he developed gold fever after hearing about Bob Womack's discovery in Cripple Creek. Count Pourtales has the distinction of being the first serious, influential investor in the Cripple Creek Gold Rush.[27]

In 1889, the Count married Countess Berthe de Pourtales, his first cousin from the French side of his family, who came to Pikes Peak Country after a failed marriage in Boston, Massachusetts.[28]

MARIA MCKEAN ALLEN loved big houses. According to one of her grandsons, she likely inherited this taste from her mother, Elizabeth Wharton McKean. Elizabeth owned an elaborate summer home in Cazenovia, New York, in addition to a mansion in Philadelphia. Since Maria Allen grew up in such palatial dwellings, she naturally expected this aspect of her lifestyle to continue when she came to Colorado Springs.

Benjamin Allen hired Philadelphia architect Horace Trumbauer to design an estate suitable for her. Mr. Trumbauer had been gaining a reputation in Colorado Springs for revival styles. The house Trumbauer designed for the Allens had the late Tudor style of seventeenth century England (also called Jacobethan). He also designed El Pomar—the Spanish-style home of Spencer and Julie Penrose, who built the Broadmoor Hotel. [29]

The Allen mansion was one of the finest residences ever built in Pikes Peak Country. Completed in 1909, it had seventy-two rooms and was virtually a castle. It was located at 8 Fourth Street on an 8-acre plot in Broadmoor, which at that time was an unincorporated part of El Paso County.

Built of red and gray brick with a cast stone trim, the magnificent house featured copper gutters, multiple front gables, fourteen chimneys, and double-hung windows. Benjamin and Maria Allen seemingly wanted to carry on the venerable tradition of English country living with this elaborate estate and its manicured grounds. [30] The following pictures, courtesy of the Chapel of Our Saviour, display its stunning elegance.

When the Allens moved into their new mansion, they called it "Cheyenne Court," as written on the upper left corner of Benjamin's personal stationery (see page 77). The cost of the lavish estate was $170,000. [31]

Maria Allen hired a governess to educate her children at Cheyenne Court. Evidently some neighbor children also attended the lessons, for Tina Chisholm, daughter of the man who managed the Broadmoor Dairy for Count Pourtales, attended class with Hope Allen. Maria also had at least four servants in her employ.

Maria had a brother named Henry Pratt McKean who also loved big houses. He built a 630-acre estate in Philadelphia called Pine Run Farms, which today is home to the exclusive Talamore Country Club. The history of this club [32] sheds the following background on

The Allen Mansion at Broadmoor (circa 1915).

Main Stairway

Hallway

Dining Room

Conservatory

Library

Study

Cheyenne Court (circa 1915). *Courtesy George Allen Jr.*

why the McKean family built large houses and estates:

In the latter part of the 19th century, during the pre-income tax, laissez-faire era of American history, wealth generated by the great industrial and commercial boom became concentrated into the hands of the very few. As these wealthy few sought refuge from the teeming, often fetid urban confines, the countryside beyond Philadelphia became highly prized as sites for gentlemen farms, summer residences, and playgrounds for expensive pastimes. To symbolize their power and social status, Philadelphia's industrial and commercial aristocracy hired noted architects to design and build grandiose architectural struc-tures and spectacular estates modeled on the majestic manor houses and estates of Europe and particularly England.

The manor house on Pine Run Farms that Henry Pratt McKean built is shown here. Notice how much it looks like Cheyenne Court! It was once described as "one of the show places in the Philadelphia suburbs" and "one of the handsomest estates in the vicinity of Philadelphia."

Henry Pratt McKean and his brother Thomas (Maria had three brothers—the third was George Wharton, and a sister Phebe Warren) became Philadelphia's premier patrons of architectural genius, hiring Frank Furness, regarded still today as Philadelphia's greatest architect, to design and build them el-

Manor house of Henry Pratt McKean. *Courtesy Talamore Country Club.*

Farms, which boarded many of his valuable horses, burned to the ground. Desiring to replace them with a new, state-of-the-art facility to house his precious horses while also conceding to the growing impact of the automobile, Henry hired Horace Trumbauer (the same architect who designed Cheyenne Court) "to design and oversee construction of a fabulous multi-purpose carriage house to serve as both stable and automobile garage. This was not to be just any carriage house or stable and garage. Indeed, it became one of the most luxuriant and expensive known to exist."

One wing of this carriage house contained an "automobile house to include a cement pit and all the appliances for maintaining automobiles," which in 1904 put Henry substantially ahead of the times. In 1900, there were fewer than 14,000 automobiles registered in the entire United States.[35]

egant homes on Walnut Street in Center City Philadelphia, near Rittenhouse Square.[33]

Before Benjamin and Maria Allen moved to Colorado Springs, Maria's brother Henry McKean was running 120 head of cattle at Pine Run Farms and owned thirty horses, including thoroughbred show horses.[34] No doubt Maria and Benjamin were aware of Pine Run Farms and what Henry was doing with it.

In 1902, Henry's large stables at Pine Run

Trumbauer, a highly gifted and extraordinarily successful Philadelphian who lived from 1868 to 1938, also designed a house for Phebe Warren McKean Downs, sister of Maria McKean Allen. Known as Fordhooke Farm, it was connected to Henry McKean's Pine Run

Cheyenne Court in winter (circa 1915). *Courtesy George Allen Jr.*

Farms estate by a private, oak-lined carriage road.[36]

One striking feature for which Trumbauer was known was his use of tree-lined entrances. Even today, his influence is evident in the entrance to Shamrock Ranch. Note the similarity shown here between the oak alley connecting the estates of Henry and Phebe McKean and the ponderosa pine entrance to the Shamrock Ranch.

As Colorado Springs socialites, Maria and

Oak-lined entrance to Fordhooke Farms, designed by Horace Trumbauer. *Courtesy Talamore Country Club.*

Ponderosa pine-lined entrance to Shamrock Ranch (2008).

Benjamin Allen were contemporaries of many other famous Pikes Peak Country personalities and traveled in the same social circles. Two that deserve mention are Spencer Penrose and Charles L. Tutt.

Spencer Penrose was another Philadelphian who came to Colorado Springs, arriving in December of 1892. "Speck," as he was known since childhood,[37] joined with Charles Leaming Tutt (also from Philadelphia) to buy the Cash-On-Delivery Mine in Cripple Creek for $20,000. It was located across Poverty Gulch from Bob Womack's original gold discovery. Through hard work, Penrose and Tutt made this gold mine (also known as the C.O.D. Mine) produce handsomely, then sold it in 1895 for $250,000.[38, 39]

They also invested in real estate ventures throughout Cripple Creek, Pueblo, Colorado Springs, and Denver, and later founded other mining and mine-processing operations, including the Utah Copper Company (now Kennecott Utah Copper—the largest copper mine in the world[40]). Tutt became president of the United States Reduction and Refining Company, which controlled most of Cripple Creek's gold ore processing. Penrose was a partner of the company. When Tutt died at age forty-five of a heart ailment, Penrose was named the executor of Tutt's will and guardian of his children—a responsibility he took seriously.[41, 42]

After marrying beautiful widow Julie Lewis McMillan in 1906, Penrose became interested in the hospitality business. Using the vast fortune he had accumulated from mining operations, he and Julie built the luxurious Broadmoor Hotel near Colorado Springs. The hotel opened in 1918 with John D. Rockefeller as its first celebrity guest. Today, this famous hotel and resort is touted as "the pinnacle of meeting locations in North America." The Broadmoor Hotel is one of the *Travel & Leisure* Top 500 Hotels in the World, and 2008 marked its 48th year as a Mobil Five-Star property and its 32nd year as an AAA Five-Diamond hotel.[43]

Cheyenne Court was situated only a few blocks from the Broadmoor Hotel.

From the title of the photograph below, "Mr. Tutt's Coach and Six on an excursion to General Palmer's Glen Eyrie, 1903," it is reasonable to infer that the Allens met General William Jackson Palmer before his tragic 1906 accident in the Garden of the Gods, and that Maria and Benjamin knew Julie and Spencer Penrose as well as the Tutts. The woman behind Maria Allen in the photograph is Varina Davis Hayes—wife of Dr. Gerald Webb and granddaughter of Jefferson Davis, president of the Confederate States of America during the Civil War.

Benjamin Allen was a banker by profession, according to the 1911 El Paso County census. In early 1904 he expanded his career interests by purchasing several thousand acres of land in the Divide Country from the Husted Sterling Live Stock Company, which included much of present-day Shamrock

Ranch. As a banker, it is likely that Allen knew of Calvin Husted's financial troubles and bought his ranch when the price was right.

Later that year, Allen also purchased additional land in section 34 (shown on page 86 as present-day Shamrock Ranch) that was between the road to Franktown and his new ranch's western boundary. He acquired this land from the Colorado Pinery and Land Company.

Benjamin C. Allen (circa 1918).
Courtesy Chapel of Our Saviour.

Allen began to raise purebred shorthorn cattle on this large ranch. He later formed the Allen Cattle Company, and eventually became president of the American Shorthorn Breeding Association—a position he held as late as 1923.

Originating in the northeastern coast of England, shorthorns were first brought to America in 1783. The *American Shorthorn Herd Book* was published in 1846—the first registry for any breed of cattle in the United States. Shorthorns—which do in fact have

"Mr. Tutt's Coach and Six on an excursion to General Palmer's Glen Eyrie, 1903"
Charles Tutt is on the right side of the driver's box. Behind him in a dark hat is his wife, and to her right are Benjamin and Maria Allen. *Courtesy Special Collections, Colorado College Tutt Library.*

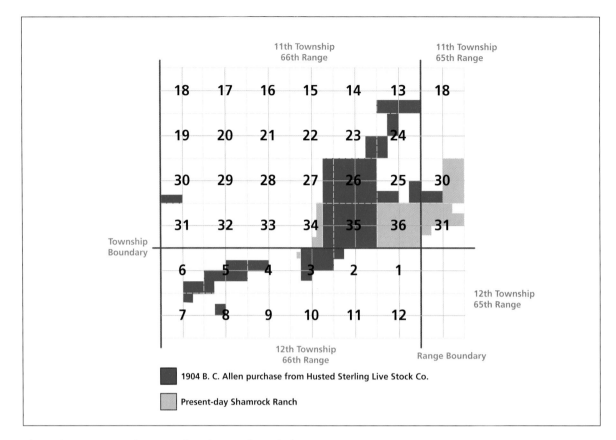

short horns—are known for their adaptability, early maturity, reproductive performance, hardiness, good disposition, and longevity.[44] The photograph here shows some shorthorns on the Allen Ranch.

The cover from a circa 1916 sales brochure titled "The Divide Pure Bred Registered Short Horn Herd" is shown here to indicate the status and seriousness of Benjamin's cattle endeavor.

Sometime prior to 1922, Allen purchased a second ranch closer to Cheyenne Court. Comprising only 310 acres, it became known as the "South Ranch" and was located near the intersection of present-day I-25 and CO 29. The northern ranch, which eventually grew to cover 3,600 acres, was called the "North Ranch," the "Divide Ranch," or the "Allen Ranch." Benjamin raised his prize shorthorn cattle on both ranches.

The year 1909 was a banner construction year for the Allens. Not only did they complete Cheyenne Court, they also built two houses (shown on next page) on their North Ranch. The family spent their summers at the main house, where temperatures are consistently five to ten degrees cooler than Colorado Springs. The smaller house was known as the

Shorthorn cattle on the Allen Ranch. *Courtesy Sam Cheesman.*

The Divide Pure Bred Registered Short Horn Herd

SCOTTISH KING WHEN 10 MONTHS OF AGE
SIRED BY CUMBERLAND MARSHALL BY KING CUMBERLAND
GRAND CHAMPION IN 1908

THE ALLEN CATTLE COMPANY

RANCH: HUSTED, EL PASO COUNTY

Office: Mining Exchange Building, Colorado Springs, Colo.

The "bungalow" (left), and main family house on the Allen Ranch (circa 1915). *Courtesy George Allen Jr.*

Garden in rear of the bungalow. *Courtesy George Allen Jr.*

"bungalow." It may have been used as a guest facility, a chauffeur's house, or as a place to isolate TB sufferers Benjamin and/or Hope during their treatment. Later on, the Allens added an ice house, a root cellar, and a playhouse for Hope that was directly behind the main house.

Today, David and Mary Anne Wismer live in the main ranch house that the Allens constructed in the early 1900s. Extensive modifications have been made to it, and the bungalow no longer exists.

Between the time Benjamin purchased the Allen Ranch (March 7, 1904) and the year 1927, there were two different barns on the

ranch, perhaps at different times. Both are shown here, courtesy of Sam Cheesman. Notice that both barns display the Allen Cattle Company brand, although one or both may have been built during the Calvin Husted era.

Barn No. 1 was located just northeast of the site for Barn No. 2 and had no side entrances for cattle. The ponderosa pines and a similar cattle shed behind it are still there today, but the barn was gone by 1927. From the numbering, it is reasonable to assume that the wooden barn was the first one constructed but it was clearly not there when the photo of Barn No. 2 was taken. Both barns included haylofts and had a strikingly similar appearance. Barn No. 2 was constructed of cement blocks, as was the small house into which the Joe Romick family moved in 1917 (see page 135). This is the same cement block house that appears in the background behind Cal Husted's original house on the ranch (see page 64). Because of the similarity of construction materials, it is possible the Barn No. 2 also existed during the Cal Husted era.

As a pioneer of the Pikes Peak Country ranching industry, Benjamin became an executive committee member of the National Western Stock Show Association in 1915. The National Western Stock Show is a Colorado tradition that was started to improve the quality

Since 1994, David Wismer has used the ice house to house his Rocky Mountain Front Range HO scale model railroad (2008).

The root cellar (2008)

Hope's playhouse is now a guest house (2008).

Allen Ranch Barn No. 1 (which no longer exists).

Allen Ranch Barn No. 2 (which still exists).

of western livestock. The first show took place in 1906. It is still held every January in Denver and is the world's largest stock show in terms of number of animals involved, hosting twenty different breeds of cattle plus horses, sheep, swine, goats, llamas, bison, yak, stock dogs, poultry, and rabbits.

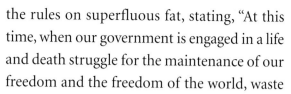

The year that Benjamin became an executive committee member of the association was the first time in the show's history that it was cancelled. A nationwide outbreak of hoof-and-mouth disease caused the cancellation. Also, the Association was at least $11,000 in debt that year, due largely to bad weather in previous years that had discouraged attendance.

Benjamin worked with other committee members to rescue the stock show financially. By the 1919 show, they had turned a net gain, thanks mainly to the generous contributions and subscriptions they had solicited. This was also the year that the Brown Palace Hotel, Denver's second oldest hotel, paid a record fifty cents per pound for the Grand Champion steer.

When World War I came along, Benjamin was still an executive committee member of the National Western Stock Show Association. During the war, the stock show became a fund raiser for the Red Cross. Ranchers donated calves branded with the letters "CRC" (Colorado Red Cross) to display their support for the war effort. The association instructed judges to observe

Red Cross emblem

the rules on superfluous fat, stating, "At this time, when our government is engaged in a life and death struggle for the maintenance of our freedom and the freedom of the world, waste of feed in preparing animals for the exhibition should be frowned upon by every patriotic citizen."[45]

More than a thousand heifers—young cows that have not given birth to a calf—were donated to the war effort, and the 1919 "Victory Stock Show" set the highest attendance and revenue records to date. The Allen Cattle Company undoubtedly contributed to this extraordinary feat. Benjamin remained an executive committee member of the association through 1925.

1914 Declaration of War by the German Empire.

Benjamin Allen at the North Ranch (circa 1915). *Courtesy George Allen Jr.*

World War I trenches

When America was about to enter the war, the Allen twins—Wharton and Curtis—who were attending the University of Pennsylvania, decided to become part of it. Wharton joined the American Field Service in France and served as an artillerist and ambulance driver there. He enlisted in 1916. Benjamin and Maria donated a car with the inscription "University of Pennsylvania" to the American Field Service on his behalf.[46] Curtis served in the U.S. Army.

A certificate heralding Wharton's "Excellent Character of Service" at the military instruction camp (dated August 5, 1916) and a certificate of appreciation for his "patriotic service with the American Forces . . . in the Great War" (dated April 26, 1919) are shown here.

The family picture on the next page was taken before the twins left for the war. Fortunately, both soldiers returned safely.

This may have been one of the last times the family was united and relatively happy—for Benjamin was not faithful to his wife.

Maria may have known this as early as 1919, as her husband deeded the Allen Ranch to her that year. If she did know of his indiscretions, she was not willing to end the marriage. But he was.

According to Peggy Hubbell, daughter of an Allen Ranch manager, Maria Allen related the following incident to Peggy's mother, to whom she was kind and friendly: "One day I returned from a visit to Philadelphia and

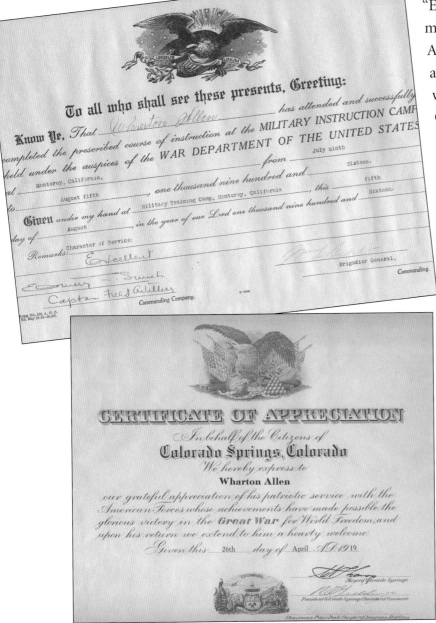

Courtesy Sam Cheesman

The Benjamin C. Allen Family (1918). Left to right front row—Wharton, Benjamin, Curtis; left to right back row—Hope, George, Maria, McKean. *Courtesy Chapel of Our Saviour.*

found another woman in my house. When I confronted Benjamin, he told me to pack up and leave. My response was, 'Oh, I'm sorry, but this happens to be my money and my house—so you can leave!' "

Benjamin did. He bought a smaller house in Broadmoor and moved into it.

This likely happened in 1922. Finding her husband with another woman in her own house must have been the last straw for Maria, for she suddenly had Cheyenne Court razed that year. According to a grandson, she wanted to get rid of Benjamin's spirit and destroy everything associated with him. The only things she salvaged were the bricks and shingles. Today, all that remains of Cheyenne Court is a piece of the south wall, which attests to its former grandeur.

On February 24, 1923, Maria filed suit for divorce in the Colorado Springs District Court. The reason given was willful desertion. A preliminary decree was granted to her on March 28, 1923, and the divorce became final on September 29 of that same year.

Ironically, virtually the same thing had happened to Maria Allen's brother Henry

McKean a decade earlier, as shown in the following excerpt from Dr. James W. Hilty's *Talamore at Oak Terrace:*

Henry Pratt McKean, for all his land and wealth, apparently found little happiness at Pine Run Farms. His wife, Marian, enjoyed it even less. In 1910 scandal struck the McKean household, which for many years had been the topic of Philadelphia gossipmongers. Marian Shaw McKean— a woman celebrated in newspaper accounts for her 'beauty' and 'diplomacy'—simply packed up one day and left her husband. That summer she went to Boston ostensibly for the purposes of settling her two sons at Harvard University, visiting her family, and vacationing at the McKean summer residence at Price's Crossing, Massachusetts. Instead, Marian McKean and her sons took up residence on Beacon Street in Boston, determined to remain.

In 1913 Henry Pratt McKean charged his wife with desertion. A divorce decree was granted in June 1914. Four months later, Marian Shaw McKean married Percy Haughton, brother of the Harvard football coach. She lived thereafter in Boston, using her father's $2 million inheritance to become, among other things, a noted patron of the arts.

The woman Benjamin had brought into Cheyenne Court was Mrs. Rosalie Cameron, a New York society woman and mother of debutante Rhoda Cameron. Rosalie and Rhoda Cameron had spent several summers in Broadmoor, where Rhoda became popular with the younger set. During those summers,

MRS. CAMERON BRIDE OF B. C. ALLEN IN NEW YORK WEDDING

Fashionable Set Here Not Surprised at News of Couple's Marriage

Mrs. Rosalie DeG. Cameron, fashionable New York society woman, sister of Mrs. August Belmont, Jr., and Benjamin C. Allen, Colorado Springs clubman and cattle breeder, were married at the home of Mrs. Belmont in New York city, yesterday, according to word received last night from Mr. Allen. The bride is well known here, having spent several summers at Broadmoor with her daughter, Rhoda Cameron, one of New York's most favored debutants and popular with the younger set here.

Mr. Allen, in addition to being president of the Allen Cattle company, whose ranch is located south of this city, is nationally known as president of the American Shorthorn Breeders association, vice president of the Western society, and a director in the National Western Stock Show association. He is a member of the Cheyenne Mountain Country club and the El Paso clubs.

News of the wedding did not come as a surprise to the fashionable society set here, as rumors of the event had been current for several weeks, the day of the event alone being lacking.

While nothing definite is known about Mr. Allen's plans for the future, it is understood that he will return here with Mrs. Allen this week.

Whether Miss Cameron will return at this time is not known.

Cameron-Allen Wedding in East Event of Interest

Announcement was made in last Sunday's paper of the marriage of Mrs. R. de Golcouria Cameron of 993 Park avenue, New York, to Benjamin Curtis Allen of this city, at the New York home of the bride's sister, Mrs. August Belmont, Jr., Saturday afternoon of last week. Concerning the marriage, the New York Times has the following notice:

"Mrs. R. de Golcouria Cameron of 993 Park avenue was married yesterday afternoon to Benjamin Curtis Allen of Colorado Springs, formerly of Philadelphia. The ceremony was performed at the home of the bride's sister, Mrs. August Belmont, Jr., 30 East Seventy-fifth street, the Rev. Robert W. Courtney officiating.

"Only the relatives and close friends of the bride and bridegroom were present.

"The bride is the daughter of Albert V. de Golcouria. Mr. Allen has a large ranch in Colorado and is the president of the American Shorthorn Breeding association.

"Mr. and Mrs. Allen will make their home at the Broadmoor, Colorado Springs.

"Mrs. Allen has a daughter, Miss Rhoda Cameron, by her first husband, W. Scott Cameron, whom she divorced in Reno, Nev., in 1920. Mr. Allen is a member of an old and wealthy family of Philadelphia, and his first wife, Mrs. Marie McKean Allen, obtained a divorce from him last March. A daughter and four sons were born to them."

her mother evidently became popular with Benjamin Allen; he married her in New York City on December 8, 1923—just seventy days after his divorce with Maria Allen was final.

Benjamin Allen and Rosalie Cameron lived in the Broadmoor area for several years following their marriage. Little is known about their life together.

A 1926 *Colorado Springs Gazette* article mentions the work of Benjamin Allen in helping to expand the ranching industry in Pikes Peak Country. He may have been recognized at that time to acknowledge his departure from Colorado Springs, since he turned over the South Ranch to Wharton about then. Additionally, 1925 marked the end of his tenure as an executive committee member of the National Western Stock Show Association.

Benjamin Curtis Allen died on March 24, 1931, in Montecito, California, today one of the wealthiest communities in the United States and home to many celebrities. He was sixty-two years old. Sadly, he died without the comfort and companionship of the children he had brought into the world and the woman who was their mother.

The photograph below shows him at his home in Montecito with his wife Rosalie, on the left, and Dorothy Allen, wife of his son Curtis, on the right.

Left to right—Rosalie Allen, Benjamin Allen, Dorothy Allen. *Courtesy George Allen Jr.*

THE MARIA
McKEAN ALLEN ERA

MARIA WHARTON McKEAN was indignant after her discovery of Benjamin's affair with Rosalie Cameron in her own house. She tore down Cheyenne Court in 1922 to rid herself of anything associated with him . . . or Rosalie. In its place she left a gigantic pile of bricks and a second large heap of shingles. Then she began to rebuild her life.

First she hired an architect, Robert Rhodes McGoodwin. Robert was a Penn State faculty member at the time and had previously worked (albeit briefly) with Horace Trumbauer, architect of Cheyenne Court.[1] Together, Maria and Robert designed and built her next house where Cheyenne Court had once proudly stood.[2]

Although not as immense or grandiose as Cheyenne Court, it was nevertheless a large, elegant mansion. She called it Cheyenne House and sometimes referred to it as a "cottage."[3] It was constructed in Jacobethan style with the same bricks and shingles that had previously been used for Cheyenne Court. The east wing housed the servants and the west wing was reserved for the family. All the children's bedrooms were upstairs, near hers.

While Cheyenne Court had seventy-two rooms, Cheyenne House had only twenty-six. According to Peggy (Romick) Hubbell, daughter of Allen Ranch manager Joe Romick, Maria told her mother, "Now that the children are grown, I don't need nurses and governesses." So she cut the number of rooms by forty-six!

The interior of Cheyenne House boasted dark oak paneling, ornate fireplaces, and heavy iron accents. Special

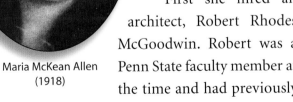

Maria McKean Allen
(1918)

Robert McGoodwin
(1886–1967).
Courtesy the University of Pennsylvania Archives.

features included Tudor-style arches, a dumb-waiter, a walk-in safe, an electric system of relays to call servants, and an impressive library.[4]

Outside, the grounds were landscaped into formal and casual gardens. The large, south-facing veranda had a goldfish pond in the middle and was bordered by rose bushes.[5]

There were enough bricks left over to build some out-buildings, the courtyard fence shown below, and an outer wall enclosing the entire estate. Every brick Maria had saved was reused, and all the buildings on the 8-acre site were given new roofs from the slate shingles of the first house.[6] Photographs of Cheyenne House provided here are courtesy of the Chapel of Our Saviour and Sam Tease.

One might wonder why Maria didn't return to Philadelphia to be with family when Benjamin left her. One answer may be that, since Hope suffered from tuberculosis, Maria believed the best treatment she could provide for her only daughter was to be found in Colorado Springs.

The next thing Maria did to restructure her life was to put her son Wharton in charge of the cattle business on the North (Allen) Ranch. She had been the sole owner of the ranch since 1919, but now she needed someone to manage it for her and ensure its profitability. According to Sam Cheesman, son of a South Ranch manager, Maria paid Wharton $300 a month to manage her ranch and cattle business.

As soon as the preliminary decree for her divorce was granted, Maria deeded a small

Hope Allen
(1918)

Cheyenne House looking north by northeast (circa 1920).

Automobile entrance off Fourth Street looking west—the gate house on the left was for the gardener; the one on the right for the chauffeur (1925).

Main entrance on the north side convenient to the garage (1925). *Courtesy Sam Tease.*

All shadows point north.
Notice that the garage is attached to the chauffeur's gate house.

Veranda with goldfish pond

Great Room

Upstairs Hallway

Dining Room

Parlor

Library

piece of land in Section 3 to Lawrence E. Burnett in exchange for a small piece of his land east of the road in Section 34. This transaction completed her ownership of the ranch adjacent to and east of the road in section 34 (see the present-day Shamrock Ranch map on page 39). Then, in 1927, both Maria and Burnett granted rights of way to El Paso County for a 60 foot strip of road, most likely when the old stage road was upgraded to a county road. Maria also had the Allen Ranch bungalow razed (see page 87), possibly to save on property taxes. The photographs here showing her ranch house appear to have been taken after the bungalow was demolished.

Wharton Allen (1918)

Lastly, Maria stopped speaking of Benjamin altogether. She was determined to rid herself of her memories of him and Rosalie. As a result, most of her children became somewhat estranged from their father after the divorce.

Wharton was the exception. In 1925 or 1926, Benjamin turned the South Ranch over to his son, who then oversaw both ranches and continued to raise Shorthorn cattle on both. Over time, Maria began to depend more and more on Wharton. As her other children grew older and married, they all left Colorado. But Wharton stayed on and cared for his mother in Cheyenne House until she passed away. He was devoted to her and never married.

The first of the children to leave was McKean, even though he was the fourth one born. McKean became engaged to Emma Louise Schwartz in June of 1920 and was married October 1st of the following year. This happened before Maria filed for divorce. McKean

Maria in front of her Allen Ranch house (circa 1930). *Courtesy George Allen Jr.*

Maria's summer house on the Allen Ranch (circa 1930). *Courtesy George Allen Jr.*

McKean Allen
(1918)

and his bride lived in Philadelphia for several years, then settled in northern California where he grew apricots. McKean and Emma had four children—a girl and three boys, including Thomas McKean Jr. and Benjamin Curtis. McKean later divorced Emma and remarried.

Maria's son Curtis was the next to leave. He married Dorothy Fox and moved to

Announce Engagement

Mr. an Mrs. Charles W. Schwartz, Jr., of Germantown, Philadelphia, announce the engagement of their daughter, Miss Emma Louise Schwartz, to Thomas McKean Allen, son of Mr. and Mrs. Benjamin C. Allen, of Broadmoor.

Curtis Allen
(1918)

Philadelphia. They raised two daughters there, Sonia and Marya. The announcement of their marriage, shown here, was published in the *Gazette and Telegraph* on June 22, 1924.

Hope left Cheyenne House next. A beautiful woman, she met and fell in love with Captain James V. Ruthven Ryan, a member of the King's Own Royal Regiment stationed in India. The September 1926 *Sunday Colorado Springs Gazette and Telegraph* photographs following announce

Invitations for Wedding.

The following invitation will be of interest to a large number of friends here:

Mrs. Charles William Schwartz, Jr., requests the honor of your presence at the marriage of her daughter, Emma Louise, and Mr. Thomas McKean Allen, Saturday, the first of October, nineteen hundred and twenty-one, at four o'clock, church of St. Martin-in-the-Fields, Chestnut Hill, Philadelphia.

Allen-Schwartz Wedding.

A wedding of much interest to Broadmoor and Colorado Springs society is that of Miss Emma Louise Schwartz, daughter of Mrs. Charles William Schwartz of Germantown, Pa., to Thomas McKane Allen, son of Mr. and Mrs. B. C. Allen of Colorado Springs, on Saturday, October 1. The wedding took place in Philadelphia at the church of Saint Martin-in-the-Fields. It was a large one, as both Mr. and Mrs. Allen are prominent in eastern society circles. Mr. B. C. Allen, Mr. Wharton Allen and Miss Hope Allen went east the early part of the week to be present.

Miss Dorothy Fox Weds Curtis Allen

The marriage of Miss Dorothy Fox of New York city to Curtis Allen of Philadelphia and Colorado Springs took place in New York city June 11. The service was read at St. Thomas church by Rev. Ernest M. Stires, and a reception followed at Sherry's. The maid of honor was Miss Virginia Fox, sister of the bride, while Wharton Allen served as his brother's best man. Miss Fox was elaborately gowned in white satin trimmed in old point lace worn by her mother and grandmother at their weddings. Her sister wore salmon pink satin.

Mr. and Mrs. Allen will spend the summer at Lake Mahopac and next fall will go to Chestnut Hill, Pa, to live.

her engagement and marriage. Captain Ryan and his bride later moved to England, where they raised Kathleen Hope and James V. Ruthven Ryan Jr.

Ruthven Jr. (pronounced Riven) reported that Hope reconciled with her father after her wedding, but she never saw him again before he died.

George, Maria's youngest son, was the last to leave. He married Edith Allison Leavens of Houston, Texas, in 1928. Her wedding announcement is shown below. They made their home in Houston and had three children.

One of George's sons, George Nelson Jr., got to know his grandmother Maria when his father started renting a summer house in the Broadmoor area in the late 1930s. He never got to know her one-on-one, he explains, because "she was a pretty stern lady and not overly fond of grandchildren. So when you were around her,

George Nelson Allen
(1918)

Wedded in Kashmir, India

CAPTAIN AND MRS. J. V. R. RYAN
Whose marriage in Srinagar, Kashmir, India, on September 21, was of interest to Broadmoor and Colorado Springs society. Mrs. Ryan was Miss Hope Allen before her marriage. She is the daughter of Mrs. M. McK. Allen of Broadmoor. Captain Ryan is a member of the Kings Own Royal regiment, stationed at Rawal Pindi, India.

MRS. GEORGE NELSON ALLEN
The former Miss Edith Leavens of Houston, whose marriage in late October was one of the smart weddings attended by Houston's elite. Mr. Allen is the son of Mrs. M. McK. Allen of Broadmoor.

you minded your Ps and Qs because you didn't want to get on her bad side."

George Nelson Jr. remembers having dinner at Cheyenne House promptly at 8:00. "You showed up at eight o'clock or else you got her wrath for not being there on time."

Maria's son George called her faithfully every Sunday night from Houston. In 1936, after the sudden death of her husband, Hope brought her children from England and stayed for an extended time with Maria, residing both at Cheyenne House and the Allen Ranch house. Ruthven was only six years old at the time, but he fell in love with Pikes Peak, the Black Forest, and Broadmoor nonetheless.

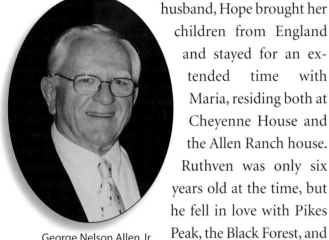

George Nelson Allen Jr.
(2007)

One summer Curtis and his family came to visit Maria at the ranch. By then his daughter Sonia was three years old. During the visit, Sonia was briefly missed from the house. After the family searched for her, they found her heading toward the ranch gates. When asked what she thought she was doing, the determined toddler replied, "I'm going to see my mountain!" pointing to Pikes Peak in the distance. Her tender feelings for this majestic mountain when viewed from Shamrock Ranch have undoubtedly been shared by most every resident and visitor.

Peggy (Romick) Hubbell, whose father, Joe Romick, managed the Allen Ranch when she was a girl, described Maria as "austere," although she also noted that she often gave lovely things to Coral Romick, her mother. One time she even gave Coral a bolt of laven-

Pikes Peak as seen from near the entrance of Shamrock Ranch (circa 2006).

der linen so that she could make herself some new dresses.

Maria proved herself to be generous and kindhearted again and again. In her later years, she gave the Romicks money to provide Christmas dinner for families in need. They bought and delivered groceries, turkeys, and all the trimmings (and perhaps gifts as well) to needy people on behalf of Maria. She also took a bushel full of "the best apples and oranges you could buy" to the Cheesman boys, Sam and Robert (sons of the South Ranch foreman), every Christmas.

Maria even sent one of her maids, Katherene Davis, to college. Katherene took care of McKean's boys—Thomas "Tommy" McKean Allen Jr., and Charles "Charlie" Schwartz Allen—when they came from Philadelphia to visit Maria and enjoy the ranch during the summertime. After she graduated from the University of Colorado, Katherene returned to the Divide Country and taught in the one-room, log elementary school that is a Black Forest historical site today (see photos on pages 144).

In 1935, a sudden, powerful cloudburst caused a flood in Colorado Springs. Dr. Charles Stewart, Maria's veterinarian, found his office on Colorado Avenue wiped out by the flood. Maria promptly gave him $1000 to rebuild. As a remembrance of her generosity, Dr. Stewart kept a picture of one of Maria's dogs in his office, along with the following caption: "Mrs. Maria McKean Allen gave me the first $1000 to rebuild my office."

Maria had three dogs. They had their own private bathroom with a bathtub in Cheyenne House near the kitchen. One was an Airedale Terrier named Aeron. The other two were Scottish Terriers. She named them Jiggs and Maggie after characters in the popular cartoon strip *Bringing Up Father,* which ran in newspapers from 1913 until 2000. This comic strip was about an Irishman living in America named Jiggs who came into wealth but still wanted to keep his old pals, eat corned beef and cabbage, and hang out at the tavern— much to the consternation of his wife, Maggie.

Sam Tease age 2 with Maria Allen and her dogs, Jiggs, Maggie, and Aeron (1924). *Courtesy Sam Tease.*

1995 U.S. postage stamp commemorating "Bringing Up Father"

One can't help but wonder if Maria chose the names Jiggs and Maggie as reflective of her marriage to Benjamin. A 1995 postage stamp commemorating the comic strip is shown here.

In 1924, Maria hired a young man from Pennsylvania, Cameron M. Tease, to be her chauffeur. He was a veteran of World War I and had a wife, Esther, and a two-year-old son, Sam.

During the summers, the Tease family lived on the Allen Ranch in a three-bedroom cottage, made all of wood, with a nice front porch that can be seen in the photograph here of Sam Tease in front of Maria's summer touring car.

Maria owned two Packard automobiles, which Cameron drove. They both had straight eight-cylinder engines and were purchased from Britsell and Stockdale in Colorado Springs. One was a four-door sedan with a canvas top. It was her summer touring car. Sam remembers it sitting on blocks in the center garage of Cheyenne House all winter long. The other Packard was fully enclosed and used for winter driving.

Sam Tease and Maria's summer touring car (1925). *Courtesy Sam Tease.*

1920 Packard touring car

1925 Model T Ford pickup truck

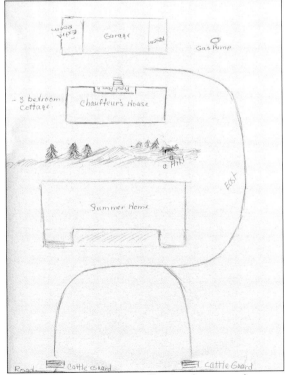

Relative positions of Maria's Allen Ranch summer home, the chauffeur's house, and the garage, hand-drawn by Peggy Hubbell.

Maria also had a Model T Ford pickup truck for use around her Broadmoor estate. It was a 1925 or 1926 model similar to the one shown here.

The Allen Ranch garage was a rather long building with rooms at each end. It could hold several automobiles. A sketch provided by Peggy Hubbell, drawn at age ninety, shows the proximity of the chauffeur's house and the garage to Maria's main ranch house. The trees indicate a low ridge that separated the main house visually from the chauffeur's house and garage, which have both been torn down.

As a young boy, Sam Tease would sit on top of an ash pit near the driveway that led to the garage courtyard, hoping that Maria would take him along when Cameron drove her for a pleasure ride. Once in a while she would stop and allow Sam to get in. They'd drive around for an hour or two, chatting and enjoying the Broadmoor neighborhood and its wondrous sights.

Sometimes, when it was spring, they would go to the ranch. Sam remembers driving to the town of Husted along the Colorado Springs and Denver Road (see the 1904 El Paso County map on next page), then turning right onto the Husted Wagon Road, which was

The old stagecoach barn that was located near the entrance to the Allen Ranch.

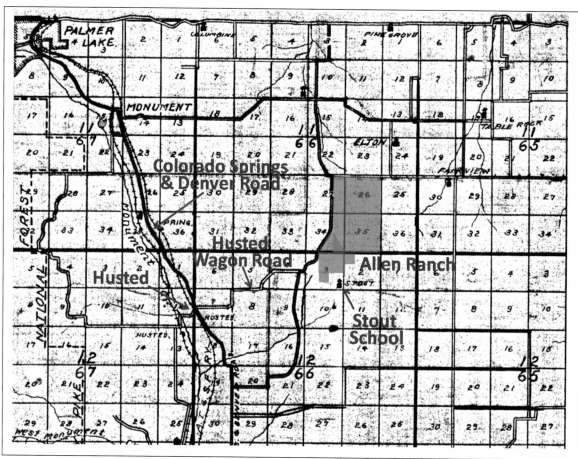

1904 El Paso County map highlighting a portion of the Allen Ranch, the Stout School, the Husted Wagon Road, and the town of Husted. *Courtesy Susan (Steppler) Koch.*

white and sandy, with grass growing between the wagon tracks. After traveling a few miles, they would come to the end of the Husted Wagon Road. After bearing left here, they would soon come to the old stagecoach barn (see previous page) that signaled the entrance to Maria's Allen Ranch.

Buzzard's Roost was located near the stagecoach barn. Because both historic buildings were falling down, Maria Allen must have had them removed sometime prior to 1943 (see Margaret Long's automobile log entry about the Allen Ranch on page 41.

The beams that were used to build the old stagecoach barn still exist today. They were hand-hewn with broad axes into rectangular beams by Leavenworth and Pikes Peak Express workers in the 1850s. A former tenant of Ben-

jamin Allen's named Lou Steppler hauled them away and used them to build the cattle shed shown here. This shed is located on what is today the Steppler Ranch (see page 125ff).

Sam Tease remembers that life on the Allen Ranch was all fun for him as a small boy. "It was

This cattle shed on the Steppler Ranch was built of logs from the old L&PP stagecoach barn that Maria Allen had removed because it was falling down (2008).

Sam Tease, age 6, with Jimmy Reed on the Allen Ranch (1928). *Courtesy Sam Tease.*

Left to right—Sam Carlson, "Long Distance," Cameron Tease, and Charlie Kelly (1925). *Courtesy Sam Tease.*

Cameron Tease at Maria's house on the Allen Ranch (1925). *Courtesy Sam Tease.*

great!" he recalls. Sam played with Ruthven Ryan, Hope's son, and Tommy Allen, McKean's boy, at the Broadmoor house. Maria purchased a pony, named Jimmy Reed, for Tommy. She kept it at the Allen Ranch. But Tommy wasn't there very often, so Sam got to ride it. "I rode the legs off the poor thing," he recalls.

Sam also played with the Romick children, Peggy and Joe Jr., whose father was the ranch manager then. One day he discovered an open wooden barrel sitting in a foyer near the kitchen. It was filled with molasses. Delighted, he tasted the sweet ingredient, then ate until he could eat no more. Of course, he was sick for the next two days!

Sam remembers a ranch worker called Long Distance who he says "must have been seven feet tall." Long Distance is the tallest one in this 1925 picture taken on the ranch. The man on the far left is Sam Carlson, Maria's head gardener at Cheyenne House. He had a

daughter in her twenties named Margaret, who lived with him in the gardener's gate house. The man to the right of Long Distance is Cameron Tease, and the one on the far right is Charlie Kelly, a friend from Broadmoor.

Sadly, Sam's father, Cameron Tease, died in 1928 of tuberculosis and injuries he had received in World War I. He was only thirty-three years old, and Sam was only six. Upon her husband's death, Esther took Sam with her back east for a short time. She later returned to work for Maria. She was probably a housekeeper, although she never wore a uniform like the other servants did. She and Sam lived on the ranch that summer

Esther Tease at the Allen Ranch (1928). *Courtesy Sam Tease.*

until school opened. Then they moved to Cheyenne House. Sam's room was directly above the kitchen. The above photograph shows Sam's mother at the ranch in August 1928.

Maria was very kind to Sam after his father died. He remembers a long corridor running down the west wing which ended in a sitting room where they sat and talked for hours at a time. He remembers it as a comforting time, and describes Maria as "a very, very kind and understanding person."

Upon leaving Maria's employ in 1932, Esther took Sam back to Bryn Mawr, Pennsylvania—a northern suburb of Philadelphia. Maria's sister, Phebe Warren (McKean) Downs, also raised a Quaker, lived there. Sam recalls that Mrs. Downs was very strict about being on time for dinner—just like Mrs. Allen.

In 1937, Maria came to visit her sister in Bryn Mawr. Sam, age fifteen then, had the opportunity to meet with her for a couple of hours while she was there. "She was still the same kind, kind lady—just a wonderful person," He says. They talked about old times and about the impending war.

It was the last time Sam saw Maria. She wrote to him occasionally and usually sent him Christmas cards. When he joined the Marine Corps and fought in the Pacific, she wrote to him now and then. "It was always good to hear from her," he said.

The chauffeur who replaced Cameron Tease was Dwight Bond, who drove Maria all the way to Bryn Mawr in 1937 when she visited her sister and Sam Tease. Sam met and chatted with Bond during that visit. Bond had a daughter, Gay Eloise, and a boy who died in childhood.

One summer, when McKean and his family were visiting Maria at the ranch, the Tom Mix Circus came to town. Maria asked her chauffeur to take Tommy, Katherene Davis (Tommy's sitter), and Peggy Romick to the circus. It was Peggy's first circus, and they all had a wonderful time with Mr. Bond.

Benjamin Franklin 1706–1790 by David Martin (1737–1797), oil on canvas, 1767. Gift of Maria McKean Allen and Phebe Warren Downs through the bequest of their mother, Elizabeth Wharton McKean. *Courtesy Pennsylvania Academy of the Fine Arts, Philadelphia.*

George Washington at Princeton by Charles Willson Peale (1741–1827), oil on canvas, 1779. Gift of Maria McKean Allen and Phebe Warren Downs through the bequest of their mother, Elizabeth Wharton McKean. *Courtesy Pennsylvania Academy of the Fine Arts, Philadelphia.*

Cheyenne House landscaping. *Courtesy Chapel of Our Saviour.*

When Maria's mother, Elizabeth Wharton McKean, died in 1912, she bequeathed two famous paintings to Maria and Phebe, her only two daughters. These remarkable oil paintings, shown here, were then given by Maria and Phebe to the Pennsylvania Academy of the Fine Arts as gifts in 1943.[7,8] Both are treasures of American history as well as memorials to the philanthropy of the McKean family.

According to her granddaughter Marya Allen, Maria loved trees. She even endowed a grove of Sequoia Redwoods to a national park in California that is still part of the park today. Maria cultivated a lush landscape around Cheyenne House and had workers come from Denver every month to tend the trees and gardens on her property.

Unfortunately, Maria's health began to deteriorate, and she become increasingly reclusive. Even though she was extremely wealthy (worth $30 million during the Great Depression, according to Peggy Hubbell) and lived in a magnificent mansion, she never remarried. She did, however, continue to spend her summers at her ranch in the Black Forest, attended by her servants. A photograph of the main ranch house in the winter of 1948 is shown on the next page. Notice that Maria had it remodeled; it shows only one dormer, and the wing on the right side has been changed to match the Tudor style of the left wing (compare with the photograph on page 87).

The last time George Jr. saw his grandmother Maria was in 1947—after he graduated from high school. He and some friends were traveling west and stopped overnight in Colorado Springs. When he went to see Maria, she was very ill, but received him anyway. They

Maria's Allen Ranch house in 1948—notice that it only has one dormer and that the bungalow is gone (compare with photo on page 87). *Courtesy George Allen Jr.*

Mrs. Maria Allen, Broadmoor, Dies

Mrs. Maria McKean Allen, 44 Elm Ave., Broadmoor, prominent in the community for many years, died at her home this morning after a long illness.

Mrs. Allen was born April 18, 1871, in Philadelphia, Pa. She was the daughter of Mr. and Mrs. Thomas McKean and came to Colorado Springs in 1898. She was a member of Grace Episcopal church.

Mrs. Allen is survived by four sons, Wharton Allen of Colorado Springs; Curtis Allen, Philadelphia; Thomas McKean Allen, Hollister, Calif., and George N. Allen, Houston, Tex.; a daughter, Mrs. James Ryan, Ilminster, England, 13 grandchildren and one great-grandchild.

Private funeral services will be held. Friends are requested to omit flowers. The Law mortuary has charge of arrangements.

The passing of Maria McKean Allen marked the end of a distinctively genteel era in the history of Shamrock Ranch—for the bounty of Maria's life harvest had graced it with elegance, kindness, dignity, and culture unique to the early 1900s.

had a nice little visit upstairs in her room that George remembers vividly.

On December 13, 1950, Maria Wharton McKean Allen passed away at Cheyenne House. She was seventy-nine years old.

Maria was interred not far from Broadmoor at Evergreen Cemetery in a dual-plot grave, shown below. The other plot was reserved for her son Wharton.

Grave plots for Maria and Wharton Allen at Evergreen Cemetery (2005).

Maria's grave cover (2005).

Junior Warden at Grace/St. Stephen's Episcopal Church in Colorado Springs.

The Allen heirs decided to move ahead with Howard's plan. They were also interested in securing a tax exemption. In 1954, the Grace/St. Stephen's Episcopal Church purchased Cheyenne House for $75,000.[9]

Because the price was so undervalued, the IRS was, of course, interested. After much negotiating, the price and deal were finally approved. A local attorney by the name of Ben Wendelken successfully represented the Allen estate in the negotiations.

When the deal closed, El Pomar, a community stewardship foundation established by Spencer and Julie Penrose in 1937, stepped in and bought back portions of the original estate that had been purchased by private owners. The foundation then generously donated these parcels to the church so that it could own the whole property free and clear.

Once the Grace/St. Stephen's Episcopal Church had paid off the first $25,000 of its debt, the Allen heirs graciously forgave the remaining balance. So the entire estate—all eight acres plus Cheyenne House—was ultimately purchased by the church for only $25,000! It is now called The Chapel of Our Saviour and serves as a parish of the Episcopal Diocese of Colorado.

Maria left Cheyenne House to all five of her children. They decided to put it up for sale. Howard Creel, a good friend and neighbor of Wharton's, became interested in the property for use as a church. Once a caddy at the Broadmoor Golf Club, Howard was a professional golfer at the time. His wife was a wealthy oil woman from Houston. Howard was also a

Spencer Penrose and the El Pomar Foundation

Since the Pikes Peak Country mountains had been so good to Spencer Penrose (see chapter 6), he left his fortune to the El Pomar Foundation, which he established and endowed in 1937. The name El Pomar, which means "the orchard" in old Spanish, was inspired by the site of Penrose's home, which was situated in an apple orchard.[10]

Spencer and his wife Julie had no children, so their holdings, including their home (El Pomar), the El Pomar Investment Company, and the Broadmoor Hotel, were bequeathed to the El Pomar Foundation. Initially Julie assumed the presidency of the El Pomar Foundation and the Broadmoor Hotel, but during 1940 she hired Charles L. Tutt Jr., son of Spencer's partner, to assume the latter position.[11]

Chapel of Our Saviour (2005)

The chauffeur's cottage and garage (2005)

Chapel of Our Saviour grounds (2005)

The gardener's cottage. The main house can be seen behind it. (2005)

In the church's early days, services were held in the great room of the main house. But it quickly filled to capacity, so the services were moved to the six-car garage. Howard then paid for and supervised an extensive and skillful remodeling project that outfitted the garage with new floors, windows, and furnishings. Howard's family foundation (The Creel Foundation) based in Augusta, Georgia, continues to support the Chapel of Our Saviour even today.[12]

The current entrance to the church is the chauffeur's cottage, where the Tease and Bond

An Allen Family Reunion

In 2000, Ruthven Ryan Jr. organized a family reunion to commemorate the fiftieth anniversary of his grandmother's death. It was held in Colorado Springs. Maria's grandchildren got to see what had become of Cheyenne House, visit Shamrock Ranch, and learn more about a wonderful lady and their fascinating family history.

Maria Wharton McKean Allen (circa 1918). *Courtesy of Chapel of Our Saviour.*

families once lived. Cameron Tease passed away in the room directly above the entrance, which is now used as a dressing room for the choir.

The Allen heirs also decided to sell the Allen Ranch. On June 30, 1951, a deed was filed that transferred ownership of the ranch from the estate of deceased Maria McKean Allen to George E. and Stella V. Hardesty. After forty-seven years, the Allen Ranch suddenly had new owners.

Maria left the land a heritage that has helped to make Shamrock Ranch the picturesque and pristine gem it is today.

Horses in a winter pasture at Shamrock Ranch (2007).

THE WHARTON
ALLEN ERA

"COLORFUL AND BOMBASTIC" is the way members of the El Paso Club described Wharton Allen. He was a short, barrel-chested, crew-cut aristocrat who dressed and looked like a rodeo performer. With sudden impulses to action, he would instigate impromptu wrestling matches in the billiard room and jump on the chests of friends to test their stamina. His antics, whether he was playing the part of a tough western cowboy or a suave Philadelphia aristocrat, kept the club entertained for several decades.[1]

Wharton Allen
(circa 1943).
Courtesy the El Paso Club.

Wharton loved to collect "firsts" at cattle shows and elsewhere. The one of which he was proudest occurred one evening when he came to the El Paso Club with his special friend Oppie Hettinger, widow of Pacific War hero Colonel Jack Hettinger. Wharton had decided that he was going to be the first member in El Paso Club history to dine with a lady in the men's grill—which was strictly forbidden.

No waiter dared serve them. After a tense showdown of wills, manager George Cahill—who, like everyone else, was fond of Wharton—finally donned a white coat and assumed the serving task.

When Wharton tipped him generously after the dinner, Cahill protested, "I'm the manager, Mr. Allen. You can't tip the manager."

Wharton roared back, "Says who? You're a waiter tonight, George! Take the tip or I'll report you to the house committee!"

Tipping at the club was as taboo as permitting a lady to pass the threshold of the venerable men's grill. But Cahill took the tip anyway to keep the peace, even though he knew Wharton was bluffing. Besides, Wharton had already committed one El Paso Club felony.[2]

Another club first that Wharton pioneered took place in 1943. Because of his reverence for ladies, he persuaded the board of trustees to create a female membership "limited to fifty at any one time." Dues were set at two dollars a month. The new club bylaws specified that "their privileges shall be limited to the use of the Ladies Dining Room, Private Dining Rooms and the Ladies Cocktail Lounge . . . They shall neither vote nor hold office." The change was resisted by some male members at first, but is still in place today.[3]

Narrye Davis became the first lady member of the El Paso Club. She was followed soon after by eight other "first" ladies, two of whom were single, Agnes Donaldson and Mary C. Sargent. One can't help but wonder if Wharton was dating one or more of them at the time.

Wharton became a life member of the El Paso Club in 1945 when he made a thousand dollar contribution to help offset property liens that were cropping up as previously-paying members went off to fight in World War II. His donation helped the club stay afloat during those challenging times. He is also listed as a "Special Honorary Member" in the club's 1962 book of rules and members.

In 1949, Wharton convinced Major General Emmett "Rosie" O'Donnell, leader of the first B-29 attack against Tokyo, to join the club. The two spent much of their time in the men's grill surrounded by admirers. "O'Donnell had a fund of amusing tales and Allen added stories of his own experiences during World War I as an ambulance driver and artillerist in France."[4]

Major General
Rosie O'Donnell
(1906–1972)

Wharton probably didn't tell them, however, why he went to France in the first place. According to Peggy Hubbell, daughter of ranch manager Joe Romick, "In the few times that Wharton had any conversation with me he said, 'I flunked geometry three times. The last time I begged the professor to give me a passing grade.' The professor said, 'All I can say to you with tears in my eyes is . . . goodbye.' Wharton continued, 'So I went and joined the French Army and drove an ambulance!'"

Peggy described Wharton as "one tough guy" and wondered if he became like that in France. But she was also quick to point out that he wasn't mean—he was good to people. "He was just a bit odd and sometimes curt." When he came to the ranch, he frequently wore tweeds and a leather jacket. "He always dressed well and looked like he was going someplace special. He was handsome in a certain sort of way and debonair."

Sam Tease, son of Maria's chauffeur, characterized Wharton as a real tough western cowboy—not one to mess around with. But he was tough in a nice way, and Sam never feared him. Sam also remembered that the open Packard touring car Wharton drove had a bronze bull as a hood ornament and unique air horns that were extremely loud. Everyone knew Wharton was coming when he sounded those air horns! He was well known around the Broadmoor area.

Wharton was also a polo fan. There was a polo field just east of Cheyenne House, off Polo Drive, that he frequented. Sam Tease became a line attender at that field when he was nine or ten years old. Somehow, he also got the job of leading the polo ponies in a parade after each game so they could cool off. Although this job paid well, it was very dangerous for a young boy since the horses were excitable and easily spooked. When Wharton saw Sam leading

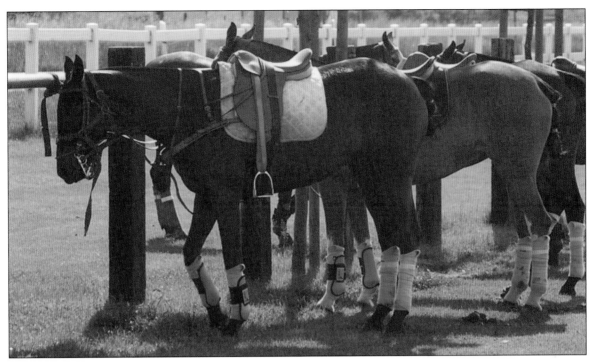

Polo ponies

the ponies one day, he expressed concern to Sam's mother about the danger involved. Although Sam had to give the job up as a result, he realized that Wharton was only concerned for his welfare.

Wharton's nephew George Jr. and his wife Bonnie visited him regularly. Both George and Wharton were golfers. Wharton belonged to the Broadmoor Golf Club and got George an invitation to play in the Broadmoor Invitational. He played in it for two or three years. Wharton was quite proud that he got his nephew accepted into this prestigious invitational for amateur golfers—and that his nephew did well enough to be invited back.

According to George, Wharton was a real character and loved to drink. Like his father, he was a man about town and made all the spots—the Broadmoor Tavern being one of his favorites. "He was gruff and rough, and cussed and drank, but he had a heart of gold." George said. "He was interested in the Olympics and had a passion for hockey."

Wharton also had an abiding affection for members of the military. Sam Cheesman, son of Wharton's South Ranch foreman, relates that Wharton would often invite his military friends to Cheyenne House late at night with the admonition to "be quiet and don't wake Mother." The purpose of these late night adventures? *"Have a snort with Whart!"*

One of Wharton's special friends was Art Hillis, a policeman covering the Broadmoor area who watched over Wharton to keep him from getting into too much trouble after visiting the Broadmoor Tavern. Wharton was genuinely interested in helping young people get to where they wanted to be in life. He had a very generous spot in his heart and provided financial support to many, including Oppie Hettinger's sons. He even sent Sam Cheesman to veterinary school at Oklahoma State University (OSU). This was an amazing feat because OSU's policy was to only accept students from states that did not have a veterinary school. Since Colorado had one, Sam thought he would never be accepted. However, because Wharton was on a very good personal basis with the head of the agricultural school there, Dean Albert Darlow, and had donated cattle and other gifts to the school, Sam was the first student in his class to be accepted!

Although Wharton dated numerous women, he never married. When asked for his opinion why, George responded, "I'm not sure anybody would have him! He was pretty tough. I think, too, that he felt devoted to his mother—to stay there and look after her when she was left alone." Peggy Hubbell described him as a Casanova.

Anticipating that he might marry someday, Wharton purchased three lots across the street from Cheyenne House (Lots 1, 2 and 3, Block 37, Broadmoor). But since this never happened, they remained vacant until at least 1958—when he gave directions for their bequeathal in his last will and testament.

Wharton ran a very successful shorthorn bull breeding operation at both of the Allen Ranches. He and his father had an office in the Mining Exchange Building located at 8 South Nevada Avenue in downtown Colorado Springs. When Benjamin Allen left Colorado in 1926 or so, he deeded the South Ranch to Wharton. Wharton maintained the Mining Exchange Building office for many years after his father left. He also went to California periodically to visit him and bolster their relationship. As a result, he was one of only two children to whom his father left an inheritance (the other was McKean, who also lived in California).

It may seem as though Wharton was strictly a playboy, but according to Sam Cheesman, he was serious about his registered bull breeding operation, checking in daily and often calling late at night. He drove to the North Ranch nearly every day, and visited the South Ranch two or three times a week to oversee the operation. In 1940, Wharton was elected president of the American Shorthorn Breeder's association, a position his father had held years earlier.

Allen Heads U.S. Shorthorn Assn.

WHARTON ALLEN

Of Colorado Springs and Broadmoor, prominent Pikes Peak region registered livestock breeder, who has just been elected president of the American Shorthorn Breeders' association. This is the highest honor within the gift of this great national breeders' organization, whose meeting was held in Chicago in conjunction with the annual International Livestock exposition. Mr. Allen is owner of the Allen Cattle company, whose Divide herd is one of the great Shorthorn groups in the nation and winner of many awards in all the big show rings. Allen Shorthorns have aided in the building up of herds thruout the country. Mr. Allen's father, the late B. C. Allen, was founder of the herd and president of the national Shorthorn association many years ago.

Colorado Springs Man Shows Champion Bull

—Associated Press Photo.

Divide Gold Prince, entered by the Allen Cattle company of Colorado Springs, was named the grand champion in the breeding shorthorn division of the national western stock show at Denver January 28-February 4. Shown here with the bull are, left to right, Wharton Allen of Colorado Springs, Courtland Jones, show manager; H. J. Gramlich, secretary of the American Shorthorn Breeders association, and Walter Davidson, a handler.

In a bull breeding program such as Wharton's, the number of cattle involved is small compared to operations that raise beef strictly for slaughter. The number of cows, calves, and bulls that Wharton kept on the North and South Ranches was capped at about a hundred. However, the amount of work that he did to provide accurate record keeping for registration purposes was significant. In fact, Sam

Cheesman said that he named each calf personally and "knew them all by name."

According to Sam, the most famous breeding bull Wharton ever owned was named The Duke of Killearn, named for a historic village in Scotland near Glasgow and Loch Lomond. He purchased this bull in Canada for $1,500.

The Duke of Killearn was an excellent sire. Many of his offspring were champions

Divide Goldpiece at the North Ranch (circa 1941).

and grand champions at shows including the American Royal and the National Western Stock Show. According to Sam Cheesman, The Duke was responsible for Wharton having, for a time, the leading Shorthorn operation in the United States in terms of the number of champions produced.

Divide Goldpiece, shown above, was another prize bull that Wharton owned. Some of his offspring are pictured to the right.

In order to group his cattle by ranch, Wharton called those sired on the North, or Divide, Ranch by the first name of "Divide." Over time he began to spend more time at the South Ranch because he had an able manager in Joe Romick at the Divide Ranch.

When Wharton was ready to sell his prize Shorthorns, he would prepare a professional sales brochure and make the sale a national event. A few pages from these brochures are shown opposite. The photograph was taken at the Divide Ranch, as can be seen from the impressive view of Pikes Peak and the Rampart Range in the background. All the cattle in this picture were raised on the Divide Ranch.

From the Allen Cattle Company Auction Sale of Divide Shorthorns held at the State Fair Grounds, Des Moines, Iowa, January 29, 1941.

SHORTHORN SIRE WINS CHAMPIONSHIP

Divide Chancellor, Shorthorn herd sire at the Northwest School and Station, was declared the grand champion Shorthorn bull at the recent Minnesota State Fair. This bull was bred by the Allen Cattle company of Colorado, and purchased at the International Livestock exposition last fall. As a senior yearling, he won first in his class at the Kansas City Royal and International Livestock show.

The Best Ten Head" at the 1935 International Stock Show, from the Allen Cattle Company Auction Sale of Divide Shorthorns held at the State Fair Grounds, Des Moines, Iowa, February 12, 1936.

A view of the barns at the Divide Ranch adjacent the Black Forest. Calves developed at this high altitu are naturally more thrifty and make hardier breedi cattle.

The Allen Cattle Company Auction Sale of Divide Shorthorns held at the State Fair Grounds, Des Moines, Iowa, January 29, 1941.

One of Wharton's buyers was the Northwest School of Agriculture at the University of Minnesota. An article from the October 1935 edition of the *Northwest Monthly* announces that one of Wharton's prize bulls was the grand champion of the Minnesota State Fair that year.

The Allen Cattle Company brand is reproduced here.

When Maria determined to raze Cheyenne Court, Wharton took all the furniture, plaques, pictures, records, and trophies from Benjamin's home office and transported them to a small office at the South Ranch. One extraordinary piece of mahogany furniture he moved was an enormous rolltop desk.

As Sam Cheesman was growing up on the South Ranch, he learned to love all these things that had once belonged to Benjamin C. Allen. So when Wharton died, Sam asked George, Wharton's brother, if he could have them. George graciously agreed, so Sam hauled the furniture and mementos all the way to Pine Bluff, Arkansas, where he lives today. The rolltop desk was recently refinished and is now being used by Sam's nephew in Colorado Springs.

Sam and his brother Robert have visited the Shamrock Ranch several times and have given to David Wismer Wharton's cattle records plus many photographs and important pictures from the Allen Ranch days. Sam Cheesman felt these treasured items should be preserved on the ranch where they originated. Many of them are reproduced in this book. One special treasure received from Sam is a watercolor-finished photograph of a Montana cattle drive titled "The Last Roundup," (see page 228).

Sam (left) and Robert Cheesman in front of a Shamrock Ranch barn door (circa 2000).

Early in 1913, the year that Wharton graduated from St. Mark's School, the 16th Amendment of the United States Constitution was ratified. Only Connecticut, Florida, Rhode Island, and Utah rejected it.[5] This Amendment states that "The Congress shall have power to lay and collect taxes on incomes, from whatever source derived, without apportionment among the several States, and without regard to any census or enumeration."

Naturally, the Allen family was affected by the ratification, which meant that paying federal income taxes would forever be required of them. According to Sam Cheesman, "Income tax time was Wharton's most miserable week . . . or two or three. He was just like a bear! So I wished he wouldn't come down to the ranch until it was all over."

Before Maria McKean Allen died, she sold the land north of Hodgen Road and west of present day State Highway 83 (the old L&PP and West Cherry stage routes) that had made up the Allen Ranch when Benjamin first bought it from the Husted Sterling Live Stock Company. But she also purchased some additional land adjacent to her holdings west of State Highway 83. The map opposite shows what the Allen Ranch looked like in 1950—the year that Maria passed away.

Comparing this map to the one on page 86, notice that the acreage north of section 26 is gone and that most of the land east of section 26 is also gone. However, the holdings west of sections 3 and 34 have changed and grown in total acreage. This western portion of the Allen Ranch was separated from the eastern portion by three-quarters of a mile and bordered on the Husted Wagon Road; Wharton and his employees called it the Husted Pasture.

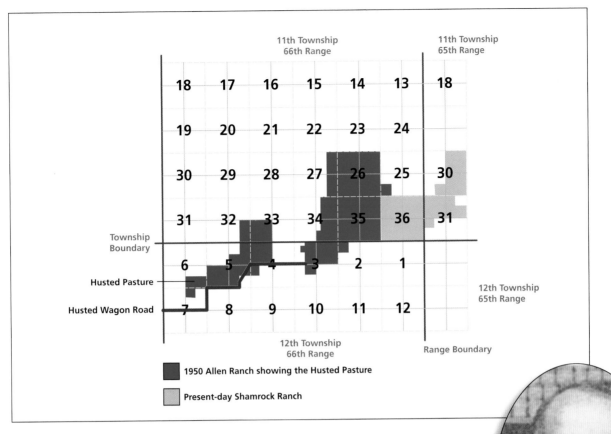

11th Township
66th Range

11th Township
65th Range

18	17	16	15	14	13	18
19	20	21	22	23	24	
30	29	28	27	26	25	30
31	32	33	34	35	36	31

Township Boundary

| 6 | 5 | 4 | 3 | 2 | 1 |
| 7 | 8 | 9 | 10 | 11 | 12 |

Husted Pasture

Husted Wagon Road

12th Township
65th Range

12th Township
66th Range

Range Boundary

■ 1950 Allen Ranch showing the Husted Pasture

■ Present-day Shamrock Ranch

After his mother passed away, Wharton moved into a one-story house just around the corner from Cheyenne House. His address was 1 Berthe Circle, the road having been named for Countess Berthe de Pourtales, wife of Count James Pourtales. Howard Creel, with whom he was close friends, lived next door to him on Elm Street.

Wharton passed away on November 21, 1963—one day before President John F. Kennedy was assassinated in Dallas, Texas. His nephew George remembers the day well because he and his wife Bonnie were on their way to Colorado Springs to attend Wharton's funeral when news of the tragic assassination broke. Wharton's funeral was held at the Chapel of Our Saviour (formerly Cheyenne House).

President John F. Kennedy
(1917–1963)

Instead of being interred in the grave next to his mother, Wharton's ashes were scattered at a place Wharton had designated on the Allen's North Ranch by Milton C. Cheesman, foreman of the South Ranch, and Willard Miller, foreman of the North Ranch.

Milton C. Cheesman
(1903–1997)

Wharton Allen's grave cover (2005). Note that his ashes were scattered on the Allen Ranch and are not interred in the Evergreen Cemetery.

Because of their close friendship, Wharton left his house on Berthe Circle to George Allen Jr. and his wife. They later sold the house, but still come to Colorado Springs every summer to play golf, visit places of historical interest to the Allen family, and attend church at the Chapel of Our Saviour.

To his special friend Oppie Hettinger, Wharton left a large radio-phonograph and all of his records, plus some stock and Broadmoor Lots 2 and 3.

Wharton also left "to my foreman, M. C. Cheesman, a most faithful and upright man, and in appreciation of his loyalty and services to me," the ten best cows and any bull from his herd that Cheesman desired. Also, he bequeathed to Sam Cheesman, whom he called "Bud" in the will, and Robert Cheesman, "the pick of one heifer or bull from my herd to each of them after their father's choice."

These bequests certainly denote the affection that Wharton had for Milt Cheesman and his sons. No wonder Sam Cheesman named one of his three children Wharton Allen! Sadly, Wharton Allen Cheesman, who went by Allen, was tragically killed in a bicycle accident in 2008, at age 46.

In addition, Wharton left financial gifts to many Colorado Springs charities, including Grace/St. Stephen's Episcopal Church, Colorado College, Post No. 5 of the American Legion, the Fireman's Pension Fund, the Police Pension Fund, the American Red Cross, the Salvation Army, the Boy's Club, and the Colorado Springs Nutrition Camp.

He also left shares of his estate to the University of Pennsylvania's Wharton School of Finance and Commerce, and St. Mark's School in Massachusetts. Lastly, he forgave all his debtors.

Per his instructions, the executors of Wharton's will (his brother George and Colorado Springs attorney Ben S. Wendelken) gave the South Ranch to Colorado College. Sam Cheesman had attempted to buy the ranch for his father first, but the wording of the will didn't allow this to happen.

However, the Colorado College Board of Trustees was kind enough to lease the ranch to Milt Cheesman for a nominal fee for a number of years. Then they sold it to the Gates Rubber Company. Today the ranch has been subdivided and has a number of industrial buildings, including warehouses, on it.

Wharton Allen
(1918)

Wharton preceded his twin brother Curtis in death. Evidently, they still looked alike when he died as illustrated by the following amusing incident. According to George Allen Jr., Curtis came to Colorado Springs several years after Wharton's passing and went to the Broadmoor Tavern for dinner and a drink. While he was eating, a waitress who knew Wharton came up to him to get a closer look. Upon studying Curtis' face, she nearly fainted—thinking Wharton had come back from the dead!

Curtis was the last of Maria and Benjamin Allen's children to pass away. He died in March of 1979.

Curtis Allen
(1918)

ALLEN RANCH
EMPLOYEES AND TENANTS

The Steppler Family

IN 1877, a young man named Christian Lewis "Lou" Steppler and his younger brother Charlie ran away from their father. Their mother had died years before while giving birth to a daughter, Minnie. After their mother's death, their father, who was a cobbler as well as an alcoholic and a card player, began to beat the two young boys. When Minnie was very young, he farmed her out as a servant and maid, but kept the boys and had them work on the family farm and at various places around their hometown of Fort Calhoun, Nebraska.

Lou was eleven years old when he finally had enough and fled. Charlie was only nine. They headed south to Omaha, then followed the Union Pacific railroad tracks west across the vast Nebraska prairie.

Before leaving home, they raided the family root cellar for glass jars of food to sustain them on this brave journey. At least one bottle was tainted with botulin, a neurotoxic prod-

uct of the bacteria *botulinum*. When the boys camped out under a railroad bridge one night and ate, they both contracted an acute case of botulism, a deadly paralytic illness caused by this toxin. They both lay unconscious under the bridge in the middle of nowhere for several days.

When Charlie finally awakened, he saw Lou lying as still as a cadaver. Certain that his brother was dead, he headed for home—feeling frantic, lost, and alone. Somehow he made it back to Fort Calhoun and reported the death of his brother, but he never stayed with his father again.

But Lou was not dead. He eventually revived to find Charlie gone. Determined to continue his way west and not knowing where Charlie was, Lou pressed on and eventually worked his way to California. For fourteen years, he roamed the West and did whatever he had to in order to eat. During this time, his family thought he was dead because of Charlie's report.

In 1888, Lou caught a train to Salt Lake City and then took the narrow gauge Denver and Rio Grande train to Ouray in southwestern Colorado. There he met Otto Mears—"Pathfinder of the San Juans" (1839–1931)—whose road building, track building, and railroads enabled development of Colorado's San Juan Country. They had much in common, both being born in the Old World and losing their mothers while very young, so Otto took Lou under his wing and gave him a job.

Lou worked for Otto until 1892, when he got on a train heading for Iowa. Lou intended to visit his sister Minnie, whom he had successfully contacted by mail. But when the train arrived in Monument, Colorado, he got off and saw a note on the station board advertising for potato pickers in the Table Rock community. Seeking to earn some money before continuing his journey, he walked all the way to the potato fields and was hired—not knowing that he would spend most of his remaining life in the Divide Country. It is likely that he boarded with the William Clark Brown family (see page 66) in Table Rock, and thus met Martha Jane "Jennie" Brown, his future wife.

When Lou had earned enough money picking potatoes, he was ready to homestead. Looking around for some available land (which was becoming scarce by then), he found a 160 acre parcel at Fondis—a small town near Kiowa.

Though he had lived in the United States since he was six months old, Lou was born in Prussia (which is now Germany), and therefore not a U.S. citizen. In order to homestead, he needed citizenship. So in November of 1894, he walked to Denver, renounced his Prussian citizenship, and became a U.S. citizen. That same day, he applied for the home-stead in Fondis that had captured his imagination. He was twenty-eight years old at the time.

Lou tried to grow beans on his homestead, but they didn't do well in the hot, dry climate. By working for his room and board, he was able to survive during the homesteading period. During this time, he traveled as often as possible back to Table Rock so he could court Jennie Brown, who was working on local farms by then. Having only one good pair of clothes, Lou stored them under his feather tick mattress to keep them clean and pressed for his next visit with Jennie.

When his homesteading requirements were fulfilled early in 1900, Lou received a patent (per the Homestead Act) for his quarter section and promptly sold the land for $600, plus a team and wagon. Then he went southeast to Calhan where he rented a farm.

On February 20, 1900, Lou and Jennie were married by a justice of the peace. They were wed at the residence of the bride's parents, which was the ranch manager's house on the Evergreen Ranch, where the Brown family was living at the time (see page 66). This is the first marriage known to have taken place on land that is now Shamrock Ranch.

Jennie Brown, wife of Lou Steppler. *Courtesy the Steppler family.*

Lou took his bride back to his farm near Calhan. Jennie was distraught when she first saw the place, but she stuck it out for four years. Then, in 1904, she and Lou moved back to Table Rock and rented the Bishop place, located near the Allen Ranch. For a year or two, they lived in a small, three-room log cabin there.

Then, Lou rented 400 acres just north of Hodgen Road from Benjamin C. Allen. They were the ranch's northernmost acres, which Allen purchased from the Husted Sterling Live Stock Company in 1904. Benjamin had recently built a two-story bunk house for ranch hands on this piece of land, and he allowed Lou and Jennie to move into it. Jennie was pleased with this new house, which had three rooms on the main floor and two more upstairs.

For the next thirty-nine years, Lou and Jennie lived in this modest but comfortable house. In the late 1960s, the road leading to it was named Steppler Road in honor of their family.

Jennie and Lou had five children, one of whom died in infancy. The other four are shown in the family photograph. In the back row of the photo are, from left to right, Charles, Irene, and William Albert "Al," the three youngest children. They were born in the house Lou rented from Benjamin Allen. The oldest daughter, Marie (front center of photo), was born at the farm near Calhan.

Over the years, Lou made improvements to the ranch he rented from Benjamin Allen— first shingling the house, then building a shed and barn, and finally planting willow trees along Cherry Creek. He also started to buy land from Allen. In 1907, he bought 160 acres south of Hodgen Road, then another 211 acres adjoining this parcel in 1917. As of 2008, these acres make up Sundance Ranch, which lies between Shamrock Ranch's current northeast corner and the High Forest Ranch subdivision (see page 18). In 1920, Lou purchased the 400 acres that he was then renting from Maria Allen—giving him ownership of 771 acres.

The Lou and Jennie Steppler family (circa 1920). *Courtesy the Steppler family.*

+ – P

Lou Steppler's Cross-Bar-P brand

Lou used some of his land to raise cattle. In 1912, he purchased the Cross-Bar-P brand, which is still in the family today. But most of the land was used for dryland, or nonirrigated, farming of wheat, oats, alfalfa, etc. When he discovered that Early Ohio red potatoes grew well on his farm, Lou began to raise them in earnest.

With only his children and a four-horse team for help, Lou planted and harvested at least 80 acres of potatoes a year. Soon he was winning ribbons and trophies all over Colorado for his dryland seed potatoes. Eventually he earned the title of "Colorado Potato King," which was fitting because he was truly a pioneer in dryland farming of potatoes. The Colorado Agriculture School in Ft. Collins even invited him to join their faculty. People came all the way from Kansas and Nebraska

to buy his seed potatoes. His son Al remembered driving to the town of Husted in a wagon drawn by a team of horses to sell the prize potatoes to town residents and train passengers. Susan Koch, Lou's granddaughter, has silver trophies and a basket full of ribbons that Lou won.

Jennie and Lou's oldest child, Marie, married a man by the name of Bill Conger when she was in her mid–twenties. She first met Bill when her father hired him to help milk cows.

Soon after their marriage in 1924, Bill and Marie moved into the small log cabin shown here, which was situated on the state-owned section of land just east of the Allen Ranch. This section has come to be known as the "school section" and is now part of the Shamrock Ranch (see page 42). At least one child (Lewis, their firstborn) was born to the Congers while they lived in this cabin.

One night, when Lewis was not yet five years old, the barn next to the cabin was

Remains of the log cabin on the school section that was home to the Conger family (2008).

Spring-fed pond on the school section (2008).

deliberately set on fire. Bill rushed to Lewis's bed, carried him outside, placed him on a milk can away from the flames, and told him to stay there. Even though he was very young, the events of that night burned deeply into Lewis's memory—he remembered all of his life being upset because he didn't have his shoes on!

Unfortunately, the only water available was a small pond that was of no use in fighting the fire. Hence the barn burned to the ground. The pond is still there today, but the barn was never replaced. Rumor has it that two men started the fire to take revenge on Bill for some perceived infraction during a night of heavy drinking.

Marie eventually had eight children. She lived a long life. One of her favorite childhood memories was of her mother hitching up the horses and taking her along to deliver butter, cheese, and eggs to the Allen Ranch. Marie was five years old then (it was 1906). As she later told her family, she loved the beautiful ride through the forest to the ranch so much she would remember it until the day she died—even if she lived to be a hundred. Well, she lived to be a hundred-and-one and never forgot that fond memory!

Jennie and Lou Steppler's youngest son, William Albert, is shown here at age fourteen. Nicknamed "Al," he was born in 1914 and followed in his grandfather Brown's footsteps by working at the Allen Ranch. Hired by ranch

Al Steppler at age 14 (1928). *Courtesy the Steppler family.*

manager Joe Romick, he started as a teenager and continued into his twenties "doing odd jobs—the dirty work."

One of Al's jobs was to fill the silo with corn silage (chopped corn stalks and grain), then stomp it down to get the air pockets out. He did this by climbing inside the silo and marching around to pack the silage down. Sometimes Joe would look in on him, and once in a while Joe's daughter Peggy would climb in to join the fun. Al earned a quarter a day from the Allens.

The silo where Al Steppler stomped corn silage (2008).

When he was still in his teens, Lou sent him to get some old fence posts from the Allen Ranch. When Al discussed the errand with Wharton, he confessed to not having anything with which to haul the posts.

Wharton gave him a wagon and told him he could take any of the posts except for the pitch ones, which have more resin in them and so are extremely hard and therefore more desirable. Al's daughter, Susan Koch, still has that wagon today.

Al Steppler standing on the wheel of a his Case steam tractor (1927). *Courtesy the Steppler family.*

Lou and Al would go to the Allen Ranch periodically to get pitch stumps. Since ponderosa pines naturally produce an abundance of resin (i.e., pitch), the wood from these trees burns extremely hot, although they also produce a lot of smoke.

Lou used these pitch stumps to run a steam tractor that pulled and powered a threshing machine, which separates grain from straw. Sometimes the threshing was done in the fields, but more often it was performed in a stackyard—an area for holding stacks of grain. After Lou cut his grain with a horse-drawn binder, the sheaves were stacked (shocked) in the field. Since the Divide Country was a close-knit community, everyone pitched in and traded labor as needed—especially during the harvest in the fall. Using teams of horses or mules to pull hay racks, Lou and his neighbors provided a steady flow of oat or wheat shocks to the threshing machine so the grain could be separated from the chaff. While they were doing this, Jennie and the other wives prepared a midday meal for the hardworking men.

The steam-powered Case tractor Lou used was state-of-the-art technology at the time. The tractor's owner and crew especially liked coming to work for Lou Steppler because he always had those hot-burning pitch stumps to fire the boiler—therefore they were able to minimize the amount of wood and work required to do the job.

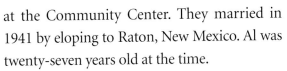

Al grew into a dashing and handsome young man. He chased a beautiful and gifted woman named Alta Elizabeth "Betty" Simpson all around Pikes Peak Country—until he convinced her to marry him. He had met her at one of the Black Forest barn dances held at the Community Center. They married in 1941 by eloping to Raton, New Mexico. Al was twenty-seven years old at the time.

Young Al Steppler.
Courtesy the Steppler family.

Al and Betty lived with Al's parents for the next three years. Unfortunately, Jennie didn't take kindly to Betty at first—after all, she had taken her baby boy away!

Jennie constantly gave Betty a hard time about household chores. For example, when Lou purchased a brand-new, gasoline-powered Maytag washing machine for Jennie, Betty was not allowed to use it. When Jennie and Lou went to California to visit Lou's sister, Minnie, Jennie went so far as to remove the spark plug from the washing machine so that Betty couldn't use it while they were gone! However, Betty happened upon the missing spark plug one

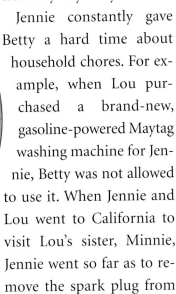

Young Betty Steppler.
Courtesy the Steppler family.

day and made good use of the washing machine. Of course, the spark plug was back in its hiding place when Jennie returned—never the wiser!

Remarkably, Betty never became bitter over the way Jennie treated her. As a result, Jennie grew to love her youngest son's gracious wife.

Al and Betty had two children—William Allen (they liked the name William and carried it on from the Brown side of the family) and Susan Elaine. Susan later married Nolan Koch (pronounced "Cook").

Al helped his father farm the Steppler Ranch until Lou died in 1944. Jennie moved to Colorado Springs after his death, so Al and Betty had the house to themselves. Then Al's sisters Marie and Irene sold their shares of the land to Al and his brother Charles. Eventually, Al ended up owning all 400 acres of the land that his father purchased from the Allens in 1920.

The Brown Family

THE LAND Benjamin C. Allen acquired on March 7, 1904, from the Husted Sterling Live Stock Company included much of present-day Shamrock Ranch. When Benjamin bought this land, there was a ranch manager's house (see page 64) already located on Section 3. William Clark Brown, Jennie Steppler's father, was the ranch manager living in this house when the Allen-Husted-Sterling deal concluded. Besides being Calvin Husted's first known resident ranch manager, William was also Benjamin Allen's first—though he didn't hold the job for long.

On June 1, 1904, William's wife, Adaline, died of a heart attack at the young age of fifty-four. Devastated by her death, William took his youngest daughter, Beulah, and moved to

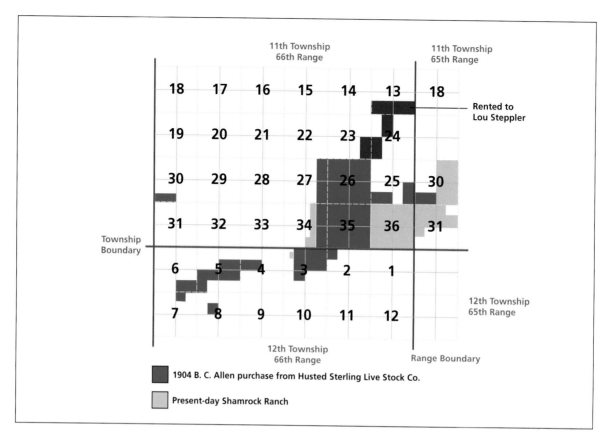

11th Township 66th Range

11th Township 65th Range

| 18 | 17 | 16 | 15 | 14 | 13 | 18 |
| 19 | 20 | 21 | 22 | 23 | 24 | |

Rented to Lou Steppler

| 30 | 29 | 28 | 27 | 26 | 25 | 30 |
| 31 | 32 | 33 | 34 | 35 | 36 | 31 |

Township Boundary

| 6 | 5 | 4 | 3 | 2 | 1 |
| 7 | 8 | 9 | 10 | 11 | 12 |

12th Township 65th Range

12th Township 66th Range

Range Boundary

■ 1904 B. C. Allen purchase from Husted Sterling Live Stock Co.

▢ Present-day Shamrock Ranch

Pasadena, California, in 1905 or 1906. The photograph of them shown here was taken in 1905 at their home on the Allen Ranch before they moved to Pasadena.

William's older daughters, Jennie and Fannie, and his son Allie were grown by then and had already left home. His son William "Billie" Lester, who was about eighteen years old, stayed on and worked at the Allen Ranch.

William Clark Brown and daughter Beulah (circa 1905). *Courtesy the Steppler family.*

Billie and Beulah Brown. *Courtesy the Steppler family.*

Allen Ranch manager Neil Wishart with one of Benjamin Allen's prize shorthorns (circa 1915).

Sometime after William Clark Brown left the North Ranch, Benjamin hired a man by the name of Neil Wishart as the new ranch manager. Neil moved his family into the house that both William and Billie Brown had occupied. An April 1916 *Colorado Springs Gazette and Telegraph* article mentions the birth of one of his sons in Husted, which was the nearest town to the Allen Ranch houses at the time; the Allen Ranch mailbox was located in Husted on the east side of its main street (U.S. Highway 85), opposite the grocery store.

Milton C. Cheesman
(1903–1997)

Billie Brown eventually became manager of the South Ranch, a position he kept until the early 1940s. He then went on to become foreman at a ranch near Glen Eyrie, and eventually caretaker of Glen Eyrie. The picture opposite shows Billie with his sister Beulah. Billie married and raised three children—two girls and a boy.

When Billie left the South Ranch, Wharton hired Milton "Milt" C. Cheesman to be the new foreman. Milt had been working at Camp Carson (now Ft. Carson), which was under construction at the time, and wanted to get back into ranching. He managed the South Ranch for approximately thirty years—even after Wharton died—until Colorado College finally sold it to Gates Rubber Company.

The Romick Family

IN LATE 1917 or early 1918, Benjamin Allen hired a herdsman by the name of Henry Joseph (Joe) Romick. Formerly a farmer in Wamego, Kansas, Joe was working in Prowers County, Colorado, when he saw an advertisement in the *Breeder's Gazette* for the Allen Ranch job. His daughter Margaret, who went by the name Peggy, was only a year or so old at the time. Peggy's only sibling, Joe Jr., was just three years older.

When Joe was hired for the job, he moved his family into a cement block house with a cement porch directly north of Neil's house. It was smaller than the Wishart house (see photo on page 64).

As the ranch herdsman, Joe was in charge of all the cattle on the ranch. His job—in which he took great pride—was a very important position involving long hours and much hard work, especially during calving time. In those days, a herdsman bred, registered, cared for, transported, groomed, and exhibited cattle at livestock shows around the country.

Over the years, each owner of the Shamrock Ranch who has had a cow-calf operation (meaning that they bred cows and raised their calves according to strict bloodlines while keeping accurate records) has employed a herdsman as well as a ranch manager or foreman. The herdsman reported to the ranch manager, whose responsibilities were broader.

Joe wife, Coral Meta Lucinda, boarded other ranch hands in their house. One of her boarders was Wharton Allen, who lived there after he returned from the war in France. Evidently, Benjamin Allen felt it was important for Wharton to learn the cattle business from the ground up by starting as a ranch hand. Wharton was very friendly with the Romicks,

and called Peggy "Le Petite Mademoiselle Fizzletip" because of her curly blond hair.

In 1918 or 1919, the most devastating epidemic in recorded world history—the influenza pandemic—reached the Divide Country. This pandemic, which was most deadly to people ages twenty to forty, was so severe it shortened the life span in the United States by ten years. Ten times more Americans were killed by this epidemic than by World War I, which was thought to have contributed to it and certainly hastened its global spread. One fifth of the world's population was eventually infected,[1] but fortunately, none of the Allens or Romicks died from the epidemic. The pandemic's effect on the Wishart family is unknown.

Wharton Allen
(1918)

It was about this time that the Divide Country began to be called the "Black Forest." Soldiers returning from the war who had seen Germany's Black Forest undoubtedly saw the resemblance between both locales and related to the more romantic name. Real estate developers probably helped establish the new name, and some attribute it to Leonard Curtis,[2] but no one knows for certain how it originated.

In 1920, Joe left the Allen Ranch for a better job in Missouri. By then he had become good friends with Wharton Allen and Billie Brown. And he must have impressed Benjamin Allen, because he hired him again in 1925 to manage the South Ranch. Pleased with this new opportunity, Joe returned to Colorado in 1925 to start a new career as a ranch manager. Fortunately, he didn't move his family—for he was only there a for few weeks.

When he found that Benjamin was reading mail from his wife, Coral, which had been sent care of Benjamin, he left in a huff, shouting "I won't work for you!"

Although normally even tempered and good natured, Joe was furious when he left. And no wonder—Benjamin told him the news from his wife before he could read her letters!

In the autumn of 1926, Wharton was showing his prize shorthorn cattle at the American Royal Livestock Show in Kansas City. He was thirty-one years old at the time. While there, he ran into Joe. Evidently Neil was no longer the manager of the Allen Ranch, or was soon to leave, because Wharton offered the position to Joe—who eventually accepted it at a salary of $150 a month. Upon leaving Wharton's employ, Neil moved to Kansas near the town of Manhattan.

When Joe moved his family back to the Allen Ranch at the end of 1927, they moved into the house that the Wishart family had occupied, shown below. The small white shed on the left was a storehouse where a cream separator was kept. This is the same house that Cal Husted built prior to 1878.

Things had changed at the ranch by then; some for the better, and some for the worse. For one thing, Joe's wife discovered that their new place of residence had bed bugs. Evidently the Wisharts had not kept it clean. After several months of enduring the bugs, Joe convinced Wharton that the house needed to be torn down and rebuilt. The next spring he moved his family into the chauffeur's house directly behind Maria Allen's house while the work was being done.

When the workers tore the house down, they found that the walls were indeed full of bed bugs. After they built a new residence in its place (the one on the left in the picture on the next page), the Romicks moved into this inviting, bug-free house that more closely matched the style of the barns behind it and to the northeast. There were three rooms, a bathroom, and pantry downstairs, and three bedrooms plus a storage room upstairs.

The Allen Ranch manager's house where the Romicks lived for a short time (circa 1927). *Courtesy the Steppler family.*

New manager's house (left) and remodeled duplex for Allen Ranch employees (circa 1928). *Courtesy Sam Cheesman.*

Next, the workers remodeled the cement block house where the Romicks lived when Joe was herdsman for Benjamin. This house appears behind Cal Husted's residence in the photo shown on page 64. Although similar in appearance to the newly built manager's house, the remodeled house was actually a duplex that housed the families of two ranch hands. The front and back entrances can be seen in the photo on page 86. Joe's daughter Peggy used to play cards with a young couple, Rosy and Pat, who lived on one side of the duplex. The Romick's storehouse was not disturbed by the construction. In the photos on the previous page, two connected chicken houses with pens are visible between the two residences, as is a privy nestled at the edge of the trees to the right of the chicken houses. There is also a windmill on the hill behind the duplex. What can't been seen in this photograph is a building with dual garages and dual woodsheds that is behind the Romick's house.

A 2008 photograph of the dual garage/woodshed building and the dual chicken houses is provided for comparison. The chicken pens are now in the rear of the chicken house.

The dual garage/woodshed building and dual chicken houses in 2008.

Chickens are still raised in the chicken houses.

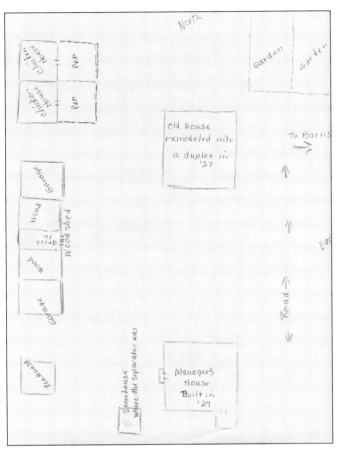

Sketch of the layout of the 1928 Allen Ranch employee housing as remembered by Peggy (Romick) Hubble at age ninety.

Another change apparent on the ranch when the Romicks returned in 1927 was the addition of a second barn and equipment annex just east of Barn No. 2 (see photo below). County records indicate that it may have been constructed in 1924. Wharton had clearly been busy since Maria appointed him director of the Divide Ranch!

The equipment annex, attached to the newer barn, was used to store farming equipment during the winter. It also had a forge and tool racks on the north end that were used to shoe horses and make repairs. Peggy remembers using a red-hot poker from the forge to do wood burning projects. Two trucks—a pickup and a flat bed—were also parked in this extension of the new barn. Wharton built another shed just east of the Romick residence to function as a shelter for horses and cattle in the wintertime.

When the Romicks moved to the Allen Ranch in 1927, they traveled by train. Joe had

Allen Ranch barns and equipment annex as they looked circa 1927 and still look in 2008.

Model A Ford (1929)

a 1922 Model T Ford, which he loaded into a box car so it could be transported along with their household goods. In 1929, he traded that Model T in for a Model A, similar to the one shown here.

Wharton met the family when they arrived at Husted Station. Peggy was ten years old at the time. She remembers sitting in the back seat of Wharton's Packard Touring car on the way to the ranch. It had side curtains to block the cold air, but the one on the driver's side was missing. Evidently Wharton liked the fresh air even in December!

The move to Colorado was difficult for Peggy since it occurred during the Christmas holiday and spoiled her eleventh birthday on January 3. She didn't want to leave her friends in Missouri, and found entering a new school in the middle of the school year to be "horrible" and living on the ranch to be "remote and lonely."

But she learned to love it there, even though she worked hard. One of her jobs was

Packard Touring Car (1927)

carrying in kindling for her family. She also worked in the family garden and cared for the chickens.

One of her favorite jobs was carrying milk to Maria's house, since it gave her the opportunity to sit in the kitchen and talk to the cooks and servants. Like George Allen Jr. (Maria's grandson), she remembers that dinner was always served promptly at eight o'clock, and that everyone, even little children, dressed for the meal. The maids and cooks told her that Wharton used to leave change lying around on the floor to test their integrity.

Peggy loved the beauty of the ranch. One day she and her mother took a walk and collected twenty-six different varieties of wild flowers. Squirrels and porcupines were common, along with coyotes and foxes. And of course there was always Pikes Peak to inspire her.

Black Forest gray squirrel

Black Forest fox

Wild columbine

Winter on the Shamrock Ranch (2007)

Pikes Peak (June 2008)

employees would cut large blocks of ice from the ponds and haul them to the ice house, where they were placed in a hole in the dirt floor and covered with sawdust. With enough ice buried this way, the ice house, which was half underground, would stay cool all summer long and provide a measure of refrigeration for milk, butter, cheese, and other foods stored there.

During the winters, Peggy and her brother enjoyed the snow—especially sledding on it. Blizzards were common, so they often missed school for days at a time when they were snowed in. Sometimes the pipes under the house would freeze and plug up the sewer, so they'd have to trudge through the snow to use a privy behind the house.

Two ponds, south of Maria's house, froze over each winter and provided ice for the ice house that was on the property. The ranch

The ice house in 2008

Of course there was no central heating in those days, so the Romicks and the other ranch employees kept warm in the winter by burning wood, which was plentiful on the ranch. Each residence had its own garage and woodshed. A covered drive-in connected them.

Kerosene lamps and lanterns provided lighting on dark winter nights. If the kerosene ran out, candles were used. Peggy learned how to trim the wicks and wash the lamp chimneys. Smaller candles with clamps were used for decorating the Christmas tree. When asked what it was like to live without electricity, Peggy responded, "I guess we were so glad to have water in the house that we didn't worry about electricity." Electricity finally came to the ranch in the 1940s.

Peggy on her horse Symphony (circa 1941). *Courtesy Peggy Hubbell.*

Kerosene lantern

A snow plow, which didn't look anything like modern plows, was kept at the ranch. The blade, made of wood and steel, was mounted at a slant to a wooden sled. The odd contraption looked like a sled with a banana attached. Horses were used to pull this strange vehicle. Peggy said she couldn't count the number of times it got stuck, but it did the job of clearing the driveway all the way to the barns.

According to Peggy, the Allen Ranch was never a showplace—it was a working ranch. For several summers, her brother, Joe Jr., got paid to ride the fences—that is, to see where they needed mending. Since the ranch consisted of a total of 3,600 acres then, he had a lot of riding to do. His salary was $25 a month. Mrs. Romick was paid to board him when he was working, like any other employee, so she put the money in the bank for him.

In addition to cattle, the Allens raised corn for silage and hay for winter feed. The growing season was too short for the corn to mature, but that didn't matter for silage. When harvested, the corn was run through a chopper and then blown up into a silo. Hay was cut off the meadows. A hay wagon with two slings served to gather it. The ranch hands would pitch hay onto one sling until it was full, then stretch out the other sling and fill it. Upon returning to the barn, they'd use a sling and pulley to hoist the slings into the hayloft on the east side of the building. Today, David Wismer stores hay in the newer barn, though now the hay is baled and a conveyor belt gets it up there much more easily.

As both ranch manager and herdsman, Peggy's father took Wharton's cattle to stock shows in Denver, San Francisco, Salt Lake City, Chicago and Kansas City. To get to these shows—which were important events to sell prize cattle—Joe, his ranch hands, and the cattle all traveled by train. The men slept with the cattle in the box cars. In order to present the animals as attractively as possible, they washed and brushed the cattle down using a curry comb, then brushed their hair back up again.

Joe Romick with a prize bull that sold for a remarkable $2,000 (1941). *Courtesy Peggy Hubbell.*

Shorthorn bull, groomed for the show ring (circa 1941).

According to Peggy, her father was a heavy smoker. He preferred Camels, and if he ran out, "We were all in trouble," she said. He truly personified the Camel advertisement, "I'd walk a mile for a Camel."

During the Great Depression, Wharton Allen cut Joe's pay from $150 to $125 a month to save money. Even so, Peggy said that, in those days of tumbling prices and burgeoning food lines, "When the house was furnished and you didn't have to pay to heat it or pay taxes, it was a very wonderful place to live."

Wharton called Joe every night to talk about the cattle. In order to do this, he had the first hand-cranked telephone in the neighborhood installed at the Romick house.

Neighbors would come by at times to use this telephone, especially if they had an emergency. Peggy remembers Bill Conger, who lived on the school section (section 36 that bordered on the east side of the Allen Ranch), coming to use the telephone when his wife was about to deliver a baby. She also remembers that someone from the school would call if the school bus couldn't make it through the snow to pick up the Allen Ranch children.

There was a school about 0.5 mile south of where the Romick children lived called the Stout School (see page 106). It was named after Sam Stout and stood on land that was once part of Sam Stout's ranch.

The Romick children were bused to Lewis Consolidated School, 12 miles away in downtown Monument. In those days, the school served all grades—elementary through high school. Mrs. Inez Johnson Lewis was the county superintendent of schools and an education pioneer in the Black Forest. This school, named after her, welcomed students from Monument, Palmer Lake, Husted, and ranches that were near enough to be serviced with buses.[3] Today it houses the district's administrative offices.

Peggy remembers riding to school in one of those buses. It had bench seats on each side and traveled here and there to pick up students scattered over the northern part of the Black Forest. If a blizzard hit—which happened quite frequently—it had difficulty making the treacherous journey to the Allen Ranch, so she enjoyed many snow days at home. Nevertheless, she graduated at age sixteen from Lewis Consolidated School as the school valedictorian. Her 1933 senior class consisted of sixteen students, five of whom were girls. Upon receiving a scholarship to the Colorado State Teachers College in Greeley, she earned a degree in education. She went on to teach at a school in Table Rock to carry on the tradition of her own beloved high school English teacher. According to Peggy, the Table Rock School consisted of two large rooms with a vestibule and a basement housing the furnace. The boys' and girls' toilets were out back and water was available from a pump in front of the building. Peggy taught eighth grade through high school in one of the rooms. Another instructor taught all grades below eighth in the other room.

Lewis Consolidated School in Monument (circa 1920).

Joe Jr., Peggy's brother, graduated from Lewis Consolidated School three years before her—in May of 1930. His graduation was postponed because a May blizzard left snow drifts taller than the fence tops!

Young Peggy Romick (1936). *Courtesy Peggy (Romick) Hubbell.*

When Peggy was growing up, her mother did most of the shopping in Husted, which was only 5 miles away and had the nearest grocery store. At the time, there was a sizeable settlement behind the train station for the railroad workers and their families. The owners of the grocery store had their house connected to the store, and several more houses were located west of town. There was also a little church there that held Youth Endeavor meetings which Peggy attended when she could.

Coral and Peggy Romick on the Allen Ranch with columbine flowers (1941). *Courtesy Peggy (Romick) Hubbell.*

On Saturday afternoons, if the weather was fair and they had time, the Romick family would take a trip to Colorado Springs. Coral would leave her shopping list at the Keystone Grocery Store, which was across the street from Phillip Smith's drug store, while the family went to dinner at the Metropole Café. It was a nice, ordinary cafe—neither fancy nor expensive. After dinner, Coral would pick up her groceries and put them in the car. Then the family would go to a movie and end the outing with an ice cream sundae at the drug store. They learned to shop well and plan ahead.

When the Romicks worked for Benjamin Allen, they didn't have a car. So if Mrs. Allen had considerable shopping to do, she would catch the train at Husted and stay overnight in the city, then ride the train back to Husted the following day.

In addition to buying groceries, Coral kept a garden and canned food to feed her family. Peggy, of course, helped her with the garden and canning. They stored the canned goods in a root cellar next to their house.

The Romick family (except for Joe, who was "always working") went to Sunday School at the old log schoolhouse in the Black Forest. There was no minister then. Frank Farmer, a poor chicken farmer who lived near the Husted Wagon Road, was superintendent of the Sunday school. Coral taught the young adults class.

Coral had her Sunday school students sit along benches lining one side of the schoolroom. There were about twenty students, including the Steppler children. When the weather was nice, Coral would invite everyone to come to the ranch after class. They would set up tables on sawhorses, have a picnic, and play softball. They all loved her.

Frank Farmer

Farmer was not only the superintendent of the Sunday school at the old log schoolhouse, but also Peggy's bus driver. She described him as a dear man, all humped over. His wife's name was Addie. When the Romicks moved to the Allen Ranch in 1927, Addie was delighted to greet them because she had taught school with Coral back in Kansas.

At one time, Coral held a contest, awarding blue and red ribbons to those students who could get friends to attend the Sunday school. The results exceeded her expectations—one Sunday a hundred and twenty-five students showed up!

Coral worked hard to get the Black Forest Community Center built. She didn't want the young adults she taught to go into Colorado Springs to dance, because she believed they might meet the wrong type of people there. First, she convinced a certain Mr. Burgess to donate some land for the building. Then, she got many of the parents to support her plan. Finally she organized Silver Tea Dances at her house to raise money for the project.

Victrola (circa 1920)

On Saturday nights, all the furniture was either moved out or pushed against the walls of Coral's 20 x 20–foot kitchen. Then the Victrola (an early phonograph) was brought in from the living room and paraffin or corn meal was spread over the linoleum floor, making for a good dancing surface.

After donating their pocket change to the cause, the Black Forest youth danced and had a wonderful time. Their mothers even served pie to help raise money.

When the kitchen became too small to hold the growing crowd, Coral moved the dances to the old log schoolhouse. She eventually raised enough money to build the Community Center, which remains a centerpiece of the Black Forest today.

When it was finally built, the hall became the gathering place for everyone. For Saturday night dances, a live orchestra played on the stage. Couples brought their small children

The old log schoolhouse where the Romicks went to Sunday School (2008).

Inside the schoolhouse (2008)

The Black Forest Community Center in 2008.

and put them to sleep on a blanket in the cloak room. Women danced together if they didn't have a partner, and children learned to square dance. Coral was its spark plug—greeting everyone who came, making them feel welcome, and inviting them over for tea. Many were Tulsa and Oklahoma City residents who had summer cabins in the Black Forest.

The community held all types of events at the hall—bridal showers, Christmas programs, club meetings, quilting socials, and holiday celebrations as well as dances. It served as a church on Sundays if a minister came to town. Peggy Romick had her wedding shower there.

The photograph here shows a community quilt on which the women in the Black Forest stitched their names in the 1920s. This photo was taken in 2008 in the old log school where it was on display. Coral's patch with her hand-stitched name is clearly visible.

Potato bakes were another type of popular socialization for Black Forest residents in those days. No doubt the potatoes grown just north of the Allen Ranch by Lou Steppler, the Colorado Potato King, were the potato of choice!

Community quilt on which Coral Romick stitched her name.

Lou grew his prized potatoes until a vicious blight attacked his fields in 1932 and then again in 1933—during the height of the Great Depression. Sadly, farmers throughout the Black Forest had to give up potato farming in the early 1930s because of this widespread disease. Many of them went out of business and had to find other sources of income.

In those simpler and more innocent days, Black Forest was a small, close community. People cared for and helped each other. They enjoyed gathering at the old log schoolhouse and the Community Center to worship, play, and dance together. The women worked in the kitchen baking pies, which were sold to help pay expenses, while the men played cards behind the stage on Saturday nights. Joe Romick and Lou Steppler were both serious pinochle players.

> Mrs. Joe Romick entertained at luncheon Thursday a group of her friends. Those present were Mrs. Thornton and Mrs. Saunders of Colorado Springs, Mrs. W. R. Brown of Monument, Mrs. Del Peterson, Mrs. Steppler and Irene, Mrs. Shiner, Miss Norma Curtis and Mrs. Frank Brown.

From the *Sunday Gazette and Telegraph*, May 28, 1939.

As down-to-earth, caring neighbors, this close community may actually have achieved the inspired vision of Psalm 133: *"Behold, how good and how pleasant it is for brethren to dwell together in unity!"*

One summer, Coral invited J.C. Truman, nephew of Senator Harry Truman, to stay with her family at the ranch because he had been exposed to tuberculosis. Coral and Joe Romick were good friends of the John V. Truman family in Missouri. Their son's summer-long visit occurred before John's brother became President of the United States.

Coral Romick was a special person who readily shared the bounty of her life's harvest. Once she even made a dress for a needy neighbor who was graduating from high school and didn't have anything to wear. According to Peggy, "She loved people and they loved her."

Coral Romick in her kitchen at the Allen Ranch with her favorite Christmas cactus in the foreground (circa 1935). Photograph taken by Smith & Morton when they came to photograph Allen Cattle Company bulls. *Courtesy of Peggy Hubbell.*

Maria Allen always invited Coral to visit at Cheyenne House during Christmastime. Peggy usually tagged along, but didn't say much. "I remember the parlor," she said. "I was impressed with the whole thing. The dining room was so formal—big oil portraits of the family were on the wall."

The Allen children also loved Coral. They stopped in to see her whenever they were at the ranch. She always had fresh-baked pie or other good things to eat in her kitchen. Many times Wharton stopped in to have lunch with Peggy's parents.

If Wharton ever came by in the morning to ask for a glass of milk, Coral knew he had been out on the town the night before. One night he got intoxicated and brought home a bunch of wild mustangs. Joe Romick had to break them all before he could sell them!

Wharton was a member of Spencer Penrose's Cooking Club—a gourmet cooking society.[4] Sometimes the club would hold meetings at a lodge built by Penrose near the top of Cheyenne Mountain. The Romicks always worried how Wharton would get down from the mountain after one of those meetings because he loved to drink.

Another occasional visitor of Coral was Billie Brown (see page 132). Brown introduced the Romicks to the gatekeepers of the Palmer castle at Glen Eyrie, which resulted in a personal tour of the castle for Peggy and her mother.

During World War II, Mr. Cheesman found it impossible to find good ranch help, so he made arrangements with the U.S. Government

Walter Davidson

The herdsman on the South Ranch was Walter Davidson. Although he was good with cattle, he was hotheaded. According to Peggy, "Walter did have a temper. One night Dad was at the South Ranch and Walter came after him with a pitchfork. We later treated the wounds when Dad got home."

Ironically, it was Joe who had gotten Walter his job on the South Ranch!

Walter used to tangle with Wharton too. Sometimes they would fight about Wharton's reluctance to let Walter buy a nurse cow—a cow that provides milk for a calf other than her own. Using nurse cows, Walter was able to get Wharton's show calves to put on weight faster than normal. This helped him win more yearling shorthorn cattle championships than anyone else at the time—which is one reason why Wharton Allen had the leading shorthorn operation in the United States.

Despite his temper, Walter was very good to Milt Cheesman's two sons. According to Sam, "We absolutely bonded with him. Every time we were home, we were out there with Walter. He was a good second dad to us and spent a lot of time with us. We couldn't have loved anybody more than Walter."

Sam Cheesman remembered Walter's temper as well. He gave an account of how fights between Wharton and Walter generally transpired. After the two began brawling, "Walter would holler for my dad to get Wharton off, so Dad would tap him on the shoulder and say, 'I think you've done enough.' So Wharton would get off. But once Walter got up, he'd attack Wharton again! Just crazy! This happened more than once. So finally my dad told Walter, 'If you want him to lay off, you need to get up and go home. You don't need to be jumping back on him.' "

In 1947 or 1948, after one particularly bad brawl, Walter left the South Ranch. He had been there for seventeen years. According to Sam, "Anytime the calves were out on the show road, everybody recognized Walter as the herdsman who did all the work. He was good at it—there just wasn't anybody better in the business than he was. It was a huge loss to the company. But I think Mr. Allen had come to a place in his life where he wasn't going to show much longer anyway." See the photo of Walter Davidson with Wharton at the National Western Stock Show in Denver, CO, (page 119).

to use German prisoners of war from Camp Carson. When the war ended, he employed braceros from Mexico.

In 1940, Peggy left the Allen Ranch to get married. As a wedding gift, Maria gave her a beautiful black alligator purse containing $25 and a handwritten note. Peggy praised Maria's handwriting as "striking and very unique." She returned to the ranch several times after her marriage.

Peggy (Romick) Hubble at age ninety (2007).

Several people were especially key to the construction of this early history. One is Sam Cheesman, who gave David Wismer many of the early photos from the Allen era, and the other is Peggy Hubbell, whose keen mind and fond memories of her life on the Allen Ranch were a constant source of information and inspiration.

Joe left the Allen Ranch soon after World War II began and the Great Depression ended. Wages were going up everywhere—except on the Allen Ranch. Wharton never offered to raise Joe's pay and Joe never asked. He was not the type to ask a favor of anyone. So when a higher paying job became available at a ranch in Laramie, Wyoming, he took it.

Wharton approached Coral when this happened and pleaded, "I don't want Joe to leave me!"

Coral chided, "Then you should have raised his wages!"

"Well, he never asked," Wharton lamented.

He never saw the Romicks again after that. They ended up working on a ranch in Ellensburg, Washington, for a Mr. Jamison, whose wife was from the Boeing family. Wharton replaced Joe with Frank Hartley, who ran the ranch until it was sold after Maria Allen's death.

Frank Hartley

According to Sam Cheesman, Frank was a widower and was raising two children at the time he was managing the North Ranch. So when he needed to come to the South Ranch, he always arrived early in the morning so that Mrs. Cheesman would invite him and his children to stay for breakfast!

"Of course, Mother was happy to have them, even though she couldn't stand old Frank because every other word was a cuss word," Sam said. "He was just hopeless. And the kids were almost like him—maybe not quite as bad, but Mother would really try to correct the kids and tell them they shouldn't talk that way, but it was pretty hopeless 'cause he was just unreal."

Joe and Coral Romick on the Allen Ranch (1941). *Courtesy Peggy (Romick) Hubbell.*

THE HARDESTY/ McCULLOUGH ERA

GEORGE E. HARDESTY was a seasoned cowboy, working ranches in northeastern New Mexico during the early 1900s. Eventually he bought his own ranch in Long Canyon, near Folsom, New Mexico. Not far away, in Watervale, Colorado, Stella Venus Starr was living and working on a ranch that her father was homesteading. She loved animals, especially cattle and horses. She also loved George Hardesty—but didn't dare marry him. That's because her mother had threatened to commit suicide if she did!

It was a difficult time for these lovers, who were both in their thirties. One day Stella's father approached her and counseled, "You'd better marry that young man because he's not going to wait around forever. Your mother won't kill herself—I'll see to it that she doesn't."

George and Stella immediately eloped. They honeymooned for a month, then settled down on George's ranch in Long Canyon. Of course Stella's mother did not commit suicide. All this happened in 1925.

Stella brought a few head of cattle to the marriage, but George was in debt from caring for his aging parents. With Stella's modest assets, the ambitious couple raised and sold cattle and turkeys for several summers, turning a fair profit.

When the couple had adequate funds, they invested in some registered Herefords. By 1942, they had developed an outstanding line that was generating handsome profits at stock shows.

Raising and showing the cattle took a lot of hard work. Stella was responsible for the registration process, which required that she

Hereford bull

keep accurate records for each cow, calf, and sire individually. She numbered all the cattle and kept track of them in the field as well. Consequently, she was in a saddle much of the time and was quite a horsewoman.

A ranch hand by the name of Ross Hamilton was working for the Hardestys in 1942. When he saw how hard Stella worked, he approached her and observed, "What you need is my daughter to help you."

Stella talked to George about the idea and he agreed with it. So they drove to Branson, Colorado, to get Oleta Hamilton. They knew nothing about her, and she knew nothing about the ranching business, but they took her under their wing anyway and she soon became like a daughter to them. They never did have children of their own.

The oldest of seven children, Oleta was fifteen when she went to live with the Hardestys. On her first day there, Stella asked her to cook macaroni for lunch. When Oleta brought the savory pasta to the table, Stella laughed and told her she had cooked enough for a week! Oleta was used to cooking for nine people and had been cooking at home since she was nine years old.

She worked for the Hardestys for two summers. Although she had never been on a horse, she knew how to work hard. In that respect she was very much like Stella, her exemplar. She learned a great deal from Stella and loved her dearly.

In 1946, Oleta married her sweetheart, Max Goodrich, from nearby Kim, Colorado, after he returned from fighting in WWII. He was the son of a farmer. They moved to Englewood, a suburb of Denver, where Max became a building contractor.

Meanwhile, Stella was getting fed up with the wind that blew relentlessly on her New

Two-story house where the Hardestys lived after purchasing their Pleasant View Hereford Ranch (2008).

Pond that George Hardesty kept stocked with trout for his visitors to enjoy (2008).

The silo and a shed still dominate the hillside of the small valley that is near the entrance to Fox Run Regional Park (2008).

Mexico ranch. She had grown up with the wind in Watervale and had come to hate it. So she convinced George to start looking for a new place to ranch where the wind didn't blow as much.

They eventually became aware of a property that was for sale in unincorporated El Paso County—about 2 miles west of present-day Shamrock Ranch. In 1950, they purchased this ranch from Channing Sweet, naming it the Pleasant View Hereford Ranch. Some called it the Hardesty Ranch. At the time, it comprised about 1,600 acres. Today it hosts the communities of Sun Hills, Gleneagle, and Pleasant View Estates (where Jennifer, daughter of David and Mary Anne Wismer, lives today).

George and Stella moved into a white, two-story house that was located on their new ranch. This house was down in a small valley and next to a pond. Some sheds and corrals, a silo, a large garden, and a playhouse were nearby. The pond and buildings were fed by a natural spring that was located about 0.5 mile to the north. George

kept the pond stocked with trout so that he could treat his guests to fishing.

Today, the entrance to Fox Run Regional Park is located near that small valley. Some of the outbuildings are gone, but the house, pond, silo, and a shed still exist.

Much to Stella's dismay, George dismantled the playhouse one day when he needed a new calf feeder to support their growing herd. He evidently did not appreciate the miniature house, which was modeled after the big house next to it, like his wife did.

The Hardestys were not wealthy people, but they worked hard and managed their money wisely. After they bought the Pleasant View Hereford Ranch in Colorado, they sold their Long Canyon ranch in New Mexico to George's brother and his wife, who lived on it until they passed away.

The photograph here shows George and Stella with some prospective cattle buyers at the Long Canyon ranch. George is holding the bull's halter rope and Stella is standing on the

Stella and George Hardesty with prospective cattle buyers (circa 1948). *Courtesy Oleta Goodrich.*

other side of the animal, which was from their Sensation line of registered Herefords. The woman next to George with her arm on the bull is Althea Hardesty—George's sister-in-law who eventually acquired the Long Canyon ranch. As Oleta remembers the Hardestys, "They were plain country folk."

Since Oleta was living not far from the Pleasant View Hereford Ranch in 1950, Stella and George invited her to join them in shopping for furniture and other furnishings for their new home. Oleta was happy to do this, but was even happier that the Hardestys had moved within fifty miles of her!

With their growing cattle business, it wasn't long before the Hardestys needed some extra acreage. Soon they were eyeing a piece of land just south of their ranch—Maria Allen's 960-acre Husted Pasture, so named because it bordered on the Husted Wagon Road to the south. In 2008, this acreage would be bordered by Old Northgate Rd. to the south and present-day Roller Coaster Road to the east.

When the executor of Maria's estate put the Allen Ranch up for sale in 1951, George and Stella bought the entire ranch, primarily for the Husted Pasture. George was uneasy about the cost of keeping up the entire Allen Ranch, so he sold all but the Husted Pasture just four and a half months later. The buyer was James N. McCullough, former mayor of Colorado Springs and owner of the Village Inn Company.

When construction of the United States Air Force Academy began in 1955, George and Stella pleaded with Oleta Goodrich and her husband to move to Pikes Peak Country. They were convinced Oleta's husband could get a job erecting the Academy buildings, but Mr. Goodrich was not prepared to move at that time. Consequently, the Hardestys had to settle for occasional visits to continue their special relationship with Oleta.

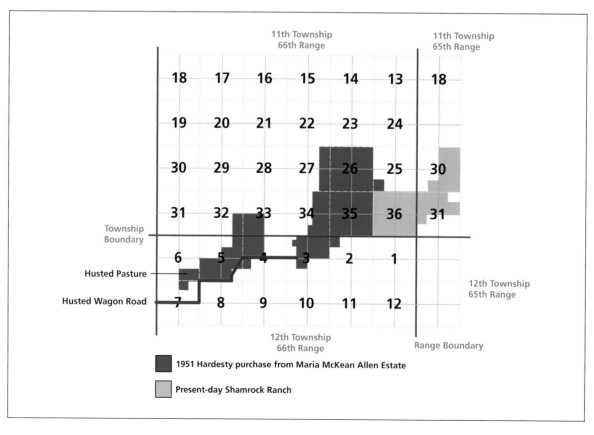

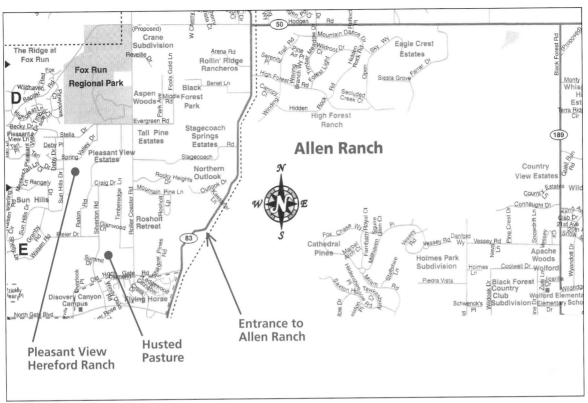

Locations of the Pleasant View Hereford Ranch, the Husted Pasture, and the eastern portion of the Allen Ranch. *Courtesy Tri-Lakes Advertising, Monument, Colorado.*

One of George's neighbors was Guy Peterson. He lived just north of the Hardesty Ranch and helped George with branding and various other demands of cattle ranching. When asked about the Hardestys, Guy reported that they were good people—down to earth.

Sadly, Stella Hardesty was only able to enjoy her Pleasant View Hereford Ranch for seven years. They were the happiest years of her life, according to Oleta. She loved the ranch and the Black Forest, and was delighted to have relief from the wind. She and George got to know everyone in the area and were active in the Black Forest Community Church. Stella was also a member of the Colorado Cow Belles Association and the Black Forest Community Club.

In April of 1957, a terrible snowstorm engulfed the Black Forest, cutting off contact with the outside world. When it finally ended,

Stella went out to milk a cow, but never returned. Worried, George began to search for her. He found her lifeless body in the shed—after she had suffered a massive heart attack.

George was devastated. He loved his wife dearly. To make matters worse, no vehicles could get to the ranch because of the blizzard, so he had an extremely difficult time making arrangements for the funeral and burial.

When the service was over, he asked Oleta and her husband to come stay with him until he could decide what to do with his life. He was sixty-eight years old at the time. Although he lived another twenty years, he never got over losing his beloved Stella, and constantly grieved over her untimely death.

George donated an electronic organ and a considerable sum of money to the Black Forest Community Church in Stella's name. As a result, an addition to the church built in 1960

Service in Folsom, N.M. For Stella Hardesty

Mrs. Stella V. Hardesty of Black Forest died Monday at her home. She was 64.

Funeral services are scheduled for 2 p.m. Thursday at the Baptist Church in Folsom, N.M. Burial will be at Folsom. Friends may call at the Law Mortuary until 3:30 p.m. Wednesday.

Mrs. Hardesty was born Aug. 31, 1893, at Watervale, Colo., and lived in Black Forest for the last seven years. She was a member of the Black Forest Community Church, Black Forest Community Club and the Colorado Cow Belles Assn.

Survivors include her husband George, and cousins, Mrs. Edith Summers, Folsom, Mrs. Julis Morrow, Borger, Tex., Mrs. Gertrude Wilbourn, Clayton, N. M., Mrs. Clara Newkirk, Folsom, Edna Tabor of California, Albert Records, Rifle, Lee Tabor, Glendale, Calif., and Arthur Tabor, Ft. Smith, Ark.

tates, Sun Hills, and Gleneagle. Stella Drive, which forms the southern boundary of Fox Run Regional Park today, was named after Stella Hardesty.

Oleta and her husband continued to live in the Black Forest after George left, raising three daughters. They became friends with Guy and Kathryn Peterson, the Hardestys' neighbors, and Alvin and Eurelle Eden. Oleta remembers how close the Black Forest community was in those days—the children all played together and the parents formed friendships that lasted a lifetime. Husted was still the nearest town, and driving into Colorado Springs for piano lessons was a major event. Oleta said, "Those were the good times, the good old days—while we still had dirt roads and you knew everyone you met because there weren't that many people out here then. It wasn't hard. We managed and did fine. I'm very thankful for that."

Oleta worked for twenty-seven years as a secretary for Academy School District 20 before retiring in 1988. Today she lives with her oldest daughter in the Black Forest.

was named Hardesty Hall. It was a welcome bounty from the Hardestys' life harvests.

Oleta and her husband were kind enough to honor George's request, and moved in with him after Stella died. They lived there for five years. Then George leased the ranch and resided alternately with his sisters who lived in Folsom, New Mexico, and Yucaipa, California. When he finally sold the Pleasant View Hereford Ranch, it was purchased by Bob and Georgia McCollom and Ed and Peggy Morast. George died in 1977—twenty years after Stella passed away.

Later, the ranch was subdivided to become the communities of Pleasant View Es-

JAMES NELSON MCCULLOUGH was Irish and proud of it. When he bought the Allen Ranch from George and Stella Hardesty in 1951, the first thing he did was rename it Shamrock Ranch.

James had ranched before. A decade earlier, he owned the Green Mountain Ranch—nestled in the foothills of the Rampart Range just north of Cathedral Rock and west of Husted. A portion of that ranch is now the property of the United States Air Force Academy.

James N. McCullough

James was the son of J. Zachariah McCullough—one of the first county commissioners of El Paso County and an owner of the National Commission Company of Colorado Springs (a food and livestock company). James followed in his father's footsteps by serving in local government and owning a share of the National Commission Company.

President Truman
(1884–1972)

After serving on the Colorado Springs City Council for a couple of years, James was elected mayor. He served two consecutive two-year terms—from April 1947 to 1951. As mayor, he had the distinct honor of reading one of President Harry S. Truman's proclamations in Acacia Park on United Nations Day, October 23, 1950.

Near the end of his second term, James sold his share of the National Commission Company and purchased the Village Inn building in Colorado Springs, which he had been leasing and operating as a restaurant since 1946 (see *Gazette Telegraph* clip, March 2, 1951, at right). At the time, the Village Inn was a large restaurant with multiple dining rooms. One room featured live music and dancing every Saturday night and was a popular gathering place for Colorado Springs residents. According to James's son Bill, "Colorado Springs was a little cattle town at that point—everybody knew everybody."

J. N. McCullough And Wife Purchase Village Inn Building

Purchase of the Village Inn building, a landmark in Colorado Springs since 1880, by Mr. and Mrs. James N. McCullough from John Ceresa was announced today.

The sale of the building, located at 125-127 E. Pikes Peak Ave., involved $110,000, based on the revenue stamps affixed to the deed.

McCullough said this morning that the Village Inn will continue to be operated as a coffee-shop, dining establishment and cocktail lounge as it has been operated since he and Mrs. McCullough leased the building from Ceresa in August, 1946. Actually, the build-will be operated by the Village Inn corporation which includes the purchasers and John Cimino, chef of the institution since August, 1946.

Cimino was trained by Louis Strada, internationally known chef at the Broadmoor hotel. Cimino is also a former partner in the Indian Grill.

"Naturally we intend to maintain the same quality of food and service that we have offered in the past," McCullough said today. "We believe that the inn's reputation has been founded in part on the excellent work of Cimino and our other regular employes."

Included in the building are the coffee shop, operated by James N. McCullough, Jr.; the Old English dining room; the Marine dining room; the Western dining room, and the cocktail lounge in the basement known as "The Pub."

The Village Inn building was originally a small church, serving in that capacity from 1880 to 1890. In the following years it served as a storeroom and a business establishment of various types. Pete Beroni operated it for a time and it was formerly known as the "Chapel Inn." Oldtimer still refer to it as the "little old church."

McCullough is also known locally as the mayor of Colorado Springs. He retires from the mayor's job and the Council in April of this year. He has announced that he is not a candidate for re-election to the Council, on which he has served six years, thus eliminating himself as a mayor candidate, a position he has held for the past four years.

The photograph below of the McCulloughs' Village Inn is taken from a postcard that reads on the back:

THE VILLAGE INN
Colorado Springs, Colorado
is housed in a beautiful old church edifice. Superb food and cocktails served in our three dining rooms and PUB COCKTAIL LOUNGE make THE VILLAGE INN the favorite and most unusual in the West. Recommended by Duncan Hines, Gourmet and Rocky Mt. AAA.

The Village Inn when owned by Mr. and Mrs. McCullough (circa 1950)

The map opposite shows the ranch property that the Hardestys sold to the Village Inn Company in November of 1951 after owning it for only four and a half months. Notice that it included only the eastern portion of the Allen Ranch (about 2,160 acres) since George and Stella kept the 960-acre Husted Pasture (compare with map on page 152).

Perhaps because he had been mayor of Colorado Springs and knew of the complications that might occur when purchasing land in the Black Forest, James McCullough required the Hardestys to obtain a court decree establishing them as the sole, encumbrance-free owners of the ranch he was about to buy from them. Accordingly, George and Stella Hardesty filed a court action on November 16, 1951 (the same date a warranty deed was recorded for the sale of the property to the Village Inn Company), to obtain the requested decree.

Defendants of the suit included the El Paso County Board of County Commissioners, the El Paso County Treasurer, and previous owners of the lands that made up the Allen Ranch—including Benjamin C. Allen, The Colorado Pinery and Land Company, George H. Bend, Calvin R. Husted, Edward H. Talbert, Samuel C. Stout, George A. Krause, Channing Sweet, surviving directors and trustees, unknown successors of such trustees, and "all unknown persons who claim any interest in the subject matter of this action."

This landmark court action resulted in a December 8, 1952, decree stating "that said defendants, each and all of them, are hereby enjoined and restrained from in any wise prosecuting, claiming or asserting any interest, claim or demand in, to or against said property or any part thereof, except such

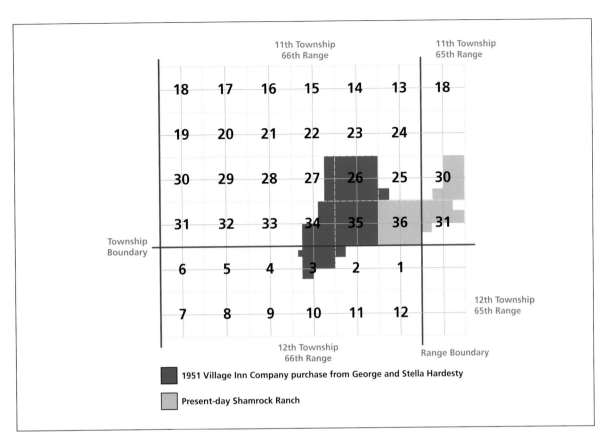

11th Township
66th Range

11th Township
65th Range

| 18 | 17 | 16 | 15 | 14 | 13 | 18 |

| 19 | 20 | 21 | 22 | 23 | 24 | |

| 30 | 29 | 28 | 27 | 26 | 25 | 30 |

| 31 | 32 | 33 | 34 | 35 | 36 | 31 |

Township
Boundary

| 6 | 5 | 4 | 3 | 2 | 1 | |

| 7 | 8 | 9 | 10 | 11 | 12 | |

12th Township
65th Range

12th Township
66th Range

Range Boundary

■ 1951 Village Inn Company purchase from George and Stella Hardesty

■ Present-day Shamrock Ranch

interest as may hereafter be acquired through the plaintiffs or their assigns."

Clearly, James McCullough obtained the assurance he was seeking.

James and his wife, Hazel Eva, married in 1919, and by the time they bought Shamrock Ranch they had four children—two daughters and two sons. Their youngest son, Bill, was fourteen years old and in boarding school when his parents bought the ranch. Upon his return home in the summer of 1952, they informed him of the change. Then his father added, "Congratulations—you're going to ride fence all summer!"

The McCulloughs raised Black Angus cattle that first summer on the ranch, and all the family except James Nelson Jr., who was in the U.S. Army Air Corp as a B-24 navigator, helped out. Hazel grew up in Calhan, Colorado, where her parents were homesteaders—first generation "sod busters," in fact—so she was familiar with ranch life. It was hard work. Bill confessed that he and his sisters sometimes complained a little. Their father would come out on Mondays, his day off from running the Village Inn, and do the mowing and baling. He also hired a foreman named Clements and a wrangler from the Black Forest named Shorty Connors to help run the business.

Mixed breed herd of predominantly Black Angus cattle on Shamrock Ranch (2008).

COLORADO LIVESTOCK BRAND
ASSESSMENT FEE PAID UNTIL JANUARY 1, 2012

Rick Wahlert

Brand number
1643275

Elp
McCullough, William J.
309 N 20th St
Colo Spgs CO 80904

CJH

Right Ear Left Ear

Validation number
30482

The McCullough Family Brand. *Courtesy Bill McCullough.*

One day, young Bill was working some heifers when lightning hit the fence and killed four head. It was an unnerving experience! Bill still owns the family brand, shown above.

The next year, James McCullough took a different approach to ranching. Rather than raise his own cattle, he summered a herd owned by another company. He was paid according to the weight each steer gained before the fall sale. Bill remembers that his family must have cared for three hundred head that summer.

James McCullough also leased some of his Shamrock Ranch land to Billy Bant, owner of a lumber company. Billy had a contract with the Santa Fe Railroad to deliver railroad ties. Using a small, portable sawmill, he set up a logging operation about a mile up a draw that goes north from the Shamrock Ranch barns. Billy felled trees, cut them to size, then shipped them to his ranch where they were soaked in creosote. The blade for his sawmill was powered by a belt that ran around the rear axle of an old truck. Bill McCullough remembers the immense pile of sawdust that Billy generated with his makeshift logging operation.

In April 1952, James recorded an oil and gas lease to C. S. McGhee for part of his ranch. About a year later, McGhee turned the lease over to the Shell Oil Company. It is doubtful that any exploration or production took place

J. N. McCullough Sells Old Allen Ranch to Texan

The famous old Allen cattle ranch, 17 miles northeast of Colorado Springs, was sold today by former Mayor J. N. McCullough to C. T. McLaughlin, a well known oil and cattle man of Snyder, Tex. McLaughlin was in the city completing details of the transaction. The consideration was reported to be about $140,000.

McLaughlin will ship Black Angus and Hereford cattle to the ranch from Texas and will operate it along with his other businesses.

McCullough has owned the ranch for two years. The cattle that he bought with it had been sold on the market but there were cattle on the ranch when the present transaction was consummated.

McCullough had made his home on the ranch since buying it, but he said today that he would move back into Colorado Springs to be nearer to the Village Inn restaurant, which he operates. The ranch is a short distance east of Husted, in the edge of the Black Forest.

on the ranch because Shell released the lease in May of 1955.

James was a devout Catholic. In order to worship on his ranch, he converted the ice house into a small chapel with pews and an altar. One of his friends, a priest, even said Mass there. Although in disrepair, this unique little chapel was still intact when the Wismers bought Shamrock Ranch.

The Village Inn kept James in town most of the time, and his wife eventually became weary of caring for the ranch by herself. Though she had been raised in the country, she preferred living in the city. Hazel asked James to sell the ranch so she could move back into town.

On September 15, 1953, he acted on her request and sold the Shamrock Ranch to C.T. McLaughlin—another Irishman. Then he moved his family back into town, about two and a half miles east of the Garden of the Gods.

During the latter part of 1956, James and Hazel decided to sell their Village Inn restaurant business as well. However, they kept ownership of the historic Village Inn building, which had served as the Grace Episcopal Church during the decade of the 1880s. This same Episcopal church purchased Cheyenne House in 1954 after Maria McKean Allen's death. The buyers went on to establish the popular and successful Village Inn restaurant chain, utilizing the name of James McCullough's original restaurant. This history is further discussed on the next page.

Sadly, James became ill shortly after selling his Village Inn restaurant business and died following brain surgery on January 22, 1957. James Nelson McCullough was a great man and an important leader in Colorado Springs during the 1940s and 1950s. His contributions to the community continue to benefit many people in Pikes Peak Country.

Ex-Mayor McCullough Dies After Brain Surgery

James N. McCullough, former mayor of Colorado Springs, died shortly before 6 a.m. today in St. Joseph's Hospital in Denver.

Mr. McCullough was taken to Denver Saturday when it was believed that he was suffering from a blood clot in the tissues of the brain.

* * *

A brain operation was performed, according to members of the staff of the attending physician, and by Monday afternoon it was believed the crisis had been passed.

Mr. McCullough was ill last week and was treated for a sinus condition. His illness prevented his appearance at the hearing of the suit brought by E. C. Bunker of the Organization for Representative Government against city officials and others over a land transaction. The ex-mayor's deposition was read at the trial. In it he denied any conspiracy was involved in the deal. The case was dismissed by District Judge John M. Meikle on the ground the plaintiff failed to prove the charges.

Mr. McCullough was a native of Colorado Springs, being born here Sept. 24, 1901.

JAMES N. McCULLOUGH

He was elected to the City Council April 3, 1945. He was elected mayor in 1947 and re-elected to that post two years later.

It was during Mr. McCullough's six years on the council that the initial steps was taken to secure Blue River water for Colorado Springs, a factor which has permitted the city to make great strides in securing military in-

(Turn to Page 8, Column 9)

James McCullough, Ex-Mayor, Dies After Surgery

(Continued From Page One)
stallations and additional industry.

At that time Colorado Springs water supplies were extremely short and quick and decisive actions had to be taken to forestall future water shortages.

He operated the National Commission Co. for 18 years and then operated the Village Inn for many years. The building was purchased from John Ceresa by Mr. and Mrs. McCullough in March of 1951.

The McCulloughs sold the establishment in November of last year to Mr. and Mrs. Jim P. Mola, Eugene, Ore., and Mr. and Mrs. Merton S. Anderson, Denver.

Mr. McCullough was a member of the Chamber of Commerce and a former leader in the Colorado Springs Junior Chamber of Commerce. He was a member of the Modern Woodmen and the Elks Lodge. He was long active in many civic and church affairs. He was a member of Corpus Christi Catholic Church.

He is survived by his wife, Mrs. Hazel McCullough; two sons, Jimmy McCullough Jr., Grand Junction; William McCullough, Colorado Springs; two daughters, Mrs. Margaret Rawls, France, and Miss Rita McCullough, Colorado Springs; his mother, Mrs. J. Z. McCullough, a sister, Mrs. Catherine Alderton, both of Colorado Springs; and five grandchildren.

Funeral arrangements will be announced later by the Law Mortuary.

Village Inn Sold In Deal Involving About $200,000

The Village Inn, 217 E. Pikes Peak Ave., a restaurant which for 10 years has been owned and operated by J. N. McCullough, former mayor of Colorado Springs, has been purchased from him by Mr. and Mrs. Jim P. Mola, of Eugene, Ore., and Mr. and Mrs. Merton S. Anderson of Denver.

The deal was made by Dick Bannister of Walker and Co., Realtors, 208 E. Pikes Peak and Ralph Armstrong of the realty firm of Morrison and Morrison, Denver.

The exact consideration in the transaction was not stated, but McCullough said it was in the neighborhood of $200,000.

The new owners will take over the business the first of the new year and McCullough will continue to operate it until that time. He said he will not then be in the restaurant business again, but will continue to reside in Colorado Springs.

It is the restaurant business and equipment and furnishings only that have been sold. McCullough retains the ownership of the buildings, which is the historic Old Grace Episcopal Church building.

Both Mr. and Mrs. Mola and Mr. and Mrs. Anderson and their children will make their homes in Colorado Springs. Anderson, who has not before been in the restaurant business, will participate in the management of the business with Mola, who for 10 years has operated Seymours Cafe in Eugene. Mrs. Anderson is Mola's sister.

"We shall retain the name Village Inn, that the restaurant now has and conduct the business as it is now conducted, maintaining the high quality and standards that Mr. McCullough has set," said Mola today.

He said he would not continue to operate the Seymour Cafe in Eugene, but that as soon as a home could be found here he would return to that city to close up his business interests there.

"We have been looking about for a new business for some time," he said. "We have looked about in California, in the Northwest in Salt Lake City and elsewhere and finally decided that we would like to live and be in business in Colorado Springs. We like the sunshine that you have here, and it looks as if this city has a great future.

Mola has been in the restaurant industry ever since his high school (Turn to Page 12, Column 8)

James McCullough sold his Village Inn to Jim P. Mola of Eugene, Oregon, and Merton S. Anderson of Denver. They went on to establish the popular Village Inn Pancake House restaurant chain. The first Village Inn Pancake House opened in Denver in 1958. Mola and Anderson's company incorporated in 1959 and began franchising in 1961. They later dropped "Pancake House" when the chain began offering lunch and dinner menus in addition to breakfast. The name of their company came directly from James McCullough's Village Inn.

Today, the Village Inn restaurant chain is owned by Denver-based VICORP Restaurants, Inc., and continues to win awards from the American Pie Council. The latest include several first place ribbons at the 2007 National Pie Championships held in conjunction with The Great American Pie Festival in Celebration, Florida.

Village Inn Sold In Deal Involving About $200,000

(Continued From Page One) days. He is a former resident of Corvallis, Ore.

Mr. and Mrs. Mola have five children, two, four, six, eight and ten years old. Three are girls and two boys. Mr. and Mrs. Anderson have three children. Mr. Anderson has previously been in the selling and printing business.

Previously to the 10 years that McCullough has owned and operated the Village Inn it was operated for nine years by Pete and John Ceresa.

The building, a landmark in the city since 1880, was purchased from John Ceresa by Mr. and Mrs. McCullough in March of 1951. That was a transaction of $110,000, according to the revenue stamps on the deed when filed for recording at the county clerk's office.

The historic church building, no longer used for that purpose after the construction of the new Grace Episcopal Church, was transformed into a restaurant in 1929, when a lease on it was obtained by Robert West from McCaffery Brothers, proprietors of the Joyce Hotel. When it was first opened as a restaurant it was called Chapel Inn.

Mayor Extols McCullough as Great Leader

Mayor Harry Blunt today characterized former Mayor James N. McCullough, who died this morning in a Denver hospital, as an "outstanding civic-minded leader" whose death was a great loss to the community. In a tribute to Mr. McCullough, Mayor Blunt said.:

"The community has suffered a tremendous loss in the death of Jim McCullough. He was a very outstanding civic-minded leader for a great many years.

"I was privileged to serve on the council for six years with him and during that time he was a councilman of exceptional ability and integrity and a capable and energetic leader. His thoughts were always for what was best of the interests of Colorado Springs.

"In his passing he leaves an indelible footprint on the history of our city. He served during the time when the Blue River water diversion was adjudicated and the project launched and he gave all his efforts and tremendous personal force to the development of that project which has proved so vital to the growth of Colorado Springs. This community owes Jim a great debt. He was a great public servant in the true sense of the word."

THE
McLaughlin Era

He was a very perceptive, intelligent, engaging personality. People liked him. They enjoyed being around him.

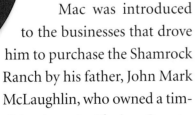

C. T. McLaughlin
(1957)

THAT'S THE WAY Mark McLaughlin describes his father, Clarence Thurston McLaughlin, who was affectionately called "Mr. Mac" by his employees and acquaintances.

Mac was introduced to the businesses that drove him to purchase the Shamrock Ranch by his father, John Mark McLaughlin, who owned a timber, coal, and oil business in Clarion County, Pennsylvania. Starting out with only a team of horses, John approached local land owners and purchased their standing timber. After harvesting it, he sold the lumber for a reasonable profit. Soon his business was thriving. He purchased more teams of horses and hired crews to work them. Before long he began strip mining for coal, then drilling oil wells and teaching his son C. T. the lumber, coal, and oil businesses.

C. T. McLaughlin was born on January 31, 1897, in Arthurs, Pennsylvania. He was the eldest of John Mark and Cora McLaughlin's children, who eventually numbered four sons and a daughter. Since he went to school near Titusville, Pennsylvania, site of the world's first commercial oil well, C. T. developed an early interest in the oil business.

When World War I came along, C. T. was assigned to the 503rd Aero Squadron and was stationed in Florida and Maryland for twenty-five months. Even though he never went overseas, his time in the Army Air Forces was an adventure; he had never traveled beyond western Pennsylvania before. C. T. was soon promoted to sergeant major, a position in which he gained both experience and respect managing men.

Upon his release from the army in 1919, C. T. took his mustering-out pay of $60 and bought a one-way ticket to Burkburnett,

Texas, where an oil boom was underway. First he worked there as a roughneck, building upon the knowledge of the oil business he had gained from his father. He soon he made friends with a young man named George Cooper. Between the two of them, they had enough money for the down payment on a Wichita Spudder (a percussion drilling rig). They soon formed their own business—the Comac Drilling Company.

Within two years, their company was operating several rigs. Mac and Cooper both worked these rigs, but they also hired other men to assist them. The photograph here shows oil derricks at Burkburnett about the time they were drilling.

Burkburnett, Texas oilfield (circa 1920)

Before long, Mac went into business for himself. He started with a single Spudder, but soon had three in operation. His next purchase was a rotary drilling rig—an expensive and bold move in those days. But it paid off for him. He was hired by drilling companies all around north Texas because he could drill wells faster than his competition. Later he went to east Texas to help with the oil boom there.

Then he met Evelyn Claire Littleton—a lovely, educated woman from Knoxville,

Tennessee. Although Claire had been a school-teacher in Knoxville, she came to Wichita Falls, Texas, as an office employee of Miller Pipeline Company.[1] Mac and Claire married on August 6, 1921, following a six-week courtship. They made their home in Wichita Falls. Three daughters and a son were born to them there. The girls were named Jean, Evelyn, and Ruth. Their son (the youngest) was named John Mark after Mac's father, and goes by his middle name, Mark, today. The McLaughlin children attended public school in Wichita Falls.

Claire McLaughlin (1957)

After starting his family, Mac was constantly on the go. His business required that he follow the oilfields, since in those day oil companies only gave out drilling contracts for locations where oil had already been discovered. Although Mac came home as often as he could, the burden of raising the children fell on Claire, who did an admirable job.

When oil was discovered in the Permian Basin of western Texas, Mac opened an office in Big Spring, and soon after moved to Midland. Then, in 1934, during the Great Depression, he was given a contract by Shell Oil Company to drill three wells in Scurry County, which was northeast of both Midland and Big Spring. The main town in that county was and is today Snyder. At the time, its population was about 2,500.

Mac stayed at a small hotel in Snyder called the Manhattan. During the evenings after supper, he'd sit in front of the hotel and greet passersby. One day a man came along who would change the lives of Mac and his family forever.

The man was Henry Bryce, an attorney who represented the Federal Land Bank of Houston. He had been given the unenviable task of foreclosing on ranches whose owners were unable to make their loan payments. Henry encouraged Mac to step into the delinquent borrowers' shoes and bring the notes up to date. By doing this, he could acquire the ranches for merely the balance owed on the notes.

C.T. McLaughlin was an astute businessman. Immediately recognizing this as a fortuitous opportunity, he acted upon it and acquired his first land in Scurry County. Then he began to buy adjoining land one section (640 acres) at a time, paying four dollars an acre. When it was known that he was buying, people began approaching him to offer their land. But once the price got to seven dollars an acre, he stopped buying—considering the price too high!

By then he had amassed a 5,200-acre ranch. He used it to raise sheep and cattle. Being a man who appreciated quality, he invested in Rambouillet sheep for fine wool and registered Hereford cattle for prime beef. By the late 1930s, Mac had a successful livestock business underway. He also experimented with new seed varieties and methods and raised gaited show horses.[2]

Rambouillet ram

After selling his home in Wichita Falls, Mac moved his family to his ranch, which was 12 miles southwest of Snyder, Texas. He called it the Diamond M Ranch. This happened during World War II—in 1943 or 1944. His son Mark was thirteen or fourteen when they moved to the Diamond M.

McLaughlin's Diamond M brand

Times had become difficult for Mac when the war started. First he began to lose his employees to the draft. Then he had trouble getting equipment—drilling pipe, cable, trucks, tools, etc.—since manufacturers were building tanks and airplanes instead. Fuel became rationed, furthering his difficulties.

No longer able to depend on his drilling business for an income, Mac sold his rigs and leased the Diamond M Ranch to the Lion Oil Company of El Dorado, Arkansas. The company paid him a cash bonus for the lease, which allowed him to continue producing oil in Midland and Howard County where he had some leases himself.

Then, in 1948, oil was discovered in the Canyon Reef formation of Scurry County. It wasn't long before the Lion Oil Company was drilling on the Diamond M Ranch. When its Number 2 McLaughlin well began producing 650 barrels a day,[3] Mac realized that his ranch was sitting on a vast reservoir of black gold!

Lion Oil Company logo

Mark, his son, was in his freshman year at Rice University when the drilling started. "When I came home at Christmas, I couldn't believe all the activity," he said. "At one time there were thirteen drilling rigs on our ranch—it was a boom!"

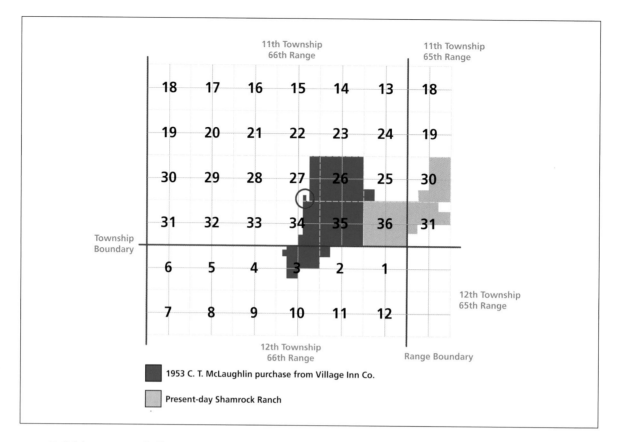

11th Township
66th Range

11th Township
65th Range

18	17	16	15	14	13	18
19	20	21	22	23	24	19
30	29	28	27	26	25	30
31	32	33	34	35	36	31

Township
Boundary

| 6 | 5 | 4 | 3 | 2 | 1 |
| 7 | 8 | 9 | 10 | 11 | 12 |

12th Township
65th Range

12th Township
66th Range

Range Boundary

■ 1953 C. T. McLaughlin purchase from Village Inn Co.

▢ Present-day Shamrock Ranch

Within a year, drilling crews on the Diamond M were bringing in a new producing well every five days. Mark remembers his dad telling him that the first royalty check he received from the Lion Oil Company was for more money than he had paid for the entire ranch! And the checks kept coming after that. In 1950, Mac built a two-story office building in Snyder to house his growing business ventures.[4]

With his newfound wealth, Mac began to buy more ranches. The first was the 6,000 acre Kuteman Ranch in southern Parker County, Texas, near Weatherford and not far west of Ft. Worth. In 1950 he stocked the ranch—which he renamed Black Ranch—with Hereford cattle and opened a successful registered cattle operation there. In 1958, he bought the vast Circle Ranch in northeastern New Mexico near Las Vegas. At 31,000 acres, it was his largest cattle ranch. Mac acquired the 1,459-acre Young Ranch in western Fisher County,

Texas, in 1965. When his oil boom tapered off, Mac sold the Black and Circle Ranches.[5]

During the summer of 1953, Mac was approached by a Denver land broker named Dawkins about the Shamrock Ranch in Colorado, which was for sale. Mac told Dawkins he was interested, so Dawkins arranged a meeting between Mac, Mac's son Mark, and James McCullough, owner of the Shamrock Ranch. Since Mac and James were both Irish, they hit it off instantly.

By then Mac had become an excellent judge of land value. When he saw the Shamrock Ranch, it didn't take him long to decide to buy. He and James McCullough made a deal right then and there, on September 15, 1953. The price was $140,000, or about $70 an acre—ten times the price that had stopped Mac from buying more land in Snyder!

The extent of Mac's purchase from McCullough is shown above. It was nearly the same

Implement shed on Shamrock Ranch

property that the Hardesty's had sold to McCullough in 1951. The only difference was a two-and-a-half acre parcel in section 27 that is circled. This parcel brought the total acreage of the Shamrock Ranch to about 2,162 acres.

The first thing Mac did after buying the Shamrock Ranch was to build some sheds for his cattle. Later on, in 1955, he built a farm implement shed, then a grain bin and another cattle shed in 1960.

Not content with this relatively small amount of property, Mac started looking around for additional ranch land in Colorado's Black Forest. Within a year, he bought the Bar X Ranch situated east of Shamrock Ranch and north of Hodgen Road. During the 1960s, he purchased the property in sections 30 and 31, shown opposite, which are part of Shamrock Ranch today. Section 36—the school section—was still owned by the state of Colorado at the time, but Mac had his son Mark, who had studied law, obtain a lease on this section so he could ranch it also. In 1966, Mac's neighbors on the east and west were the Flying Horseshoe Cattle Company and the Flying Horse Ranch, respectively.

In 1966, a decree resulting from a court action instigated by AT&T required Mac to provide an easement on his property near Highway 83 for telephone lines. The easement was a little over 16 feet wide and was used to lay a special telecommunications cable that is believed to have serviced the North American Air Defense Command (NORAD) inside Cheyenne Mountain.

Years later, when the Pendletons owned the Shamrock Ranch, some of Mr. Pendleton's workers were digging in the easement and inadvertently cut the cable. Within minutes, military helicopters were dispatched to find the source of the cable break and were soon flying overhead. Luckily, a national emergency was quickly averted!

It wasn't until the 1960s that natural gas and modern phone service came to the Black Forest. Natural gas was not piped to the Shamrock Ranch until the Wismers became its owners in the 1990s. In 1968, Colorado State Highway 83, the west border of Shamrock Ranch, was first paved.

By January of that year, all the parcels that make up present-day Shamrock Ranch were owned by Mac—except the school section, which he leased from the state of Colorado. Mac also bought a considerable amount of land in Douglas County and leased some other land around Shamrock Ranch. He then bought a ranch in Ramah, which is near the northeastern corner of El Paso County. Before he was through, he was ranching approximately 10,000 acres in Colorado.

In the 1960s, energy fever hit Colorado. A common saying heard everywhere was "Colorado will become the fuel capital of the world!" A uranium mining company in Pitkin County helped fuel this fever. The company

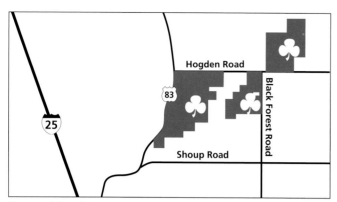

Shamrock Ranch in 1980. Despite the identifying shamrock, the upper right corner maintained its identity as the Bar X Ranch. Neither the Douglas County parcels nor the lands Mac leased are included.

sent agents all over Colorado to lease land for uranium exploration. Evidently they approached Mac, for in 1969 he issued a permit and option to Robert E. Melin for uranium exploration. Melin assigned it to Intercontinental Oil Corporation soon after.

However, as people learned of the health dangers of pitchblende (uranium ore), enthusiasm for mining it faded quickly, and nothing came of Mac's uranium ambitions.

Based on the legacy of uranium mining that is still affecting the states which encompass the Colorado Plateau today, it is fortunate

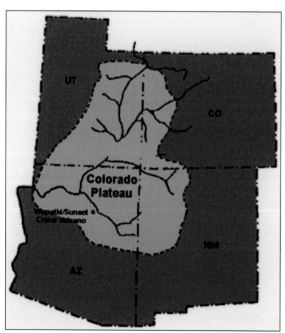

Extent of uranium deposits in the Colorado Plateau

for visitors and residents of Shamrock Ranch that Mac did not mine the dangerous, radioactive mineral here. Incidentally, Colorado is considered to have the third largest uranium reserves of any state in America, behind Wyoming and New Mexico. [6]

Mac and Claire McLaughlin loved to entertain. According to their son Mark, it was their pleasure in life. They loved to throw parties, and their guests always had a good time. Soon after they bought Shamrock Ranch, the McLaughlin's, along with the mayor of Colorado Springs, hosted an open house which was attended by the governor of Colorado among other notable figures.

The open house was held on December 27, 1953. Miss Amy Johnson, Mark McLaughlin's sweetheart at the time, was one of the attendees. Mark was in his final semester of law school and had invited her to stay with the family during the Christmas holidays. He proposed to her during that visit and they became engaged. They were married in June of 1954. Mark had graduated by that time and was a Judge Advocate in the United States Air Force. Another guest who attended that open house at the Shamrock Ranch was Doak Walker, a 1948 Heisman Trophy winner, who played for SMU and helped lead the Detroit Lions to two NFL football championships. Doak was living in Denver at the time. Today he is immortalized by the annual Doak Walker Award, given to the best college running back with good academic standing.

Mac become interested in politics as early as 1946. In 1956, he served on the Texas Democratic Executive Committee and was the party's director of finance. He often hosted parties at the Diamond M Ranch for state and national Democratic Party leaders, such as

Open House at Shamrock Ranch

Top: Governor of Colorado and Mrs. Dan Thornton (left), and Mr. and Mrs. C.T. McLaughlin (right). Above: Colorado Springs mayor and Mrs. Harry Blunt (right), and Mr. and Mrs. H.T. Fordyce of Camdenton, Missouri.

The Camp Carson commanding officer, General and Mrs. George Keyser (left), Mark McLaughlin (standing), and Miss Amy Johnson (seated).

Texas Governor Coke Stevenson.[7] Mac had many important political friends, including Lyndon B. Johnson.

According to a February 19, 2004, *Snyder Daily News* article, C.T. was quoted as saying, "I am interested in politics because I want to help good men in office. There are no bargains in men for public office."

His son Mark describes his political leanings this way: "I wouldn't call him a staunch Democrat, although he was a delegate to several national conventions for the Democratic Party. We used to call ourselves 'Texas Democrats.' The name survives in Washington today, only they call them 'Blue Dogs' there—always conservative Democrats."

The McLaughlins became well known as entertainers of friends, both local and international. Their parties were renowned. One reporter wrote, "Probably the thing which made C.T. and Scurry County known from Austin to Washington to London is the guest list at his famous parties. He'll give a party at the drop of a hat—especially if the hat is dropped into the political ring. All the Texas

President Lyndon B. Johnson (1908–1973)

Governors from Coke Stevenson on have been to the Diamond M Ranch, and so many minor state officials that they would have repopulated the town if all had stayed." [8]

Mac's history of entertaining dates back to 1938, when he held a horse show at the Diamond M Ranch. A gaited horse owner himself, he enjoyed the comradery and friendship of people who were in the gaited horse business. His guests stayed at the ranch and filled his house. The show included a barbeque and a live cowboy band, and was such a success that he repeated it the next summer. Eventually he had the best attended horse shows in Texas.[9]

When World War II came along, he made friends with several officers at Webb Air Force Base near Big Spring, which was 50 miles away from his Diamond M Ranch. He invited them to a barbeque and was soon hosting airmen regularly.

Then, when the Women Auxiliary Service Pilots (WASP) came to Avenger Field in Sweetwater, Texas, in 1943, Mac invited them for a party as well. Formed by Jaqueline Cochran, the WASP were among the first civilian female pilots employed to fly military aircraft under the direction of the U.S. Army Air Forces during the gender-sensitive days of World War II.[10] Mark remembers "having all those young aviatrixes come to the ranch for a barbeque."

A class of WASP with Jackie Cochran in the center is shown here. Jackie eventually received the U.S. Distinguished Service Medal for her work with the WASP. In 1964, she set a flight speed record of 1,429 mph in an F-104 Starfighter, and was inducted into the International Aerospace Hall of Fame a year later.

Mac and his wife thoroughly enjoyed hosting parties for those in the service of the United States. Claire prepared all the food and

A class of World War II Women Airforce Service Pilots (WASP) taught by Jackie Cochran (middle of group) (circa 1943).

engaged Mark and his sisters to put up the tables; decorate them with red, white, and blue tablecloths and napkins; and serve the guests. The whole family was involved in hosting some very memorable and distinguished events.

In Mark's words, "Mac was gregarious and had a very engaging personality. People instinctively liked him. He was generous but could be firm, too. He was very kind and generous to underprivileged people and particularly admired young men who were trying to get a start. He'd go out of his way to help someone he thought was really trying. If approached right, he'd send some kid to college. He was instinctively good about judging character. On the other hand, if somebody was a little bit shifty or wasn't true to his word, my father knew in a minute and was very hard on him. You didn't get a second chance to cheat him!"

Mac and Claire were interested in art and enjoyed sharing it with others. In 1936, they bought their first oil painting, *The Rancher's Daughter* by Philip R. Goodwin. This was during the Great Depression and well before they became affluent. Claire collected music boxes and crystal glasses, among other things, from her honeymoon on. Mac loved western art, particularly bronze statues of animals. Once his oil money came in, he began to buy paintings and other forms of fine art.

His favorite place to shop was Taos, New Mexico. Besides paintings, he bought numerous Navajo rugs and used them to decorate the Diamond M and Shamrock ranch houses. Very fortuitously, he began collecting the works of the great American illustrator N.C. Wyeth. Then he met Wyeth's pupil Peter Hurd and became good friends with him. Peter visited the Diamond M Ranch frequently and likely visited the Shamrock Ranch as well. Mac purchased a number of Hurd's paintings.

When Claire and Mac entertained, they always showed their art collections to their friends, who expressed admiration and encouragement. So they bought more and more, including paintings by Remington, Russell, Koerner, Acosta, and Hoffman. Eventually their collection grew too large for the ranch houses, so they turned Mac's office building in Snyder into the Diamond M Museum. It opened its doors to the public on April 1, 1964. They later built an addition onto the museum to accommodate their ever-growing collection.

The museum had a record number of visitors in 1967, when it previewed Peter Hurd's official portrait of President Johnson that had been rejected by the president himself to a

Artist Peter Hurd (1904–1984). *Courtesy Wyeth Hurd Gallery.*

great deal of media attention. Today this painting hangs in the Smithsonian Institution's National Portrait Gallery in Washington, D.C.

Mac loved to give young, talented artists a chance to succeed. He did this by throwing parties for them at the museum, where he put their works on display. By inviting everyone he knew plus the local newspaper editor to come and meet these rising stars, he created for them both publicity and notoriety. He also purchased some of their works to keep them encouraged and working. His parties were always well attended because he was such a good entertainer. More than one lucky artist owes his early success to C.T. McLaughlin!

In 1949, Mac and Claire established the Diamond M Foundation to offer financial assistance for various charitable, educational, and philanthropic undertakings. Mac also spent time serving on the Texas Hospital Board, the Texas Technological College Board of Regents, the Texas Department of Public Safety Commission, and the advisory board for the Southwest Legal Foundation. Because of his interest in western art, he was named to the art committee of the National Cowboy and Western Heritage Museum in Oklahoma City. He was also on the first board of directors of the Petroleum Museum, Library and Hall of Fame located near Midland, Texas.[11]

Mac was also a sponsor of Snyder Area Canyon Reef Operators' Committee (SACROC) —a model success story of an oil producing cooperative. About twenty miles long, the Canyon Reef oilfield has several thousand wells in it. Each lease is owned by a different operator. When oil production began to wane in 1951, Mac and a few other owners led the implementation of a plan to unitize all the leases and have a single operator instigate oil recovery—by injecting carbon dioxide into the formation to increase the pressure and thereby increase the yield. Each lease owner was then paid according to his percentage of the total wells involved. In 1973, SACROC oil companies recovered their billionth barrel of oil. Today, Scurry County is still one of the major oilfields in Texas, thanks to SACROC and Mac's leadership.

Because of the inspiring beauty and cooler temperatures Shamrock Ranch offered Mac and Claire, they got in the routine of spending their summers there. They would arrive in May and stay until Labor Day. However, since Mac was operating three other ranches in New Mexico and Texas at the same time, he was constantly on the go, either by private airplane or automobile.

By this time, Mac had switched from Hereford to Angus cattle on some of his

Hereford calf

Belted Galloway cattle

Mixed herd of Black and Red Angus cattle

To facilitate his business dealings, Mac purchased a DC-3 airplane manufactured by the Douglas Aircraft Company. Because of its speed and range, the DC-3 revolutionized air transport during the 1930s and 1940s, had a profound impact on World War II, and is regarded as one of the most significant transport aircrafts ever designed.[14] The picture here shows Mac and a group of his friends in front of the aircraft as they prepare to depart from Peterson Field in Colorado Springs after a visit to the Shamrock Ranch. Mac's faithful and loyal driver, bartender, waiter, and butler—Arthur "Dutch" Ward—is standing on the far right. The two men closest to Arthur are Mac's pilots, and the lady standing in the doorway wearing a white sweater is Claire McLaughlin's sister.

Mac McLaughlin (leftmost) with his DC-3, a group of friends, and some employees (circa 1950). *Courtesy Mark McLaughlin.*

The C.T. McLaughlin Shamrock Ranch brand, as registered in Colorado's El Paso and Douglas Counties.

ranches. He did this for several reasons. One was that Angus are naturally polled cattle—meaning they have no horns. As a youth, Mark's hardest job was polling (dehorning) the Hereford calves at Diamond M. He described this loathsome task as "traumatic."

Another reason for the switch was that Hereford are more difficult to care for since their white faces and pink pigmentation are subject to sunburn. Mother cows get sunburned udders. Also, they often develop pink eye, a condition which causes their eyes to run from irritation and infection.

Angus cattle are not subject to these drawbacks. Today, Black Angus is the most popular breed of cattle in the United States due to advanced genetic selection. In 2005, nearly a third of a million Black Angus cattle were registered in the U.S.[12]

In his later years, Mac raised Belted Galloway cattle, which have the advantage of being winter hardy. Due to their unique white belt, they are often called "Belties" or "Oreo cookie cows." Both Angus and Galloway cattle originated in Scotland and were named for the respective regions where they were first bred. Hereford cattle were also named after their place of origin, which is Herefordshire County, England.

Because Mac spent a portion of each year at the Shamrock Ranch, he made many friends at the Air Force Academy, which is headquartered about 10 miles southwest of the main ranch house. As Mark characterized his father, "He was the kind who would meet somebody

the first time and say to him, 'Why don't you come over for supper? Claire and I would love to have you for supper. Bring your wife. Bring your friend over and his wife.' They'd come over to the Shamrock and have a very enjoyable visit—just talk. My father could talk about any subject intelligently. They got to be friends. Then a new superintendent would come in and they'd have a reception and do the same thing all over again. He had dozens of friends at the Academy."

One of Mac's military friends was General Robin Olds, a famous "triple ace" who achieved the required sixteen victories in World War II and the Vietnam War. Olds was commandant of cadets at the Academy and is remembered for saying, "There are pilots and there are pilots; with the good ones, it is inborn. You can't teach it. If you are a fighter pilot, you have to be willing to take risks."[13] Olds was also known for his marriage to Hollywood actress Ella Raines.

Triple Ace Robin Olds (1922–2007)

Another of Mac's friends was General Earle E. Partridge, Commander in Chief of the North American Air Defense Command (NORAD) and its Air Force Component, the Air Defense Command, located at Ent Air Force Base in Colorado Springs. Early in his career, Partridge was a test pilot at Wright Field, flying many of the planes which were later used in World War II.

General Earle E. Partridge (1900–1990)

He went on to become a key commander of that war as well as the Korean War. When he retired from active duty in 1959, he was a four-star general.

According to Mark, Mac's best friend was a man from Ft. Worth, Texas, named Fred Korth. He came to the Shamrock Ranch many times. Korth was assistant secretary of the army during Eisenhower's administration and secretary of the navy under President Kennedy. Once he brought Frank Pace with him to visit Shamrock Ranch. Of course, Mac immediately befriended Pace, who served in many prestigious positions, such as secretary of the army, CEO of general dynamics, first chairman of the Corporation for Public Broadcasting, and as one of the Eisenhower Ten—a secret group created by President Eisenhower in 1958 to serve in the event of a national emergency. Pace appeared on the cover of *Time* magazine on January 20, 1958.

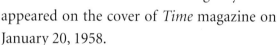

Fred Korth
(1909–1998)

Left to right—C.T. McLaughlin, Claire McLaughlin, and Frank Pace (August, 1957). *Courtesy Mark McLaughlin.*

The United States Air Force Academy

U.S. Air Force Academy emblem

In addition to being a friend of politicians, artists, cowboys, and others, C.T. McLaughlin was a great supporter of the military and especially the cadets at the United States Military Academy, which was constructed during the 1950s only a few miles west of the entrance to his ranch. The Academy plays such an important part in the life of the Pikes Peak Country that it is worthwhile to include some of its history here. The need for such an academy was first voiced in 1918 when Lieutenant Colonel A.J. Hanlon wrote, "As the Military and Naval Academies are the backbone of the Army and Navy, so must the Aeronautical Academy be the backbone of the Air Service. No service can flourish without some such institution to inculcate into its embryonic officers love of country, proper conception of duty, and highest regard for honor." [15]

Then, in 1925, General Billy Mitchell testified on Capitol Hill that it was necessary "to have an air academy to form a basis for the permanent backbone of your air service and to attend to the . . . organizational part of it, very much the same way that West Point does

U.S. Air Force Academy cadets

President Dwight D. Eisenhower shaking hands with Secretary of the Air Force Harold E. Talbott (1954). *Courtesy U.S. Air Force Academy McDermott Library, Special Collections.*

for the Army, or the Naval Academy for the Navy." But it was not until the late 1940s that the concept of the United States Air Force Academy began to take shape.[16]

After the National Security Act of 1947 provided for the establishment of a separate Air Force, Secretary of Defense James Forrestal established the Service Academy Board. In January 1950, this board, headed by Dwight D. Eisenhower (who was then president of Columbia University), concluded that the needs of the Air Force could not be met by the two existing U.S. service academies and that an Air Force Academy should be established.

In 1954, Congress passed legislation to begin construction of the Academy, and President Eisenhower signed it into law on April 1 of that year. He is shown here shaking hands with Secretary of the Air Force Harold E. Talbott after the signing.

The legislation established an advisory commission to help determine the site of the new school. Among the panel members were Reserve Brigadier General Charles A. Lindbergh—the first pilot to fly solo and nonstop across the Atlantic Ocean; General Carl Andrew

Spaatz, commander of the U.S. Strategic Air Forces in Europe and Japan who directed the bombing of Germany and the atomic bombing of Hiroshima and Nagasaki; and Lieutenant General Hubert R. Harmon, deputy commander of air forces in the South Pacific Area who later became the Academy's first superintendent.

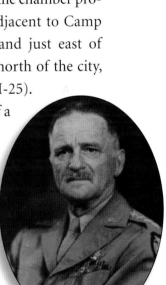

Charles Lindbergh (1859–1924)

After preliminary investigations, the original 580 sites considered for the United States Air Force Academy were winnowed down to three—Alton, Illinois; Lake Geneva, Wisconsin; and Colorado Springs.[17]

The Colorado Springs Chamber of Commerce worked very hard to win the decision. Early on in the negotiations, the chamber proposed two sites. One was adjacent to Camp Carson, south of the city and just east of Broadmoor. The other was north of the city, directly east of U.S. 85 (now I-25). During a visit by members of a preliminary Academy Site Selection Board, the two sites proposed by the Colorado Springs Chamber of Commerce were rejected, primarily because neither met the requirement for scenic beauty. But fortunately for Colorado, the board members' plane back to D.C. was delayed, forcing them

General Carl Andrew Spaatz (1891–1974)

to spend an extra weekend in the area. During this time, Lieutenant Colonel Arthur E. Boudreau, recorder of the Site Selection Board, drove to Boulder, Colorado, to visit

General Hubert R. Harmon (1892–1957)

with a professor at the University of Colorado. On the way, he "was impressed by the beauty and grandeur of the area on the west side of the highway south of Husted and Monument."[18]

When he told representatives of the Chamber of Commerce that the west side of the highway would have a better chance at being acceptable to the Site Selection Board, they adopted his recommendation.

Among the criteria for the selection decision were the following:

- At least 15,000 acres (for a modern flying field, room for expansion, etc.)
- Safe flying conditions
- Natural beauty and availability of water
- Proximity of cities within a fifty-mile radius and accessibility
- Climate (no extremes of heat or cold) and health conditions
- Accessibility by rail, air, and highway systems

The Colorado Springs Chamber of Commerce had serious negative perceptions to address for three criteria—health conditions, water availability, and flying conditions. It had been reported by the Army surgeon general that strep throat and rheumatic fever incidents were higher in Colorado than anywhere else in the United States. To address this concern, the chamber had local medical studies performed by University of Colorado and Lowry Air Force Base medical personnel (Lowry Air Force Base was located in Denver). The results showed that respiratory conditions are not a concern when treated properly.

To address the water concern, the City of Colorado Springs purchased water from the Blue River on Colorado's western slope, had it piped into Colorado Springs for potential Academy use, and built a water treatment plant adjacent to the proposed Academy site. This was a farsighted move by the city as it supported rapid population growth. City Councilman James McCullough, who purchased Shamrock Ranch in 1951, helped to make this happen (see newspaper clip, page 159).

The flying conditions concern was addressed by Charles Lindbergh, who was a strong proponent of the Colorado Springs site. Two members of the Site Selection Board, Mr. Merrill C. Meigs and Dr. Virgil M. Hancher, were concerned about the proposed site's elevation (which ranges from 6,380 to 8,040 feet above sea level), air currents, and nearby mountain ranges for takeoff and landing safety. Lindbergh suggested an aerial survey to decide the matter and they agreed. He drove them to the Pine Valley Airport, located 2 miles south of the Town of Husted, where a small flying school was operated. Dressed in his civilian clothes, Lindbergh approached the manager of the airport, who did not recognize him. What happened next was described admirably by Meigs:

"Do you know how to fly?" asked the airport manager.

"I think I can fly," Lindbergh answered quietly.

"Do you have a license?" was the next query.

"Yes, I have a license," said Lindbergh.

"Well," said the manager, "I'll have to see your license. If you will come into my office, I'll look over your papers."

We walked into the little office with its broken-down furniture and cracked walls. The manager seated himself importantly at a desk, got out some papers, and said to Lindbergh, "Let's see your license."

Lindbergh, of course, has about a dozen licenses from all over the world. Each bears his photograph. When he laid them out on the desk, the airport manager's neck began to redden. The color mounted to his face as he stared incredulously at Lindbergh, then back at the licenses.

"You ain't Charles Lindbergh, be you?" he stammered.

"Yes, I am," said Lindbergh.

*"My ***!" exclaimed the manager and almost collapsed on the desk in embarrassment.* [19]

Lindberg's aerial survey convinced both Meigs and Hancher that the Colorado Springs

Cover of the 1954 brochure prepared by the Colorado Springs committee to bring the Academy to Pikes Peak Country.

site was safe for flying. General Lindbergh also concluded that the site was suitable for flight training. This pronouncement, made by one of the world's most famous aviators, silenced any objections to Colorado Springs as the Air Force Academy site.

While the final site decision was being made by Secretary of the Air Force Harold E. Talbott, local opposition was building both in Alton and Lake Geneva. Irate taxpayers concerned about having to sell their property below market value inundated state and federal officials with indignant letters and telegrams. Noisy demonstrations were held and site visits were met with pickets.

However, many residents of Denver and other Colorado cities united with those of Colorado Springs to promote Colorado as the best site, and local newspapers carried their message. As a result, virtually no local objections were raised to government officials.

On June 24, 1954, Secretary Talbott announced Colorado Springs as the winning site. Under the direction of Governor Dan Thornton, the state of Colorado responded by contributing a million dollars towards the purchase of the property, which included the southern portion of previous Shamrock Ranch owner James McCullough's Green Mountain Ranch.

Governor Thornton had previously established the Colorado Land Acquisitions Commission to oversee the land purchases should the Colorado Springs site be selected. His foresight was commendable because land speculators attempted to drastically increase land values when the site was announced. The commission engaged three appraisers to evaluate each parcel of land, but instructed them to use 1954 land values. This saved the federal government millions of dollars in land costs

Town of Husted, Colorado

One of the consequences of the Air Force Academy coming to Pikes Peak Country was the need to remove a number of historical structures. This included the entire town of Husted, which had been the closest town to the Shamrock Ranch for more than a half century. Cal Husted, for whom the town was named, had been one of the first owners of Shamrock Ranch land and built the first house on the property. Moreover, the town of Husted was connected to his ranch by the Husted Wagon Road, which traversed the ranch's Husted pasture. So the demise of this small quaint town had a sad bearing on the history of the Shamrock Ranch.

Husted's Kinner Store and Filling Station (1956)

The photograph here shows Husted Station on the Santa Fe Railroad, just two days before it was demolished in 1956. Its weathered front sign read "HUSTED, elevation 6596 feet. Denver 62 miles. Ogden 720 miles."

Close by, a few other buildings had survived to mark the once-busy sawmill operation, lumbering center, cattle loading point, and passenger station on the Denver and Rio Grande Railroad. It was at that station where Lou Steppler and his family had once sold his prize Early Ohio potatoes, and where the Joe Romick family arrived in 1927 to be met by Wharton Allen, on their way to a new life on the Allen Ranch.

Today, the freeway cloverleaf comprising the north entrance of the Air Force Academy is located where the town of Husted once stood.[20] (For more on Husted, see Appendix B.)

Husted Station—center of the town of Husted (1956).
Courtesy U.S. Air Force Academy
McDermott Library, Special Collections.

and prevented the highly undesirable use of eminent domain.

The first property purchased for the academy was the 4,630-acre Cathedral Rock Ranch. It sold for $300,000—or $65 an acre. This benchmark set the general price for the remaining parcels. Of course, oil and mineral leases, buildings, and other improvements were also considered.

Initially the goal was to acquire 12,500 acres. However, the site grew to a total of 18,500 acres. Today's Air Force Academy is one-third the size of Washington D.C. and larger than New York's Manhattan Island, which is home to more than 1.5 million people! The academy property is also a wildlife preserve where hunting is essentially banned.

The first architectural model of the campus was unveiled in May of 1955. Because of its modular, futuristic appearance, it instantly elicited negative reactions from members of Congress as well as the public. However, most

Rare photograph of the Cadet Chapel under construction (circa 1962). *Courtesy U.S. Air Force Academy McDermott Library, Special Collections.*

United States Air Force Academy Air Gardens with Cadet Chapel in the background.

American architects defended the design, which was created by Skidmore, Owings and Merrill Associates. Frank Lloyd Wright, who had been skipped over as the site's architect, was a notable exception. In July of that year, the American Institute of Architects released a supportive statement, saying the buildings were "among the most significant productions of American professionals." [21]

However, Secretary Talbott wanted the Cadet Chapel design—which was the most controversial—revised. The architects returned with a new design that had fewer aluminum spires than the original and now included

extensive stained glass separated by buttresses. When the new design was revealed in March of 1957, reaction was still negative, but the U.S. Senate voted $3 million to fund it anyway.

When the cadet chapel was dedicated on September 22, 1963, almost all criticism of its design immediately ceased. Today, this chapel, with its seventeen spires soaring 150 feet into the deep azure sky, is one of the most popular tourist attractions in the state of Colorado.

Since the new academy facilities could not be ready for the inaugural Class of 1959, all 306 cadets were sworn in at Lowry Air Force Base in Denver. They were housed there in renovated World War II barracks until the new campus was completed. The swearing-in ceremony occurred in July of 1955.

To achieve a distinctive uniform for the cadets, Secretary Talbott wanted "imagination" in the design—and he was unhappy with pattern created by the military tailors he initally granted the job to. As a result, the academy's first classes wore temporary uniforms while the official uniform was being developed.

Talbott sought out legendary Hollywood director Cecil B. DeMille for help. DeMille's designs—especially his cadet parade uniform—won praise from both Air Force and academy leadership. His uniforms

The falcon is the Air Force Academy's mascot.

are still worn by cadets to this day. [22]

The Class of 1959 established many other important traditions that continue today. Most notably, they adopted the Honor Code (*We will not lie, steal, or cheat, nor tolerate among us anyone who does)* and chose the falcon as the academy's mascot.

In 1957, the Air Force Academy cadet wing marched in the second inaugural parade of Dwight D. Eisenhower, 34th President of the United States. President Eisenhower (Ike), whose wife Mamie was raised in Pueblo, Colorado Springs, and Denver, loved Colorado and vacationed there frequently. In fact, the Headquarters Building at Lowry Air Force Base served as the "Summer White House" for the Eisenhowers. While in Colorado in 1955, Ike suffered a heart attack and was rushed to Fitzsimons Army Hospital. Denver virtually replaced Washington D.C. as the capital city while the nation anxiously awaited word of his progress.[23] Not long after his recovery, Ike was instrumental in the adoption of "In God We Trust" as the motto of the United States of America.

President Dwight David Eisenhower (1890–1969)

The 1,145 cadets temporarily housed at Lowry Air Force Base transferred to the present Air Force Academy site in August 1958. They were bused to the north entrance, from which they proudly marched the five miles to the academic area, accompanied by a blaring band. Less than a year later, the academy received accreditation.

The first Air Force Academy class graduated on June 3, 1959. Both Mac and Mark McLaughlin and their wives attended this graduation. Conducted in Arnold Hall, it was the only one ever held indoors. Two hundred and seven members of the Class of 1959 were commissioned. Superintendent General James

President Dwight D. Eisenhower addressing the first class of Air Force Academy cadets (1959). *Courtesy U.S. Air Force Academy McDermott Library, Special Collections.*

E. Briggs conducted nineteen weddings in his quarters over the next two days.

Academy officials had wanted Ike to give the first commencement address, but his physicians frowned on him spending time in Colorado's high elevation. Instead, he made a brief, informal visit to the academy on Armed Forces Day, May 16, 1959.

Ike is shown here addressing the cadets in the dining hall. During this visit, the Cadet Wing Commander presented him with the first academy diploma and enrolled him as an Honorary Member of the Class of 1959.

Moved by this gesture, Ike told the cadet wing, *"I was on the Board, as a matter of fact, when they decided that there should be an air academy, and behind the scenes and clandestinely not saying anything about it, I was very anxious that the academy be in the state I love so much."* [24] Ike returned to the academy in 1961 to dedicate a golf course named in his honor.

When it was decided in 1954 that the United Stated Air Force Academy should be built in Colorado Springs, Mac showed his support by becoming a director of the Air

Force Academy Foundation, a private foundation dedicated to promoting the welfare of the Academy Cadet Wing. Governor Dan Thornton was president of the foundation from 1954–1961 and undoubtedly influenced Mac's decision to become a director. One of the foundation's notable contributions to the academy was a $1.75 million gift that enabled the Barry Goldwater Visitor Center to be built.

Construction of the United States Air Force Academy

When ground was first broken at the academy site in 1955, the academy construction project represented the largest single educational building program ever undertaken in the United States. Overseen by the Air Force Academy Construction Agency, this huge task boasts impressive statistics.

- More than 5,000 workers, many from Pikes Peak Country, were employed by 20 major construction firms.
- Nineteen million cubic yards of dirt were excavated from the academic complex alone.
- More than 800,000 cubic yards of concrete were poured and 250,000 square feet of tile were installed.

- The academic complex buildings cover 4 million square feet of floor area.
- With more than a million square feet of glass, these buildings have four times the amount of glass as New York City's Empire State Building
- Initial construction cost of the academy's facilities was $145 million.
- Today, the academy property contains housing and other essential facilities for a population of 10,000, including support personnel and their families.[25]

Impact on the city of Colorado Springs

It is impossible to assess the full impact that the United States Air Force Academy has had on Pikes Peak Country. After World War II, the future of Colorado Springs became very bleak. For one thing, automobile travel had drastically changed the lifestyle of tourists. Instead of staying an entire season in one resort area, they stayed only for a few days and then moved on to other vacation spots. As a result, Colorado Springs's famous Broadmoor Hotel began experiencing difficult times. And with the introduction of miracle drugs, the number of peple suffering from tuberculosis

The United States Air Force Academy under construction (circa the late 1950s). *Courtesy U.S. Air Force Academy McDermott Library, Special Collections.*

Colorado Springs greeting sign off Interstate Highway 25 (2007). Photograph by Richard Seeley. *Courtesy the Experience Colorado Springs at Pikes Peak Convention & Visitors Bureau.*

decreased and sanatoriums were closing down after fifty years of steady business. Alarmed over the declining economic outlook of the area, trustees of Colorado College—one of the city's largest employers—considered closing its doors.

However, after the United States Air Force Academy came to Colorado Springs, the city began to grow. From a quiet little resort community of 45,000 in 1942, its population exploded to over 360,000 in 2000. In *Money* magazine's 2006 "Best Places to Live" edition, Colorado Springs was selected as the No. 1 Best Big City.[26] Today, it is one of the nation's foremost military-aerospace centers, and the Air Force Academy is one of Colorado's leading tourist attractions.

MAC OPENED his Shamrock Ranch home to cadets, who came frequently for a reprieve from their intense training program. Many of them spent afternoons and evenings with him. Former Academy Superintendent General Thomas S. Moorman said, "He was a great friend of the Academy and the Air Force."[27]

The 1962 Air Force Academy graduation featured United States Vice President Lyndon B. Johnson (LBJ), as the keynote speaker. The Vice President was scheduled to have lunch at a formal affair on campus following the graduation exercises. However, he decided that he wanted to see his good friend Mac McLaughlin first, so he flew to the Shamrock Ranch for a short visit. Meanwhile, guests at the function he was scheduled to attend sat down to eat. The band was ready to play *Ruffles and Flourishes*, but LBJ was nowhere to be seen—he was still visiting his friend Mac at the Shamrock Ranch!

Vice President Lyndon B. Johnson giving the 1962 United States Air Force Academy commencement address. *Courtesy U.S. Air Force Academy McDermott Library, Special Collections.*

Vice President Lyndon B. Johnson congratulating cadet graduates (1962). *Courtesy U.S. Air Force Academy McDermott Library, Special Collections.*

In the best Western Tradition

By Kay Woestendiek

Rodeo week, traditionally a high point in the Colorado Springs summer season, was no disappointment this year. It reached its peak of excitement with the presence of a majority of the board members of the Cowboy Hall of Fame who gathered in the Springs for meetings and socializing.

Colorado Springs has three dedicated members on that board: Robert Norris, Jasper Ackerman, and C.T. McLaughlin. Each contributed notably to the pleasures of the week, and to the hospitality extended to their fellow board members.

Thursday evening, Akerman entertained the group at dinner at the Broadmoor Hotel's Penrose Room, and later at the rodeo. Friday morning the board met for a formal meeting, then were royally entertained that night by C.T. McLaughlin and his daughter, Mrs. Jean DeFord of Austin, Texas, at a marvelous barbecue party at McLaughlin's Shamrock Ranch in the Black Forest.

It was quite a party. The guest list resembled a "Who's Who" of the West. Joel McCrea and his super-charming wife Frances (Frances Dee) were among the honored guests. Each reached motion picture stardom and fame years ago, and for some of us who have admired the couple since we were kids, but had never met them, the evening provided particular interest. They are a handsome couple, but better, they are warm, friendly, down-to-earth, people. McCrea, who has generously supported the Hall of Fame both with his energy and money, is chairman of the organization's board of directors this year—he followed Jasper Ackerman in that position.

Mr. and Mrs. John Kirkpatrick of Oklahoma City were among the guests, as was Mrs. Charles Bennett (from the same place) who left early to meet Mr. Bennett at the airport. Retha Martin and Mrs. Martin were in from Lubbock, Texas for the event, as were Mr. and Mrs. Harold Shaffer, of Bismarck, N.D.; Mrs. Nova Payne of Pampa, Tex.; former U.S. Senator from Kansas City, Kan., Harry Darby and Mrs. Darby; Mr. and Mrs. Robert Rockwell of Corning, N.Y.; and Dean Krakel of Oklahoma City. Mr. and Mrs. E.W. Schrader of Snyder, Tex., were there, as were so many others from Snyder—where McLaughlin resides when he is not in the Springs—that one wonders who's keeping the store down there this week.

Among the local guests were Mr. and Mrs. Robert Norris, Mr. and Mrs. Dennis O'Rourke; and Mr. and Mrs. Archibald Barron.

In addition to supporting the Air Force Academy, Mac was also a promoter of the annual Rodeo Week in Colorado Springs. In 1973, he and his daughter Jean hosted a barbeque party at the Shamrock Ranch that was quite a success. A *Colorado Springs Sun* article about the party stated, "It is said that a party is only as good as the guests who attend . . . this was a good 'un."[28]

As a staunch supporter and board member of the Cowboy Hall of Fame in Big Springs, Texas, Mac hosted three of his fellow board members, their wives, and others at the ranch barbeque in 1973. Board members present in addition to Mac were Robert Norris, Jasper Ackerman, and Joel Mc-Crea, the organization's chairman. Mr. and Mrs. Archibald Barron, neighbors of the McLaughlins, also attended.

Mac and Claire McLaughlin continued to spend their summers at Shamrock Ranch until Claire passed away in 1971. After that, Mac still came to the

Party for Pardners

The honored guest at the Pikes Peak or Bust Rodeo was Joel McCrea, star of western movies, pictured above left with his wife, former actress Frances Dee. The couple were also honored at an outdoor barbecue at the ranch of C. T. McLaughlin, lower left, hostessed by Jean DeFord, above right. Several members of the board of directors of the Cowboy Hall of Fame—including Robert Norris—lower right with his wife Jane, also attended the party.

(SUN Photo by Tom Strongman)

Jasper Ackerman

Jasper Ackerman was a prominent cattle rancher, banker, and business leader in Colorado Springs from the 1940s to the 1980s. He founded the Air Academy National Bank and was named the Premier Banker of Colorado by the Colorado Bankers Association in 1967. Instrumental in bringing Ft. Carson, NORAD, and the United States Air Force Academy to Colorado Springs, he was a longtime friend and supporter of the Air Force Academy and Pikes Peak Country. He funded the Air Force Historical Art Museum in Fairchild Hall at the academy and raised funds for the Veterans Memorial in Memorial Park, Colorado Springs.

Mr. Ackerman was a founder of the Pikes Peak or Bust Rodeo and was founding trustee and director of the National Cowboy and Western Heritage Museum in Oklahoma City.[29] He was undoubtedly involved in recruiting Mac McLaughlin to serve on the museum's art committee. In 1963, he founded the Anna Keesling Ackerman Trust in honor of his mother. This trust is now a charitable fund administered by the El Pomar Foundation.[30]

The National Cowboy and Western Heritage Museum in Oklahoma City and the ProRodeo Hall of Fame in Colorado Springs have both hon-

ored Jasper Ackerman. Famous sculptor Edd Hayes created a life-size portrait bust of him that is on display at the ProRodeo Hall of Fame in the Jasper Ackerman Room.[31]

Edd Hayes' sculpture of Jasper Ackerman.

Joel Albert McCrea was a famous American movie actor from 1929 to1962. He was especially popular in Westerns, including Cecil B. De-Mille's *Wells Fargo* and *Union Pacific*. He reached the peak of his career in the 1940s, starring in films such as Alfred Hitchcock's *Foreign Correspondent* as well as *Buffalo Bill* and *The Virginian*. One of his later movies was *Ride the High Country*. In 1969, he was inducted into the Western Performers Hall of Fame at the National Cowboy and Western Heritage Museum, which Jasper Ackerman founded. He also has a star on the Hollywood Walk of Fame. After retiring from acting, he enjoyed ranching in Ventura County, California.[32]

In 1933, Joel met actress Frances Marion Dee on the set of the movie *The Silver Cord*. The attractive couple married later that year after a whirlwind courtship. They raised three children, including actor Jody McCrea, and were married until Joel's death in 1990. Frances's movie career took off when she was given the leading

role opposite Maurice Chevalier in *Playboy of Paris*. Her other major screen credits include *Little Women*, *Of Human Bondage*, *Becky Sharp*, and

Joel McCrea

Payment on Demand.[33] She co-starred with her husband in the 1948 film *Four Faces West*, which won a 1949 Writers Guild of America screen award for Best Written American Western.[34]

ranch until he developed a heart condition and was hospitalized in Colorado Springs. Upon regaining his strength, he returned to the Diamond M, but passed away there on July 29, 1975, just four years after his beloved wife had died.

Dean Krakel, Cowboy Hall of Fame Managing Director, said the following at Mac's passing:

"The West has lost a true champion today. Mr. Mac always said and stood up for what he believed. I know the Cowboy Hall will miss his excellent guidance and the wonderful sense of humor he brought to all the board meetings."[35]

In 2004, the National Ranching Heritage Center in Lubbock, Texas, dedicated the C.T. and Claire McLaughlin Arbor and Memorial Garden. The facility was made possible by a grant from the Diamond M Foundation and Mac's surviving heirs. It "honors the McLaughlins, who founded the Diamond M Ranch, museum, art collection and foundation, all of which brought international attention to Scurry County and West Texas during their lifetimes."

The arbor was selected by the foundation because of its significance to the history of the Old West. In former times, a brush arbor was a gathering place where the community and settlers came together from far

C. T. McLaughlin

Benefactor, rancher C. T. McLaughlin dies

Nationally-known Western art. philanthropist, Texas oilman and Colorado Springs area rancher C. T. McLaughlin died Tuesday in Snyder, Texas. He was 78.

McLaughlin was best known as the financial benefactor and a member of the board of directors of the National Cowboy Hall of Fame and Heritage Center in Oklahoma City.

At the time of his death from a heart attack, McLaughlin also was chairman of the board of trustees of the National Academy of Western Art. He began buying art, especially Western art, in 1936 and owned a collection worth several million dollars.

In the Colorado Springs area, McLaughlin was known for his support of the U.S. Air Force Academy and the operation of the 20,000 acre Shamrock Ranch in Black Forest, which he bought in 1950.

McLaughlin was a director of the private Air Force Academy Foundation. "He was a great friend of the academy and the Air Force," said former academy superintendent Gen. Thomas S. Moorman (ret.).

At the giant Shamrock Ranch, 15555 Colo. Highway 83, McLaughlin raised nearly 1,000 head of Angus and three breeds of Galloway cattle.

McLaughlin lived in Colorado Springs off and on for about six months each year. Academy cadets were among those who were invited to spend afternoons and evenings at the ranch here.

He left Colorado Springs last Saturday to return to Snyder.

In Texas, he also owned and leased thousands of acres of ranch land centering in the Diamond M Ranch near Snyder.

He purchased the ranch in 1936 and his vast art collection was housed nearby in the Diamond M Museum. Many pieces also went to the National Cowboy Hall of Fame.

McLaughlin promoted many Western artists and others through funds he established in the Diamond M Foundation.

"The West has lost a true champion today," said Cowboy Hall Managing Director Dean Krakel. "Mr. Mac always said and stood up for what he believed. I know the Cowboy Hall will miss his excellent guidance and the wonderful sense of humor he brought to all the board meetings."

Clarence Thurston "C. T." McLaughlin was born in Shippenville, Pa., in 1897 and

(See BENEFACTOR, page 2)

(Continued from page 1)
went to Texas after World War I to work in the oil business. He was a personal friend of former President Lyndon B. Johnson.

He is survived by a son, Mark McLaughlin, San Antonio, Tex.; three

daughters, Evelyn Knox, Houston, Ruth Riddle, Paris, Tex., and Jean DeFord, Austin, Tex.; two brothers, J. R. McLaughlin, Beaver, Pa., and Harold McLaughlin, Shippenville, Pa.; a sister, Mrs. Doris Filer, Grove City, Pa.; 14

grandchildren and seven great-grandchildren.

He was preceded in death several years ago by his wife.

Funeral services are pending but they have tentatively been set for Thursday.

and wide to socialize and to observe holidays and special events. The latticework canopied shelter was constructed of saplings and brush gathered from native flora.

The dedication ceremony also placed the Diamond M brand permanently at the National Ranching Heritage Center. According to Jim Pfluger, executive director of the Center, "The arbor was the perfect place to pay tribute to a couple who was known for their hospitality and the enjoyment of their friends."

The McLaughlin Arbor features a large, open-air expanse with a roof and patterned concrete floor. Lighting is provided by eighteen hanging kerosene lanterns modified for electricity. Inside the arbor, visitors can relax on oak benches as they enjoy the historical park area of the Center's museum.[36]

Mac passed on two ranches to his children when he died—the Shamrock and the Diamond M. He had deeded the Shamrock to all four of them in 1972. In 1979, his daughter Evelyn lost her husband and was very nostalgic, so she asked her siblings for the Diamond M as her part of the inheritance. Mark and his other sisters were happy to accommodate this request, so they jointly took ownership of the Shamrock Ranch in a trade that was formalized with an exchange deed.

Mark's sisters looked to him to manage the Shamrock Ranch once it was deeded to them. Mark did his best, but it was very challenging. He had three children in college, was operating a bank, and was practicing law. On top of all that, he was running two other ranches—the Double M Ranch in Nolan County, Texas (a large operation with over a thousand mother cows), and the Cold Creek Ranch just south of San Angelo, Texas.

In 1978, he discharged the resident ranch help and shut down the Shamrock's cattle business. At a dispersal sale in Denver, he sold several hundred mother cows. He then leased the ranch to Leonard Traylor and his son Richard for grazing. They were from San Antonio, Texas. Richard and his wife lived in the main ranch house during the summertime, but Leonard only came by occasionally.

Mark finally decided to sell the Shamrock Ranch because he didn't have enough time to manage it, even though it was not a financial burden. He never listed the ranch with a broker, although he was approached by many of them. Instead, he told them to produce a buyer and then he'd talk about a commission.

Somehow Ed Pendleton of Denver heard it was for sale and approached Mark directly. He agreed to the price Mark wanted and bought the Shamrock in July of 1980 with an installment land contract that required annual and semi-annual payments. Unfortunately, Pendleton was consistently late with his payments and eventually defaulted on them.

Even though he was an attorney himself, Mark hired a lawyer in Colorado Springs who was more familiar with Colorado law to foreclose on the ranch. His attorney advised him that, under Colorado law, anyone operating an agricultural property has six months after foreclosure to redeem the property. Needless to say, Mark was not happy about stringing the foreclosure along for another six months.

Literally hours before the six-month grace period was about to expire, Pendleton came up with the money he needed to redeem the note. Not only was Mark surprised, he was disappointed because by then he wanted the beautiful ranch back where he and Amy had become engaged.

The picture at right shows Mark during a visit with the Wismers in the Great Room at the Shamrock Ranch. He and Amy have three children—a daughter who works for the Controller of the state of Texas, a son who practices law in Midland, and another son who trades oil and gas futures on the New York Mercantile Exchange and the Chicago Board of Trade. In 2007, Mark was honored as a University of Texas Distinguished Alumnus. Interestingly, he was also a pledge fraternity brother of George Nelson Allen, Jr.

John Mark McLaughlin (circa 2005)

McLaughlin's
Employees and Neighbors

Ranch Manager Cecil Winfrey and workers Richard Geiger and Willie Moreland (1953–1956)

NOT LONG after Mac bought the Shamrock from James McCullough, he hired Cecil Winfrey to run it. Mac knew Cecil from Texas. He was tall and lean, and he wasn't afraid of Mac. In fact, he told Mac exactly what he thought in no uncertain terms.

Cecil and his wife Millie moved into the Shamrock Ranch manager's house, where the families of Joe Romick and Frank Hartley lived during the Allen Ranch era. After getting settled, Cecil launched Mac's cattle business and took on the task of cleaning up the ranch and getting it into good repair, which was no small undertaking.

In 1956, Cecil hired Richard Geiger to help. Richard's first job was trimming the lower ponderosa pine limbs so the cows couldn't get to the needles, which contain turpentine and cause them to abort their calves if consumed. This took a great deal of time. Later on, he assisted with forestry and fences. He also helped brand, vaccinate, and poll the cattle.

Sometimes Richard would come home tired, sunburned, and windburned from building fences on a ranch that Mac had acquired near Karval, Colorado—some 75 miles southeast of the Shamrock Ranch. Rumor has it that Mac won this ranch in a poker game—a game he loved to play.

Richard quickly found that although Mac paid good wages, he expected a good day's work. Richard was more than willing to deliver—he was known around the area as a good worker, which was why Winfrey hired him in the first place.

And he was always willing to help others in a bind. As Iola remembers, "Back then, it was all about being good neighbors." She also remembers Mac McLaughlin fondly and says "He was as common as an old shoe."

Richard drove a school bus for the Cherry Valley schools in Douglas County for twenty-seven years. He always kept a footlocker on the bus that was filled with gloves, jackets, and boots his own children had outgrown. If a student about to get off the bus needed protection from the cold, Richard was quick to loan him or her something from the footlocker.

When bringing students involved in sports home after dark, he refused to drop the girls off at their normal stops. Instead, he drove them straight to their homes to ensure their safety, even though district officials chastised him for breaking the rules.

One afternoon he came across a pregnant woman who was struggling to carry feed to her calves. Evidently her husband was not at home. Richard stopped the bus and told his young passengers to wait while he helped the lady. A number of the children jumped out with him and helped to feed and water the calves.

With Iola's help, Richard gave every one of his "kids" a birthday gift each year as well as a Christmas present. He loved them all. One day a blizzard kept the parents of a new student confined to town. Richard willingly took the girl home with him and Iola cared for her all weekend until her parents could make it back and claim her.

The Geiger's neighbors reciprocated the good treatment. In an incident that occurred

Richard and Iola Geiger (1976). *Courtesy Iola Geiger.*

shortly after Richard's father died, Iola noticed that some clothes she had hung on the clothesline were missing. But they soon appeared again—expertly ironed and folded by a thoughtful neighbor. Some ladies cared for her smaller children and cleaned her house while she was seeing to the funeral arrangements.

The Winfreys also proved themselves to be good neighbors. According to Iola, Millie "had the most beautiful white hair you ever saw. If anyone had trouble, she was the first one there to help. I never heard her say anything bad about anyone." This tall, large woman had a commanding presence. "You always called her 'Mrs. Winfrey,'" said Iola.

She was also an exceptional cook. Richard used to eat with the Winfreys when he was working for Cecil, and Millie would often pack him a lunch. She repeatedly invited Iola and her children to dine with her. She may have not been the best seamstress, however. One day Cecil got a hole in one of his western-style shirts. Being very particular about his appearance, he gave it to his wife for mending. She repaired it with a piece of cloth she had cut from inside the shirt's yoke. The next time Cecil wore that shirt, he got a perfectly square sunburn where the patch had been removed!

Although unlicensed, Cecil was an excellent veterinarian. His education came from long, practical experience. He had a box of tools that he kept handy inside one of the Shamrock barns, and used it more than once to help the Geigers' cows give birth when Richard was away.

The Winfreys had at least five children. Evidently they were a challenge for Mrs. Winfrey because they often exasperated her and "nearly ruined her health." In Cecil's later years, after the physical work of ranching had taken its toll, he moved up north to be closer to his children.

Another worker Cecil hired was Francis Wilford "Willie" Moreland. Willie worked on the Shamrock before he married in 1957. He still has an alarm clock that Mac gave him as a humorous wedding present—with two faces, it was designed for twin beds!

Willie spent many days trimming Mac's trees along Highway 83—all the way to Hodgen Road. He did this while Cecil worked the cattle. When he was a teenager, Willie worked power lines, so climbing the trees didn't bother him at all. In fact, his fiancée, Ann, said he looked like a monkey swinging from tree to tree.

According to Willie, "Cecil Winfrey was sure a good guy. He was an excellent guy. So was his wife. We went over to their house and ate dinner with them after I got married."

Willie, whose father owned land that bordered on Shamrock Ranch, also knew Mac personally. Regarding Mac, he said, "He was sure a marvelous guy. And he was quite a cowboy. He knew what work was. He was friendly to everyone and made it a point to get to know all his neighbors.

"He had a station wagon at the time and a great big poodle. The poodle would ride in the front seat next to him and his wife would always ride in the back seat! She was really an amazing woman. He loved to tickle her!

"One day he bought a registered whiteface cow in Texas for $31,000. He brought it to the Shamrock and it died just two days later. When Cecil called him about it, Mac said, 'Well, things like that happen.'

"He didn't get a bit mad. He didn't blame no one."

On another occasion, Mac brought a stallion to the ranch that had killed a cowboy who was trying to break it on the Diamond M Ranch. Mac told everyone at the Shamrock to stay away from the dangerous horse, but Cecil decided he was going to break it anyway. So one day he climbed on and did just that—but he was the only one who could ever ride it. He rode it to do his work until the day it died.

Apparently Mac had some peculiar ways. Whenever he purchased a pickup truck for the Shamrock Ranch, he bought it in Texas and then flew either Cecil or Willie to the Diamond M to drive the new truck to Colorado. And when he purchased a new truck for the Diamond M, Mac shopped in Colorado and asked Willie or Cecil to drive it to Texas.

"We could never figure that out!" Willie chuckled.

Ranch Manager Alvin Eden (1956–1959)

Mac eventually hired a third full-time worker named Alvin "Al" Eden to help Cecil and Willie. Later Al would replace Cecil Winfrey as ranch manager. The three of them did a good job of handling Mac's ranches, which totaled 2,970 acres at the time. Cecil would also hire younger fellows to do odd jobs as needed.

Soon after Alvin was hired, he was assigned to build a new fence. Wanting to impress his new boss, he told Willie to stretch the fence wires tighter. Willie knew from his power line days that a certain amount of slack is required to compensate for temperature differences, and both he and Cecil warned Alvin that the fence would break come winter. But Alvin wanted it tighter anyway. So Willie complied, tightening and tightening until Alvin was happy.

Reported Willie, "In the wintertime when it got cold, you know how they shrink—man, it started snapping like bullwhips or something! And I had to go patch that all up for him. Alvin said, 'I should have listened to Cecil!' "

Mac held a number of parties at the Shamrock Ranch that Cecil, Alvin, and Willie attended. They also were around when he was visited by some of his influential friends, including Lyndon B. Johnson. Alvin took the picture below during one such visit when five small helicopters landed in front of the main ranch house. It shows Mac in the middle dressed in a white suit. The younger civilian (second from left) in a suit is Frank Pace, whose portrait appeared on the January 20, 1958 cover of *Time* when he was CEO of General Dynamics. The older civilian (extreme left) is Harold Hinn, President of Harvest Queen Mill and Elevator Company of Plainview, Texas. Hinn was Mac's house guest at the time.

In 1956, Mac purchased two small ranches in Douglas County that were 7 miles north of the Shamrock. One of them, the County Line Ranch, had a big white house on it. Mac asked Cecil Winfrey to move into this house and run the grade (unregistered) cattle there. Cecil and his wife obliged, relocating to the new ranch, which was east of Highway 83 and bordered on the north side by County Line Road.

Willie moved to the other ranch, which was about 2 miles east of Cecil's house. But he didn't stay there long because the house was full of mice!

As the newest manager of Shamrock Ranch, in 1956 Alvin and his family moved into the house that the Winfreys had just vacated. They stayed there four years, during which time they had a son named Bret. He was Alvin's and his wife Eurelle's third boy. The older two were named Mark and Paul. Alvin was responsible for all the livestock and property on the ranch. The cattle took most of his time, but keeping the place attractive was also important. Although he worked long hours, life on the Shamrock Ranch was pleasant for Alvin and his family.

Alvin remembers that Mac ran 150 head of both registered and unregistered Herefords on his various ranches in those days. In the fall of 1957, a blizzard dumped 4 feet of snow on the pastures, so the ranch managers had to round up the cattle and bring them in close to the barns. They dragged bales of hay from the barns by horse and rope to feed the animals. Alvin remembers that terrible blizzard to this day.

When he was forty, Alvin left the Shamrock and went into the insurance business. He moved his family to Colorado Springs, where a daughter Leah, their last child, was born in 1965. Reminiscing about the Shamrock, Alvin stated, "It was and is a ranch that inspires one to give thanks to God for living in America."

Alvin and Eurelle Eden (2007)

Ranch Manager Willard Miller (1959–1976)

Iɴ Nᴏᴠᴇᴍʙᴇʀ ᴏꜰ 1959, Mac hired Willard Miller to take Alvin's place as Shamrock's manager. Miller was raising cattle on a ranch near the northeastern corner of El Paso County when he heard about the job. Born in Kansas, Willard had farmed and ranched his whole life. When he arrived at the Shamrock, he and his wife, Ila Belle, had three children and a fourth on the way. They moved into the manager's house that had recently been vacated by the Edens.

Integrating into the schools was a cultural shock for the Miller children, who had just come from a school of sixty students ranging in grade from kindergarten to twelfth. Linetta, age twelve, attended the 1,500-student junior high school at the Air Force Academy while Deanna, the Millers' ten year old, went to an elementary school with 365 students.

But they did well in school anyway. In her senior year, Linetta had the star role in the high school's production of *The King and I* by Rodgers and Hammerstein. Willard and Ila were 4-H leaders. They sponsored a girls' softball team that practiced on the Shamrock Ranch. They also hosted a barbeque at the ranch every Thursday evening in the summer for family and friends. Linetta and Deanna were both enrolled in 4-H and were involved in statewide square dancing competitions. Looking back, Willard reflected, "What a great opportunity it was to raise our family on the Shamrock Ranch!"

18 USC 707

4-H emblem

The only boy the Millers had was named after Willard, but they called him "Woody."

When Woody was three years old, he considered himself big and old enough to be his father's right-hand man. One day, while helping to feed the cattle, he found a long alfalfa pellet. Pretending it was a cigar, he put it into his mouth and got out of the pickup truck to look the cattle over, claiming to be a "cattle buyer." Almost immediately, one of the Hereford cows charged right up to the frightened young lad to protect her calf.

With incredible calmness, Willard spoke quietly, "Woody, don't move and don't cry. Stand still and look at her."

Woody obeyed. The cow stared at him for a while, then walked away.

"Too close for comfort!" Willard remembered with relief.

When Willard Miller first came to the Shamrock, his monthly salary was only $250. However, the house was furnished and he didn't have to pay for electricity or propane. He was also provided with beef in the freezer, a cow to milk, laying hens, and gasoline. Regarding the fuel, Mac told him, "Use this gasoline—I sell it." At the time, Mac owned 130 oil wells in Texas!

Mac also told Willard, "If you're the right people, your wages will be the smallest part of our deal." He proved it to the Millers over and over again in many ways. For example, when Deanna needed spinal surgery at age twelve, Mac helped with the medical bills. He also provided scholarships for both Linetta and Deanna when they were ready for college.

According to Willard, "Mac took great pride in the way the ranch looked. Every spare moment was used to improve the looks of the ranch, which he called his 'front yard.'"

The only farming Mac did was putting up native grass hay. But it wasn't enough to get them through the winters because they had no winter pastures for the cattle. Instead, they trucked in hay and fed the cattle protein pellets.

Mac brought part of his staff with him when he came to the Shamrock during the summers. This included Arthur "Dutch" Ward, his butler, chauffeur, and handyman around the house; two pilots for his DC-3 airplane; and a full time cook who lived in Castle Rock and drove to the ranch every morning.

Around the time that Willard came to the Shamrock, Mac began to loose interest in Hereford cattle. Many ranchers were raising more exotic animals that grew faster and larger. So Mac sold his Herefords and bought some Belted Galloways. He had about 350 grade (mixed breed) cattle and 100 registered Belted Galloways. After he switched breeds, Mac no longer showed his cattle in competition.

During the years that Miller was ranch foreman, many bad storms battered the Shamrock. One October, an early blizzard hit just as Mac was flying into Colorado Springs. When his car got stuck in the snow, he couldn't make it out to the ranch. Fortunately someone gave him a ride to the Broadmoor Hotel, where he stayed overnight. The next morning he called Willard to come get him. Willard picked him up at the Broadmoor Hotel and they made it safely back to the ranch. The next morning, Willard drove Mac to the airport.

After a few days, Mac called again and asked Willard to go into town and get his car. But he couldn't explain where to find it nor did he get the name of the good neighbor who had rescued him from the storm. According to Willard, "It took some detective work on my part, but I did find his car."

Another memorable blizzard blocked the roads between the Shamrock and Bar X

Ranches. Mercifully, a snowmobile dealer brought Willard a snowmobile so he could take care of the livestock. The next day the dealer brought him an even bigger one. Willard never lost any cattle in that storm.

Unfortunately, the spring of 1961 was a different story. A terrible blizzard hit right at calving time. Lee Hendrix, a herdsman working for Willard at the County Line Ranch, picked out thirty or so cows that he thought were ready to calve and put them in the barn to keep them out of the weather. When one of the cows gave birth, he set up a heat lamp to keep the new calf warm. Unfortunately, the lamp caused a fire that burned the barn and all of the cows in it.[1]

Another spring blizzard that Willard will always remember occurred in April of 1967. He had been out in the storm all day long at the Bar X Ranch. The snow was 3 feet deep on the level.

When he arrived at the Shamrock entrance on his way home, he found the snow so deep there he couldn't drive in it. He got out and shoveled for a while, then drove the truck forward a few feet. After repeating this process several times, he ran out of fuel but still had 0.75 mile to go before he would be home.

Setting out on foot, he found himself so exhausted that he couldn't lift his legs. So he selected a nearby tree as a goal and pushed the snow out of the way with his hands. By doing this over and over again, he somehow made it to Mac's house, which was empty. By then he was completely exhausted, sopping wet, and had violent cramps in his arms and legs. After calling his wife to tell her he was safe but unable to travel the next 1,200 feet to their house, he found a can of soup, borrowed some of Mac's clothes, and went to bed. A very close call indeed!

But nothing was more refreshing and uplifting to the Miller family than springtime at the Shamrock Ranch. The wildflowers were spectacular. First to bloom were the anemones and wild iris. Then came yucca blooms and Indian paintbrush. Finally, the long-awaited Rocky Mountain columbine appeared—Colorado's state flower. Later, wild gaillardias bloomed along with many other flowers that Willard never identified.

Barn Burned
Sixty Cattle Die in Black Forest Fire

Thirty head of purebred cows and 30 calves died early Saturday when fire razed a large barn at the Shamrock North Ranch at Black Forest. The loss was nearly $19,000.

Lee Hendrix, caretaker of the ranch, discovered the blaze about 2:30 a. m. His wife was unable to contact the Black Forest Volunteer Fire Dept. because telephone lines were down as a result of a blizzard.

A Denver telephone operator unexplainedly got on the line and contacted Willard Miller, ranch foreman. He summoned the BF VFD. Chief Richard Humphrey and 22 men went to the scene after they were notified about 4 a. m. Blinding snow and clogged roads prevented the firemen from reaching the barn until 4:38 a. m.

Firemen, including about 12 members of the Elbert Volunteer Fire Dept., were at the scene several hours. They could not save the livestock because the barn was almost destroyed when they arrived.

In addition to the livestock, valued at $7500, the barn contained a tractor and loader worth some $1200, and miscellaneous items such as saddles and bridles. The barn, 60x100 feet, was worth $10,000. About two years ago the barn was modernized at a cost of $4000.

Owner of the ranch, C. T. McLaughlin of Texas, will rebuild the barn.

Miller said the fire probably was caused by a heat lamp near a new-born calf.

(Note: the article mistakenly says the fire occurred on the Shamrock North Ranch.)

Yellow anemone

Wild iris

Indian paintbrush

Rocky Mountain columbine

Gaillardia

There were also many species of birds that frequented or lived at the ranch during the summer, hummingbirds were everywhere. The Millers also saw deer, antelope, raccoons, black Abert's squirrels, coyotes, muskrats, and porcupines frequently.

Hummingbird

Nuthatch

Melanistic (black) Abert's squirrel
Abert's squirrels have tufted ears and are often melanistic (black) in the Black Forest. They are named after Colonel John James Abert, an American naturalist and military officer who, in the 1800s, headed the Corps of Topography Engineers and organized the mapping of the American West. Abert's squirrels are native to the Rocky Mountains with concentrations found in Arizona, the Grand Canyon, New Mexico, and Colorado —where ponderosa pines grow to provide them with food.[2]

The biggest annual event held on the Shamrock Ranch was Mac's 4th of July party. His Texan friends came days ahead to start the celebration. On the afternoon of the 4th, they all congregated at the ranch for a big Texas-style barbeque. To do it right, Mac brought caterers in from Dalhart, Texas. The grand finale was always apple or cherry southern fried pies, which were deep-fat fried just before serving time.

Willard remembers many notable guests at those celebrations, including Texas Governor John Bowden Connally, some Texas Rangers, Secretary of the Navy Fred Korth, and many Texas state legislators. He also remembers Vice President Lyndon B. Johnson coming to the ranch.

In 1973, Willard was involved in a ranch accident that put him in hospital traction for 121 days. Mac not only paid for him to have a private room, but also paid him his monthly wage on top of workers' compensation. By then Willard's salary was $1,000 a month. When Mac passed away in 1975, he bequeathed to Willard a stipend to be paid over a ten-year period. This generous gift allowed Willard to purchase a nice house when he retired in 1990, and the accrued interest has helped him and Ila through their retirement.

In 1976, After seventeen years of working the Shamrock Ranch, Willard and Ila Miller moved to Larkspur, Colorado. Regarding his time at the ranch, Willard said, "It was a busy, happy, fulfilling time in my life. I have many wonderful memories."

One of the most tragic events to cast a shadow of gloom over the residents of Shamrock Ranch—as well as the entire nation—took place on November 22, 1963, when John F. Kennedy, 35th President of the United States, was assassinated in Dallas, Texas.

Just an hour and thirty-eight minutes after President Kennedy was pronounced dead, Lyndon B. Johnson took the Oath of Office aboard Air Force One and became the 36th President of the United States of America.

As people throughout the nation and the world struggled to make sense of a senseless act and to articulate their feelings about President Kennedy's life and legacy, many recalled these words from his inaugural address, which had suddenly acquired new meaning: "All this will not be finished in the first one hundred days, nor in the first one thousand days, nor in the life of this administration. Nor even perhaps in our lifetime on this planet. But let us begin."[3]

Because of Mac's association with the Democratic Party and his personal friendship with (now) President Johnson, these events undoubtedly had additional impact and pathos for Mac, his family, friends, and employees.

President Johnson taking the oath of office, November 22, 1963.

President
John F. Kennedy
(1917–1963)

Housekeeper Opal Pauline Reese

To care for the main ranch house, Mac hired a housekeeper in 1969 by the name of Mrs. Opal Pauline Reese. She lived in a room adjacent to the kitchen.

Opal came to Colorado Springs in 1959 when her husband's health was failing. They had just sold their farm in southern Iowa. When Mr. Reese passed away only a year later, Opal took an "amusing" job chauffeuring dogs in a Cadillac owned by an older, wealthy woman. Later she became a nanny for three small girls and effectively raised a second family for several years. The girls loved her like a grandmother and she loved them.

When Mac hired Opal, she immediately fell in love with Shamrock Ranch because she missed her farm in Iowa so much. She also enjoyed her independence and the fact that two of her four daughters—Wanda and Vivian—lived in Colorado Springs. She was very happy at the ranch.

Besides caring for the McLaughlin's ranch house, Opal took care of Buffy, one of their dogs. She loved this dog as it provided welcome companionship when she was alone in the ranch house—which was most of the time, since the McLaughlin's were only there

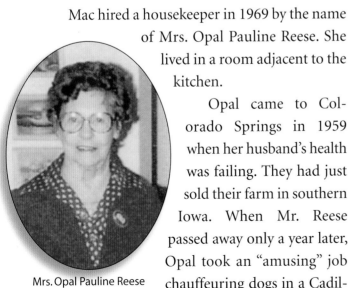

Mrs. Opal Pauline Reese
(circa 1970).
*Courtesy Doreene
(Reese) Wiley.*

The McLaughlin's dog Buffy. *Courtesy Doreene (Rees) Wiley.*

sporadically during the summer months. But when they did come, they treated her kindly and took her with them to many different places in Pikes Peak Country.

In 1975, the year that Mac died, all four of Opal's daughters convened in Colorado Springs to celebrate her seventy-fifth birthday. Doreene, her youngest, stayed with her at the ranch and relates the following memories:

Mother showed me her room, the kitchen, and the chapel. She did not show me the rest of the house as it was the private part for the McLaughlins. I slept in a small room somewhere back where Mother's room was. We were visiting in the kitchen when one of the McLaughlin girls came in to greet me. In the afternoon, the lady who was the wife of the foreman at the time (Ila Miller) invited us over for homemade peach ice cream—it was really good!

Later in the evening we were sitting on the deck. It was getting dusk and the coyotes started to howl. Mother told me that, coming home one evening, a mountain lion crossed the road in front of her car as she turned onto the path leading to the ranch house. She also told me that some raccoons had built a nest in one of the fireplaces and

that a baby coon had gotten into the living room. She also mentioned mockingbirds and black squirrels. I loved the ranch—it was very quiet and peaceful. I'm sure Mother loved every minute she was there also.

Coyote

Mountain lion

Raccoon

Mockingbird

Employee and Neighbor, Al Steppler

Richard and Iola Geiger were close with Al and Betty Steppler (see page 129ff). Iola said "Al was a nice guy and a lot of fun," and that Betty was her role model.

When Al's mother Jennie moved to Colorado Springs in 1944 after her husband Lou had died, Betty took over the house on the Steppler Ranch and made it her own. She painted, decorated, built kitchen cabinets and bookcases, and with the help of her son, Allen, planted willow trees in the west creek. She even cut a hole in the wall so that the family's first television set would not protrude into the living room. It made a good table in the bedroom on the other side of the wall—a built in table! Later in life, she also became an accomplished wood carver—crafting different kinds of beautiful, lifelike birds and animals, which she sold.

During the 1940s and early 1950s, Al farmed the 400-acre ranch that his parents purchased from Maria McKean Allen, raising grain and potatoes just like his father had. He also ran black Angus cattle under the Cross-Bar-P brand and dairy farmed—selling milk to the Meadow Gold creamery in Colorado Springs.

His son helped him do the milking, which was accomplished by machine unless the power went out—then young Allen had to do it by hand. The milk was poured through a filter into ten-gallon milk cans, then the cans were placed into a vat that was cooled by running spring water. Twice a week, the milk man, Dennis, would stop by to pick up the chilled milk cans and return the empty ones that had been collected earlier.

During the mid 1950s, the U.S. Department of Agriculture (USDA) raised standards for sanitary dairy farming in America. This happened in multiple phases. One new standard required Al to purchase a cooler to replace the spring-fed vat he used to cool and store his milk.

When the Air Force Academy was under construction, Al decided to purchase a D-4

Al Steppler's D-4 "Cat" (circa 1957–1962). *Courtesy the Steppler family.*

Caterpillar bulldozer and start a sideline business doing earth moving. Construction of the academy required millions of cubic yards of earth to be excavated, and Al wanted to capitalize on this unique business opportunity.

It was fortuitous that he made this investment. The next USDA mandate for dairy farmers required them to invest in a costly new system to keep the milk from being exposed to open air, and Al was not willing to make the investment. He got out of the farming and dairy businesses altogether and went full time into the soil excavation and conservation business. He built dams, diversion ditches, and basements for new houses. Some of his first dams, built between 1957 and 1962, were on the Steppler Ranch. Al's daughter Susan Koch estimates that at the time these dams were being built, 90 percent of all the subdivision roads in the Black Forest were cleared and graded by Al and his famous D-4 Cat.

As construction of the Air Force Academy proceeded in the second half of the 1950s, land values around it began to soar. So did property taxes, which were based on the number of buildings on a property. As a consequence, residents throughout northern El Paso County began to tear down unneeded structures in order to lower their tax bills.

Mac McLaughlin was no exception. After Cecil Winfrey introduced him to Al Steppler, he hired Al to raze Maria Allen's garage along with the chauffeur's apartment that was north of the main ranch house. Then he had Al build some diversion ditches, which continue to prevent flooding on the Shamrock Ranch to this day.

When Allen Steppler was a young boy, part of the Shamrock Ranch's forested area caught fire. This happened before Mac McLaughlin bought the ranch. Allen remembers coming home from school one day and seeing the orange flames and billowing black smoke. Fortunately, the fire was confined to a relatively small area, but it left an unsightly scar of dead, sooty trees standing in what is today the northwestern corner of High Forest Ranch.

Wanting to make his newly-purchased Shamrock Ranch a showplace, Mac hired Al Steppler to clean up the mess. Initially he paid Al $5 an hour, but later he raised the rate to $6.50.

Using his D-4 Cat, Al would push the blackened ponderosa pines down, then either push or drag them with chains into huge piles that were later burned—virtually eliminating the unsightly aftermath of the forest fire.

Mac enjoyed watching him do this. Whenever he had guests stay at the ranch, he would take them to see Al pushing over trees. Al always put on a good show!

Mac was famous for driving around the Shamrock Ranch in his Cadillac. To keep the stumps from scraping the bottom of his prized car, he hired Al to remove them. One day, while Al was at work on the stumps, Mac drove up with Lyndon B. Johnson in the car. After interrupting Al's work, Mac asked him to push over a tree so LBJ could watch—only this time Mac wanted him to push down a live tree! Of course, Al did it easily, to the delight of both Mac and LBJ.

Before long, Al upgraded to a larger D-6 Cat. He also bought a front end loader and a dump truck. Business was booming!

In 1965, Betty and Al remodeled and added on to the original Steppler house. Benjamin Allen built this residence without any insulation because he intended it for summer living only—considering the winters on the Divide too harsh for ranch living. But when Lou and Jennie Steppler—Al's parents—moved into it, they lived there year-round. During blizzards, snow came through cracks in the walls, and they had to stay next to a wood-burning stove in order to survive the relentless, biting cold. At one point, they climbed into the attic and stuffed anything they could find down into the walls to provide a measure of insulation from the severe weather.

When Al's family began their remodeling project, Susan and Allen found all sorts of interesting things inside the house's walls. Among the treasures they recovered were Lou Steppler's mouth harp, Al's baby blocks, and some corsets, newspapers, and magazines. They also found personal letters to Lou from his sister Minnie.

When asked about her most prominent memories growing up, Susan, who was born in 1948, responded:

The snow! Back then very few families lived here. I went to school in Monument. When it snowed, they couldn't come get us. When they finally did come, it would be down a one-lane road plowed just wide enough for the school bus. You couldn't see anything but a snow tunnel as you went down it.

We had a really short growing season here. You could count on snow for Labor Day. Now it's Halloween—the weather has changed.

This was famous hunting ground for the Arapaho and Cheyenne. Grandma Jennie would tell how, when they first arrived here and lived in the Hodgen place, the Indians would come riding up. I guess they didn't have any real battles, but it was scary. They had a little crawl space underneath the floor where they kept their butter and things like that cool—they would get in there to hide occasionally when the Indians would come around. We've found arrowheads around so we know they were here. We even found a large spear head.

We got our first TV in 1954. I don't think my parents got electricity until the early 40s. They had the old crank telephones. My mother would talk about hearing voices coming through the radio.

Now I'm an old timer—I was born and raised here. You can't take the land out of my blood!

In 1977, Al became nostalgic and wanted to plant potatoes again. So he sent away for some Early Ohios and planted 20 acres. His children Allen and Susan, along with Susan's family, helped him harvest them with some old horse-drawn potato equipment—it was hard work! But they got some really good potatoes that year. Despite the blight of 1932 and 1933, the Black Forest is still a good place to grow potatoes today.

Al and Betty Steppler (1996). *Courtesy the Steppler family.*

Al and Betty became good friends of the McLaughlins and were invited to a number their parties. Al enjoyed the big tents and live bands. He considered the parties to be fun and memorable events.

He and Betty are shown here in their later years. Al died in 1998 and Betty passed away in 2004. They were the salt of the earth.

Following in his father's footsteps, Allen thinned trees on the Shamrock Ranch during the 1960s, '70s, and '80s. The forest management he performed then has helped to make the Shamrock Ranch the showplace it is today.

Neighbor Bob Norris

ANOTHER NEIGHBOR who attended Mac's parties was Robert C. "Bob" Norris (see page 184), the original "Marlboro Man,"[4] who became the largest individual landowner in El Paso County. In the 1950s, Bob went to a livestock sale in California. He noticed that ranches there were selling for more than a hundred times Colorado prices. In a visionary move, he started to buy up ranches, anticipating that the price of land in Pikes Peak Country would eventually escalate. At one time he owned more than 110,000 acres.[5] One of his ranches was in the Black Forest, which explains why he and Mac knew each other. It was called the Bridle Bit Ranch, now a subdivision, and was south of the Shamrock Ranch and just north of Shoup Road (see map, page 18).

In 1965, some Chicago advertising executives on a scouting trip discovered Bob and his Bridle Bit Ranch. They contracted with him to use the ranch as the background for a photo shoot for the Marlboro Man advertising campaign, which has been hailed as one of the most brilliant ad campaigns of all time. Photographers arrived for the shoot with agency models wearing brand-new western wear, but they opted to photograph Bob in his own authentic clothes instead! The ads in which he appeared over the next twelve years were phenomenally successful. However, when Bob's children started questioning the health risks of cigarettes, he stopped advertising them.[6]

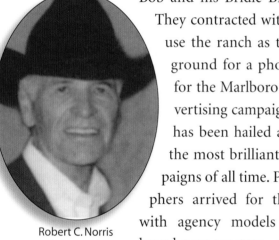

Robert C. Norris
(1929–)

Today, Bob Norris raises quarter horses and more than 1,200 head of cattle on his T-Cross Ranch south of Colorado Springs. He also holds key roles in several rodeo organizations and oversees a charitable foundation that supports dozens of charities.[7] Recently, he was the subject of a newly released book titled *The Cowboy and His Elephant,* by Malcolm MacPherson. All of his proceeds from this book are donated to the Autism Treatment Center of Texas.[8]

Bob is still active in the cattle business and rides regularly. He hosts an annual branding that is well attended by his many friends, who come from far and wide, bringing their own horses to the event.

Neighbors Ned McLean and Gloria Hadrick McLean Stewart

ANOTHER CELEBRITY who settled down near the Shamrock Ranch was Edward Beale McLean Jr., son of Edward Beale McLean Sr., who was born into a publishing fortune founded by his paternal grandfather, Washington McLean, who owned the *Washington Post* and the *Cincinnati Enquirer.* In 1908, Edward Sr. married Evalyn Walsh, the only surviving child and sole heiress of mining millionaire Thomas Walsh—who made his fortune from the Camp Bird Gold Mine in Ouray, Colorado. (For a full discussion of this interesting family, see *Father Struck It Rich* by Evalyn Walsh McLean, Bear Creek Publishing Co., Ouray, Colorado, 1981).[9] On a whim, Edward Sr. purchased the Hope Diamond for his bride. When the couple eloped, they did so with $200,000 in "pin" money for honeymoon expenses, only to find part way through that they were broke and couldn't pay a Paris hotel bill. Their parents, happy that they hadn't done anything drastic such as buying the hotel, happily wired them money. The couple eventually returned to Washington D.C. and settled at the McLean family's house "Friendship" along Wisconsin Avenue.[10]

Evalyn Walsh McLean
(1886–1947)

MCLAUGHLIN'S EMPLOYEES AND NEIGHBORS ♣ 203

As their frivolous spending accelerated during their marriage, their inability to understand the basics of money management resulted in virtual bankruptcy toward the end of their lives. Together, they wasted two family fortunes worth millions of dollars (billions in today's cash value) by splurging on such exotic things as a million dollar birthday party for their dog, who was allowed to wear the Hope diamond on his day of honor.[11]

Ned was the third of their four children. He met and married Gloria Hatrick, a Manhattan model from Larchmont, New York, in 1943 after divorcing his wife of five years.

Evalyn Walsh McLean is shown opposite wearing the 46-carat Hope Diamond. When she died in 1947, she willed this mysterious, supposedly cursed gem to her grandchildren, but her trustees sold her jewels to settle her debts.

She also owned the 94-carat Star of the East diamond.[12] Today, this striking blue diamond, which has belonged to King Louis XIV, Marie Antoinette, and King George IV of Great Britain, is currently housed in the Smithsonian Museum of Natural History.

In 1942, Gloria and her husband Ned built a pink, Spanish-style stucco mansion on a small ranch, located just south of the Shamrock, that was originally part of Sam Stout's ranch. Their plan was to raise artichokes, but it was a fruitless venture because of the Black Forest's climate and short growing season. Their sons, Ronald and Michael McLean, were born in Colorado Springs in 1943 and 1946, respectively.

The woman who the McLeans had hired as a housekeeper, Mrs. Mable Hensley, lived in the house and was friends with the Romicks and Stepplers. After she was married and returned to Colorado for a visit, Peggy Romick Hubbell got to tour the McLean mansion with Mrs. Hensley as a guide. No one was living there at the time. Peggy remembers that every room was painted a different color.

Unfortunately, Ned McLean was an inveterate womanizer and a bad alcoholic, whose skirt-chasing and drinking both increased after they were wed.[13] Gloria divorced him in January of 1948. Ned settled the divorce, granting a considerable sum to her and their two sons. In August, 1949, Gloria married the revered, Oscar-winning actor Jimmy Stewart. Jimmy adopted Gloria's two sons, Ronald and Michael, and together they had twin daughters, Judy and Kelly, in 1951. Gloria and Jimmy had a fondness for Colorado Springs and the Broadmoor Hotel in particular. They are shown here during their honeymoon at the Broadmoor.

Gloria Stewart did not follow in the ways of the McLean family. In contrast, she was one of the few Hollywood types who planted and

The Hope Diamond

Jimmy and Gloria McLean Stewart during their honeymoon (1949). Bob McIntyre photo. *Courtesy Broadmoor Historical Collection.*

False Legends

Their are four false legends connected with the Shamrock Ranch that bear mentioning. The authors have tried unsuccessfully to confirm them, and yet they occasionally appear in newspaper articles and in casual conversation about town.

One is that Jimmy Stewart courted his bride Gloria McLean in the pink house that adjoins the Shamrock Ranch, and that both Jimmy and Gloria attended one or more of Mac McLaughlin's famous parties. While this story is intriguing to consider and was considered true by at least one now-deceased source, the facts seem to say otherwise.

Another fable tied to the McLean house is that the Hope Diamond actually resided there for a time. This is made all the more believable by the large walk-in bank safe that was in the home until it was demolished in 2008. However, the history of the Walsh-McLean families seems to say that Evelyn Walsh McLean, mother of Ned McLean, never lived in Colorado Springs during the period that she owned the Hope Diamond and the Star of the East Diamond. Also, she lost possession of these precious gems late in her life, but before her death, when they might have been inherited by her offspring. The only thing that can be said with confidence is that Evelyn's life ended in misery whether or not that misery can be attributed to the fabled curse of the Hope.

Another famous and oft printed tale is that President Eisenhower stayed as a guest of Mac Mclaughlin at the Shamrock Ranch. In fact, during their initial visit to the ranch, the Wismers were shown the Eisenhower Room displaying a photo of Ike where supposedly the president had slept. Despite serious attempts to confirm such an intriguing story by contacting the Eisenhower Museum in Abilene Kansas, Ike's boyhood home, as well as the Archives at the U.S. Air Force Academy, no verifiation could be found.

And finally, it is commonly held that before coming to Colorado, Benjamin C. Allen was publisher of the *Saturday Evening Post* magazine. This seems plausible, since the *Post* was published by the Curtis Publishing Company in Philadelphia and Benjamin's middle name is Curtis and he was from Philadelphia as well. The most that may be concluded is that there may have been some family connection between Benjamin and his mother's family, the Curtis's.

tended her own garden. She and Jimmy would take the excess vegetables to their neighbors. After the heartbreak of her first marriage, Gloria told friends that "she was looking for a decent man with a strong character . . . a proper father who could help raise her sons." [14]

The trainable and naturally domestic Jimmy Stewart fit her bill as much as she did his. [15]

Jimmy and Gloria were faithful and devoted to each other and their children for nearly forty-five years—until the day Gloria died in 1994.

According to actress Shirley Jones, "Gloria's death was a shock he (Jimmy) never got over." [16]

Neighbor John Ben Snow

AFTER GLORIA AND NED'S DIVORCE in 1948, the McLean's Black Forest property was sold to another personality by the name of John Ben Snow. Snow entered the F.W. Woolworth (Five and Dime Store) firm after graduating from New York University in 1904. He rose rapidly through the ranks—from stock boy to corporate director. In 1939, he retired from Woolworth after amassing a small fortune. He devoted the remainder of his life to building the Speidel chain of newspapers and publishing *American Horseman* magazine. When he first came to Colorado Springs in 1939, Snow took up residence at the historic Antlers Hotel and joined the El Paso Club, where he dined on excellent food. No doubt he knew Wharton Allen! His favorite hobby was raising thoroughbred race horses.

John Ben Snow
(1883–1973)

Throughout his life, Snow gave generously and freely to causes and people he cherished. He preferred to invest in people, especially the young, by providing financial assistance. In 1948, he founded the nonproft Snow Foundation to distribute funds for educational, religious, scientific and community causes in central New York State, where he had grown up. Snow died in 1973.[17]

The Barron Family

A MAN NAMED FLINT bought the pink mansion from Snow in 1958. Then Archibald and Gloria Barron purchased it in 1965. The sales brochure, courtesy of their son, Thomas Barron, that led to this purchase is the source of the photographs provided here. The scenic view shows the land looking west, toward the Husted Pasture, before Highway 83 was paved. The Barrons attended the barbeque Mac McLaughlin held during Pikes Peak or Bust Rodeo Week in 1973, along with Bob Norris, Jasper Ackerman, and the McCreas (see page 183).

The pink, Spanish-style stucco mansion built by Ned and Gloria McLean in 1942 (photo 1965).

View from the mansion looking west (1965)

North view of the patio (1965)

Aerial view of the mansion (1965)

THE PENDLETON
EQUESTRIAN ERA

ED PENDLETON and Beverly Haun were high school sweethearts. In fact, they attended the same grade school together in Wichita, Kansas. They married young and have had an extraordinarily eventful and notable life together.

Beverly's father, William George Haun, served overseas as a first lieutenant during World War I. After his return from the war, he married Christine Ross, a graduate of the National Park Seminary—an elite girls' fin-

Ed and Beverly Pendleton (1983).

ishing school in Forest Glen, Maryland, that operated from 1894 to 1942. As a polished and sophisticated lady married to a wealthy businessman, Christine naturally became a Wichita socialite.

In 1921, the Hauns lived on North Waco Avenue—next to Central Riverside Park and the Little Arkansas River. Christine was a member of the Wichita Pioneer Society, which means that members of her family were living in Sedgwick County, Kansas, prior to 1880.[1] She and William George had at least two daughters. Beverly was born in the 1930s toward the end of the Great Depression.

Mr. Haun became a successful oilman and was well known around Wichita. He was also interested in horses—especially American saddlebreds, which he raised. Beverly and her sister rode when they were young, but it is not known if they or their parents competed in horse shows.

About the time Edmund Pendleton married Beverly Haun in the mid1950s, he went to work for his father-in-law and began to learn the oil and gas business. Then, in 1969, he moved his family to Littleton, Colorado, and started his own oil and gas business—the Pendleton Land and Exploration Company. By then, he and Beverly had two young sons. Alan was twelve years old and Louis was ten.

As Ed's business grew, he became wealthy, although he was highly leveraged financially. Beverly also had money that she had inherited from her father. Being a city girl, she enjoyed living in Littleton, but Ed liked ranch life and had ambitions to raise cattle. It wasn't long before he bought a cattle ranch in Elizabeth, Colorado.

As their cumulative wealth increased, Ed decided to please his wife by getting into the horse show business. He built an equestrian center in

Pendleton equestrian facility in Versailles, Kentucky (1983).

Fourteen of Pendleton's horse stalls are visible here—seven on each side (1983).

Kentucky—home to some of the world's leading horse farms and auctions—and began to raise American saddlebreds, just as his father-in-law had. Ed named this state-of-the-art facility Pendleton and hired Don Brookshire to manage it. Located on Shannon Run Road near the town of Versailles, Pendleton sat on more than one hundred acres of bluegrass pastureland. Built in the tradition of Kentucky's finest horse barns, it included 28 stalls finished in fine wood, an indoor arena, and an apartment.

Under Don Brookshire's leadership, Pendleton became a successful breeding operation. The advertisement from a January 1983 *Saddle & Bridle* magazine shown here highlights Titleist—one of the Pendleton's prestigious stallions. Trainer Bobby Gatlin is riding Titleist.

Pendleton also became home to the Shannon Run Sale Company, managed by Donna Moore and Don Brookshire, and was used to host three premier horse sale events. The January 1983 *Saddle & Bridle* advertisement

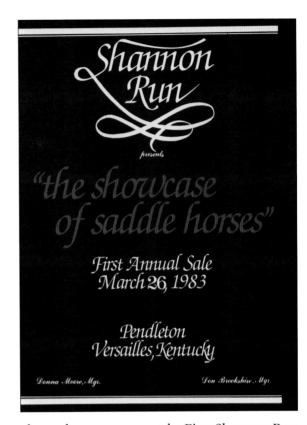

shown here announces the First Shannon Run Sale at Pendleton. The text reads as follows: "The Showcase of Saddle Horses" will be presented in the first annual Shannon Run Sale on March 26, 1983 at Pendleton, Versailles Kentucky. This premier presentation will include champions, world champions, select breeding stock and the outstanding young prospects of tomorrow. Over fifty of the finest saddle horses in the country have been personally selected by Donna Moore and Don Brookshire for this classic event."

This first Shannon Run Sale was a historic event and a huge success, as recorded on the following pages from the May 1983 issue of *Saddle & Bridle.* The event set two new records: the most ever paid for an American saddle horse ($1.2 million for Preferred Property), and the highest sales total for a public horse auction ($5.46 million). At that time, Preferred Property was the undefeated 1981 World Champion two year old in the Fine Harness class, and the

Shannon Run Sale

"*The Showcase of Saddle Horses*" *will be presented in the first annual Shannon Run Sale on March 26, 1983 at Pendleton, Versailles Kentucky. This premier presentation will include champions, world champions, select breeding stock and the outstanding young prospects of tommorow. Over fifty of the finest saddle horses in the country have been personally selected by Donna Moore and Don Brookshire for this classic event.*

The following examples represent what will truly be a "Showcase of Saddle Horses."

1. *Preferred Property* - Undefeated, 1981 World Champion two-year-old Fine Harness. 1982 National Sweepstakes three-year-old Fine Harness Champion.

2. *C.M. High Rise Marches On* - Yearling out of World Champion Meadow March and sired by World Champion High Rise Spirit.

3. *From This Moment On* - Half sister to Multi-World Champion La La Success. 1982 National Sweepstakes Junior Three-Gaited. 1982 Three-Gaited Champion at Kansas City.

4. *Sultan's Matchmaker* - 1981 World three-year-old Five-Gaited National Futurity Champion, 1981 National Sweepstakes three-year-old Five-Gaited Champion, 1982 Reserve World Junior Five-Gaited Champion.

5. *Courageous Decision* - 1980 World Champion Ladies Fine Harness, 1981 World Champion Ladies and Amateur Fine Harness, 1982 Reserve World Champion Ladies Fine Harness.

6. *Pride's Starmaster* - 1982 Reserve World Champion Ladies and Amateur Harness Pony. 1982 Ladies Harness Pony Champion at Lexington. 1981 Ladies Harness Pony Champion at Kansas City and Indiana.

7. *A Chariot Afire* - Half brother to Imperator. Third in the 1982 gelding stake at Louisville, behind Valley Venture and Imperator in one of the strongest classes ever.

Shannon Run Sale

8. *Fortunate Commander* - 1982 World Champion Ladies Three-Gaited Horse.

9. *First Choice* - 1982 All American Reserve Juvenile Three-Gaited Champion (15-17). 1982 Juvenile Three-Gaited Champion at Rock Creek. 1982 Juvenile Three-Gaited Champion at Lexington. 1982 Reserve World Champion Juvenile Three-Gaited Stake.

10. *Romantic Event* - 1982 over 15.2 Champion at Santa Anita and Monterey. Ladies and Amateur Three-Gaited Champion at Tulsa. 1982 Amateur Reserve Champion over 15.2 at St. Louis.

11. *Sultan's Sweet Lorraine* - 1981 National three-year-old Three-Gaited Futurity Champion at Kentucky State Fair.

12. *Supreme Attraction* - 1981 Ladies and Amateur Five-Gaited Champion at the American Royal. 1982 Ladies Five-Gaited Reserve World Champion.

13. *Evening In New York* - 1982 Junior Three-Gaited Champion at Rock Creek. 1982 Junior Three-Gaited Champion at Lexington. 1982 All American Junior Three-Gaited Champion.

14. *20th Century Fox* - 1981 under 15.2 Three-Gaited World Champion Junior Stake at Louisville. 1982 Amateur Three-Gaited Champion at Madison Square Garden. Three-Gaited Champion at Lexington, Pin Oak, River-Ridge and Indiana State Fair.

15. *Cavalleria* - 1981 World Champion Juvenile Three-Gaited Horse. 1982 Amateur Three-Gaited Champion at Rock Creek. 1982 Ladies Three-Gaited Champion at Lexington.

16. *Fashion's Carina* - 1982 World Champion Junior Five-Gaited Mare. 1982 National Sweepstakes Junior Five-Gaited Champion.

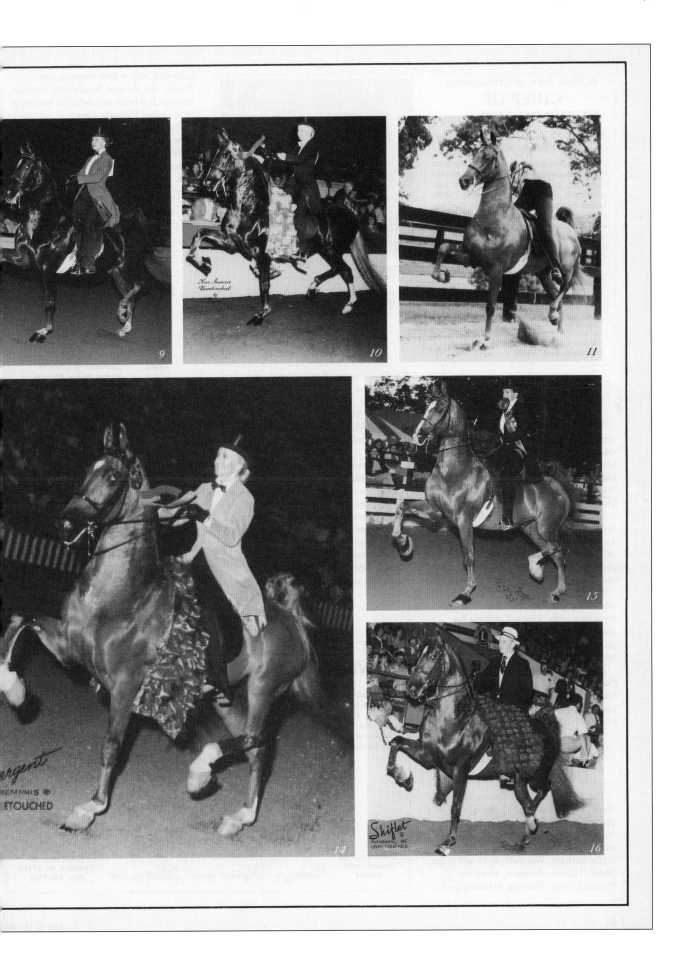

1982 National Sweepstakes Champion three year old in the Fine Harness class.

Ed participated strongly in the Shannon Run Sale. Not only was he a member of the syndicate that purchased Preferred Property (see brochure, page 216), but he also bought Fashion's Carina, a world-champion mare, for $105,000 (see page 217, horse #14). Ed sold four colts sired by Titleist for an average price of $26,100.

Fortunate Commander

Shannon Run Sale... Tops Five Million Dollars

Sultan's Matchmaker

Story by Maureen Jenner

Photos by Avis Girdler

"Progress, innovation, new horizons. . . a growing industry with great potential" was the theme of an opening speech presented by Kentucky's Lieutenant Governor, Martha Layne Collins, at the first annual Shannon Run Sale, held Saturday, March 26, at Pendleton in Versailles. Martha Layne Collins was most gracious in welcoming buyers to this premier presentation of "The Showcase of Saddle Horses". As the American Saddlebred industry enters into an era where "the monetary and aesthetic value of the American Saddlebred show horses is tremendous in scope," the first annual Shannon Run Sale will go down in history as the milestone to this most exciting era. The Shannon Run Sale presented excellence in bloodlines. . . excellence in American Saddlebreds, bred the best to be the best; broodmares with proven records, dams of, or full sisters to, World Champions; World Champions; prospects with World Champion potential and bloodlines.

Shannon Run Sale managers, Donna Moore and Don Brookshire, achieved their ultimate goal and brought to public auction the most glorious and truly inspiring legion of American Saddlebreds ever to grace the sales arena. The presentation of the sale horses was absolute perfection. Each horse was turned out without a flaw, even the broodmares appeared ready for the show ring with their sleek coats and proper condition, evidence of many long hours of labor.

People from all over the country attended this history-making, record-breaking public sale with total sales of $5,461,250, an average of $91,021 per head — what more can be said? Never have American Saddlebred broodmares brought higher prices, averaging $39,934 apiece.

All kinds of records fell with the auctioneer's hammer, but probably most impressive were the prices for the three outstanding stallions.

May 1983

Preferred Property, the gorgeous World Champion son of High Rise Spirit, has matured beyond belief, and with Donna Moore in the jog cart, he was acquired by a syndicate for the world record price for an American Saddle Horse, $1.2 million.

Dale Milligan came from Texas to team the spectacular Sultan's Matchmaker, and when the gavel came down, this leg - waving five-gaited son of Supreme Sultan commanded $675,000. Milligan was also aboard the last stallion in the sale, Family Jewels, himself a World Champion. This highly colorful son of Grape Tree's Fox went for $380,000.

Shannon Run Sale offered to an American Saddlebred public sale the bid board, a scoreboard which shows exactly where the bidding is, most professional and definitely needed. A bus shuttle service was offered to the Campbell House by Shannon Run Sale Company, and valet parking was provided at Pendleton.

There was excellent television coverage for the sale on two Lexington television stations. Pre-advertising television commercials were compiled and edited by Carolyn Brookshire and Donna Moore.

Friday evening, a cocktail party and buffet dinner was held at Kentucky Training Center in Lexington, with over 1500 people in attendance. Turf Catering from Lexington catered this social event with burgoo, cornbread, cole slaw, and dessert. A swinging Dixieland band, the Sound of Swing, entertained, while Diane Austin and Deedee Gatlin showed videotapes of the sale horses to guests in the pavilion at the center.

Saturday morning Sari Levine hosted a brunch, complete with champagne and delicate croissants, starting the day off with a bang!

During the sale, Hammond Productions of Lexington professionally videotaped the sale, and anyone interested in purchasing a tape should

Walt Robertson, Martha Layne Collins and Bill Carrington.

Supreme Attraction

contact Hammond Productions. For future use, the American Saddlebred Horse Association will choose to use the tapes for documentary and educational purposes and promotional needs.

Not only was the sale presented in a first-class manner, the horses sold left Pendleton in first-class style, with custom-fitted RaDon blankets and custom-fitted leather halters with sheepskin covering and name tags. From the very beginning to the very end, Shannon Run Sale, "The Showcase of Saddle Horses," was a first-class, innovative presentation of American Saddle Horse bloodstock offered at public auction, excelling to date any public offering of American Saddlebreds.

PREFERRED PROPERTY SYNDICATE

The Shannon Run Sale Company congratulates the Preferred Property Syndicate on the purchase of the undefeated four-year-old fine Harness champion, Preferred Property, for a new world record price of $1,200,000. The members of the Preferred Property Syndicate are:

1. Carolyn Brookshire, Versailles, Kentucky
2. Donna Moore Stables, Inc., Versailles, Kentucky
3. Burton W. Greenwald, Akron, Ohio
4. Linda Kerr Johnson, Lexington, Kentucky
5. LeHigh Sales and Products, Inc., T/A LeHigh Farm, Allentown, Pennsylvania
6. Ed Pendleton, Littleton, Colorado
7. Anne Phillips, Brewton, Alabama
8. Ann Trimble D/B/A Ponjola Farm, Versailles, Kentucky
9. Jerry D. Vanier D/B/A Meadow Muffin Farm, Salina, Kansas

The syndicate members have elected Donna Moore to train and show this undefeated world champion stallion during his show season of 1983. They have also elected to restrict his book to nine mares only so that he might be shown for the 1983 season.

Announcement of the Preferred Property sales syndicate. Note that Ed Pendleton is a member.

HORSES IN ORDER OF SALE

Hip No.	Name	Purchaser	
1.	Sultan's Matchmaker	J.W. York, Raleigh, N.C.	$675,000
2.	Cocktail Time (broodmare)	William J. Dutel, New Orleans, La.	$39,000
3.	Woodland Magic (broodmare)	William J. Dutel	$23,000
4.	Sunami (yearling)	Ann Trimble, Versailles, Ky.	$27,000
5.	Wing's Gay Lady (broodmare)	Jimmy DeMaret/Broodmare Syndicate Boulder, Colo.	$31,000
6.	Manhattan Man (three-gaited)	A.L. Viles, Flying V Farm, Lincolnton, N.C.	$42,000
7.	Heavenly Heritage (broodmare)	William J. Dutel	$20,000
8.	*Leanne's First Choice	consigned by Fred Davis, Miami, Fla.	RNA
9.	Pendleton's So Rare (five-gaited)	J.W. Taylor, Athens, Ga.	$50,000
10.	Night's Enchanted Evening (broodmare)	Nancy Hudlow, Versailles, Ky.	$50,000
11.	Casual Elegance (yearling)	B.G. Hudson, Atlanta, Ga.	$13,500
12.	Fortunate Commander	Kay Ward, Baltimore, Md.	$125,000
13.	*Oak Hill's Desert Rose (broodmare)	consigned by Anna Marie Knipp Jefferson City, Mo.	RNA
14.	Fashion's Carina (five-gaited)	Ed Pendleton, Littleton, Colo.	$105,000
15.	Titleholder (yearling)	Jimmy DeMaret/Broodmare Syndicate	$23,000
16.	Symbol Surprise (broodmare)	Jimmy DeMaret/Broodmare Syndicate	$21,000
17.	*Twentieth Century Fox	consigned by Carolyn Garrett, San Antonio, Tex.	RNA
18.	Tiffany Style (five-gaited)	Elmo Greer, London, Ky.	$32,000
19.	Frisco Faye (broodmare)	William J. Dutel	$42,000
20.	Courageous Decision	Bill Ley, Buffalo, Ia.	$80,000
21.	A Chariot Afire	Woods L.B. Farm, Tampa, Fla.	$40,000
22.	Princess Trigg (broodmare)	Donna Moore, Versailles, Ky.	$25,000
23.	Pride's Starmaster	Jackie Ramos, Ashleigh Stud, Paris, Ky.	$55,000
24.	*Evening In New York	consigned by Dr. David Thomas, Paducah, Ky.	RNA
25.	Ace's Captain Bernard	Owen Clayton, Kansas City, Mo.	$32,000
26.	High Rise Marches On (yearling)	Herb Kohler, Kohler, Wisc.	$75,000
27.	Meadow March (broodmare)	A.L. Viles, Flying V Farm	$58,000
28.	Pro Staff (three-gaited)	Gail Heslep, Brownsburg, Va.	$35,000
29.	Supreme Attraction	David C. Loughlin, Wilmington, N.C.	$100,000
30.	Sweet Georgia (broodmare)	Jack E. Weih, Travers, Mich.	$41,000
31.	*Cavalleria	consigned by Frank Ogletree, Greenville, S.C.	RNA
32.	*Greystone's Best of All	consigned by W.L. Sigmon, Newton, N.C.	RNA
33.	Comedienne (broodmare)	Jimmy DeMaret/Broodmare Syndicate	$54,000
34.	Preferred Property	Preferred Property Syndicate	$1,200,000
35.	*Fashion's Wind Chime	consigned by W.L. Sigmon	RNA
36.	Gallant Provocations (five-gaited)	J.W. York	$35,000
37.	Sultan's Sweet Lorraine	Jerry Vanier, Meadow Muffin Farm, Salina, Kans.	$50,000
38.	Nearly Famous	Jerry Vanier, Meadow Muffin Farm	$165,000
39.	*Romantic Event	consigned by Anna Marie Knipp	RNA
40.	Sultan's Desert Prince	Ernest D. Key, Jr., Atlanta, Ga.	$84,000
41.	Sultan's Great Day	Linda K. Johnson, Tuscon, Ariz.	$170,000
42.	Morning Time Gold	Honey Baked Ham, Cleveland, Ohio	$122,500
43.	*Highborn Admiral	consigned by Stonetree Farm, Versailles, Ky.	RNA
44.	Kilarney's Parading Promise	David Goodstein, Los Angeles, Calif.	$32,000
45.	Reverie's Mayday (broodmare)	William J. Dutel	$16,000
46.	From This Moment On (three-gaited)	Ann Trimble/Linda Johnson Lexington, Ky.	$100,000
47.	Gold Gold (five-gaited)	Roy R. Carpenter, Hilton Head, S.C.	$42,500
48.	Exclusive Princess (yearling)	George Gwinn, Danville, Ky.	$6,250
49.	Hellacious (road pony)	Jack E. Deeter, Colorado Springs, Colo.	$17,500
50.	Treat Treat (five-gaited)	Joe Dana, Lafayette, Ga.	$25,000
51.	BNB's Delta Magic	Connie Swanson, Colonial Farm, Edwardsburg, Mich.	$150,000
52.	*Our Mandolin Wind	consigned by Pendleton, Versailles, Ky.	RNA
53.	*Time Machine	consigned by Shannon Run Sale Co.	RNA
54.	BNB's Winter Folly (two-year-old)	Ann Trimble	$35,000
55.	Greystone's Selection (five-gaited)	Arthur Simmons, Mexico, Mo.	$22,000
56.	Wild Promises (broodmare)	William J. Dutel	$45,000
57.	Sensational Sue (fine harness)	Ann Trimble/Linda Johnson	$59,000
58.	Sharon Hope (broodmare)	William J. Dutel	86,000
59.	Amber Cascades (broodmare)	Jimmy DeMaret/Broodmare Syndicate	$35,000
60.	Family Jewels	William J. Dutel	$380,000

*indicates No Sale

Sales recorded for the first annual Shannon Run Sale. Note that Ed Pendleton bought Fashion's Carina.

Donna Moore, Don Brookshire's partner in Shannon Run Sale Company. She trained many champion horses during the 1980s.

Pendleton advertisement from the May 1983 issue of *Saddle & Bridle* featuring four colts sired by Titleist.

"The Showcase of Saddle Horses"

The Shannon Run Sale Company extends a sincere thank you to everyone for their support in our first sale . . . history and record-breaking prices were made!

The Shannon Run Sale Company
Managers
Don Brookshire   Donna Moore

Beverly and her son Louis enjoyed riding and training at Pendleton, and before long they were competing in horse shows around the country. A new era had begun for the Pendleton family. It would eventually include the Shamrock Ranch, Opal Rees, and Jeannette Billings.

BARBARA JEANNETTE BILLINGS, who goes by Jeannette, was born November 10, 1950, in Sweetwater, Tennessee. She grew up in a rural historic community called Hiwassee, which was founded soon after the United States Government's 1817 Hiwassee Purchase forced the area's Cherokee inhabitants to exodus.

The name Hiwassee is taken from the Cherokee word *ayuwasi*, which means "meadow place at the foot of the hills."[2] A delightful and enchanting region, Hiwassee lies at the foothills of the Great Smoky Mountains.

Among the early settlers of the Hiwassee Purchase frontier were a large number of Methodists. Fortuitously, they set aside some prime land near a bubbling spring for a camp meeting place.[3] The Great Revival, which swept the United States in the early 1800s, had made such camps popular—they were used to convert early Americans to various denominations of Christianity; the Methodists were especially active in this Great Revival.

This Methodist camp meeting place became known as the Bat Creek Campground. For years, Methodist preachers known as "camp riders" or "circuit riders" visited this campground periodically to hold revival meetings.

In 1845, the trustees of Bat Creek Campground allowed Dr. M. W. Gibson, a Presbyterian educator, to move his overcrowded academy to the camp. But when he left in

The Great Smoky Mountains

Entrance to Hiwassee College, established 1849

1848, the trustees had to make a decision regarding the future of the camp. In March of 1849, they decided to establish Hiwassee College. Its primary mission at the time was to train sons of farmers for the ministry.

As the oldest private, two-year institution in the State of Tennessee, this small college survived at least four major financial crises as well as the Civil War to become a notable United Methodist college that has enabled many rural students of modest means—including Jeanette Billings—to obtain a higher education.

Dr. John Hamilton Brunner (1825–1914)

In 1854, Jeannette's great-grandfather, Dr. John Hamilton Brunner, became the second President of Hiwassee College. He married the only daughter of Reverend John Key, leader of the trustees who established the college. Until his death in 1914, Brunner was an able leader for both Hiwassee College and the surrounding community. He served in official positions at the college for nearly thirty-three years.

Brunner's wife, Elizabeth Key, inherited her father's farm, Lark Meadow, where the Brunner family lived. It later became known as the Brunner Place. Jeannette's grandmother was born there and eventually inherited it. Jeannette virtually grew up in the Brunner house "because it was a small community then and the family was so close."

Jeannette's grandfather died when she was only five years old. Her grandmother continued to live at the Brunner house until the early 1960s, when she had the old house torn down and erected a new, smaller one that had the luxury of modern electric heating.

Hiwassee College was central to Jeannette's young life. Both of her parents worked there—her father as the maintenance engineer and her mother as a cafeteria worker. For financial support, the College board ran a meat packing plant and a dairy as well as a farm. This allowed the school to supply most of its own food, including meat, potatoes, and dairy products. It also allowed Jeannette to grow up around fields, cows, and horses. She rode regularly and became proficient at it.

Jeannette described herself as a "faculty brat," attending all the basketball games and participating in many of the school activities, which usually had a religious orientation. Her Sunday School teachers were Hiwassee College professors.

When she first started to attend Hiwassee College, Jeannette worked as a secretary for the head of the agricultural department. Not long before she started this job, the board had decided to turn some of the college's best farmland into a faculty subdivision. Half-acre lots were given to faculty members free of charge. Naturally, the professors considered this a very generous gift. But Jeannette, who was concerned about the long-term effects of losing productive land, decided to give a lecture in her speech class about how the subdivision was destroying the farmland and hurting the farmers. Her boss was kind enough to give her details about the size and impact of the development.

What Jeanette didn't know at the time was that her speech teacher had just built the second house in the subdivision. No wonder she ended up with a C- in that class, even though she was passionate and gave a very good speech! She didn't do so well in her economics class either—because that teacher didn't like her "no work, no eat" economics!

Jeannette graduated from Hiwassee College in 1970 with an associate's degree. She then went to Knoxville to attend the University of Tennessee. Two years later she graduated with a bachelor's degree in animal husbandry. This enabled her to get a job working with horses as a groom at Happy Valley Farms in Chattanooga. As she remembers, "In 1972, that was the only job a female could get in the animal-related industries."

However, this job didn't last long because the trainer who hired her was fired for taking commissions under the table. Before long Jeanette got another job working with a very capable horse trainer in Georgia. His name was Bobby Gatlin.

1979, Ed Pendleton offered Bobby a job training horses at Pendleton. Bobby took those of his crew who would go with him to Kentucky, but Jeannette was not among them. She didn't want to go to Kentucky, so she began working in a nursing home in Chattanooga instead. But Bobby wouldn't forget about her in the years to come.

Not long after hiring Bobby, Ed Pendleton bought the Shamrock Ranch from Mark McLaughlin. He immediately set out to remodel the main ranch house and to upgrade

The black wooden fences on Shamrock Ranch were constructed during the Pendleton era (2007).

the newer barn with horse stalls similar to those at Pendleton. First, he brought in Kevin Loftus, who had been working for him at his cattle ranch in Elizabeth, Colorado, to clean out the cattle pens, supervise the upgrades, and put up the sturdy, black, Kentucky-like fencing that still exists on the Shamrock today.

Then he hired contractor Howard Battista. Howard worked at the Shamrock for more than two years, along with his helper Ed Folger. Together, they remodeled the newer cattle barn to resemble Ed's horse barn in Kentucky. The upgrades they completed include eleven horse stalls, an office, rest rooms, a tack room, and a large indoor riding arena complete with propane heat for winter riding and training. The knotty pine tongue and groove stalls they built included tail boards to protect the tail sets of the expensive American saddlebred horses the Pendletons owned (see discussion of tail setting, page 226). They even affixed small green Shamrocks to the top of each stall door.

One of the fine Shamrock Ranch horse stalls built by Howard Battista and Ed Folger. Note the carved and painted shamrocks on the door (2008).

A sample of their fine work is shown above. At the time, the Shamrock Ranch stables were the finest stables in all of Colorado. A number of people have visited the Shamrock since to learn how to design their own horse stalls.

Howard and Ed also remodeled the trainer's house and the kitchen and bathrooms in the main ranch house. With Kevin's help, they built over a mile of three-rail fence between the barns and Highway 83. Then they built a gazebo on skids that could be moved to any location Ed chose. All these improvements still enhance the Shamrock Ranch today.

Howard has nothing but praise for Ed Pendleton. His insights give us a glimpse of this remarkable man, whose fortunes ebbed and flowed during the last two decades of the twentieth century. "Ed was a great man," Howard said. "He was a family man and was really great

to work for. It was a pleasure to work out here. It was so serene and such a pleasure that I would almost have done it for free."

Ed Pendleton was very generous and gave the two carpenters a side of beef at Christmas. He often provided them with steaks, which they would cook in Howard's camper at noon and eat together. According to Howard, "It was such a great atmosphere. You enjoyed everything you did out here."

Ed also provided Howard and his family with tickets for his boxes at the National Western Stock Show in Denver, where Beverly, Louis, and his horses were performing. Additionally, Ed frequently invited Howard to

Kevin Loftus with two of Ed's draft horses, Pat and Casey (circa 1981).

Howard Battista celebrating his birthday at Shamrock Ranch (December 5, 1981).

Ed Pendleton riding one of his favorite mares, Libby Lanes (circa 1983).

bring his boys to the ranch on weekends to ride motorcycles. To summarize his experience at the Shamrock, Howard stated, "It was the greatest job I ever had!"

When his horse stalls were completed, Ed hired Terry Malone to be the head trainer at Shamrock Ranch. Terry likely came from

Kentucky, Georgia, or Tennessee because he and Bobby Gatlin knew each other. It was the end of 1980 when Terry moved into the ranch manager's house that Willard Miller had vacated in 1976.

Of course, Terry needed help with the horses. Bobby contacted Jeannette and asked her if she would like to come to Colorado and work with Terry as a groom. Jeannette agreed and arrived in March of 1981. She has been at the Shamrock ever since.

As a groom of Saddlebreds, Jeannette was involved in all the intricacies of saddle seat competition. She became very close to Beverly, who competed in numerous shows during the first part of the 1980s.

In 1982, Terry Malone left the Shamrock and Bill Field replaced him as head trainer. Ed then shipped his top horses from Kentucky to the Shamrock for Bill to train and transport

Shamrock Ranch Manager's house (2007).

The American Saddlebred and English Saddle Seat Riding

Sometimes called "peacocks of the horse show world," American saddlebreds can be trained to be flashy, high-stepping animals. Developed by Kentucky plantation owners from Thoroughbreds and native stock, they are most often seen in horse shows that feature English saddle seat riding. This style of riding, for which Beverly and Louis Pendleton trained, is designed to show off the horse's extravagant gaits.[4]

The trot is a two-beat gait. Notice that the two legs with white stockings are about to contact the ground at the same time.

American saddlebred

United States Equestrian Federation logo

In America, the United States Equestrian Federation creates and maintains the rules for most breeds shown in saddle seat competition. American saddlebreds may be entered into either three-gaited or five-gaited show classes. The three-gaited class displays the walk, trot, and canter—all "natural" gaits that are exaggerated and fine-tuned by careful training.

The walk is a four-beat gait (i.e., each hoof strikes the ground at a different time) that averages a speed of about 4 mph. In contrast, the trot is a two-beat gait that averages nearly 8 mph. Legs diagonally opposite each other move forward together.

The canter is a three-beat gait faster than a trot but slower than a gallop. It can range in speed from 10 to 17 mph, depending on the stride of the horse. Typically the left hind leg and right foreleg strike the ground at the same time, creating the second beat of the gait.

For the five-gaited show class, two additional gaits are added—the slow gait and the rack. These are called "ambling" gaits because they are not natural to most breeds and require meticulous training.

The slow gait, precursor to the rack, is sometimes called a "stepping pace," which means that two legs on the same side of the animal move simultaneously. However, the hind foot contacts the ground slightly before the front foot.

Slow gait speed is then gradually increased until it transitions into the most exciting gait of the five-gaited show class—the rack.

continued next page

continued from previous page

At rack speed, each foot hits the ground separately in a four-beat cadence. The ability to learn this special gait was inherited by the American saddlebred from one of its ancestors, the Narragansett pacer.

Saddle seat competition has other requirements. For example, riders use a special saddle—shown here—not seen in other English riding disciplines. It has very little padding and is placed farther back on the horse to avoid restraining its movements. The specialized tack also includes a double bridle, which has two bits and four reins. Saddlebreds are fitted with heavier shoes that have longer toes to encourage higher stepping.

Saddle Seat-style English saddle

The United States Equestrian Federation also regulates competition riders' attire. For both men and women, this attire is modeled after the tuxedo.

Another aspect of high-action show horse competition is tail setting—i.e., lifting the tail to an abnormally high position so it can flow more freely and increase the horse's flair. The stallions shown on the previous two pages have their tails set.

During the 1980s, tail setting was accomplished with a nicking operation, which involved partially cutting the tail's retractor muscles and ligaments, and the installation of a tail set. A tail set is a harness-like device with straps that loop from the chest to the underside of the tail in order to support a crupper, which does the lifting. A tail set holds the tail up and stretches associated muscles and ligaments, preventing the tail from gradually sinking down. Once the nicking operation heals, the tail will retain most of its movement and function, such as swatting flies, but it can no longer be clamped down hard against the buttocks. Today, the more-common method of tail setting uses a "bustle" to stretch the tail muscles in a more natural position, thus eliminating the need for nicking.[5]

Set tails require constant attention. If not cared for properly, even a nicked tail will drop to a more normal position in a few months. The tail set is often worn the entire time a horse is kept in show shape. And since it is dangerous to turn a horse out to pasture wearing a tail set, horses in active competition must stay in a stall—except when being schooled or exercised under direct supervision. Tailboards mounted to the walls of the stall prevent the horse from rubbing its tail set off, hence the need for stalls like those Ed Pendleton built for his prize Saddlebreds at Shamrock Ranch.

to shows from coast to coast. The Pendletons continued to use both of their ranches as bases of operation for showing. From the Shamrock, they transported one trainer, three grooms, and nine horses with all their tacking. Horses, tacking, and grooms were also trucked from the Kentucky barn. Ed and Beverly used their private airplane (flown by a hired pilot) to arrive a couple of days before the show so that Beverly could prepare for the competition. As soon at the socializing and celebrating were over, they flew back home.

Beverly and Louis were excellent riders and the Pendleton trainers—Bobby Gatlin, Terry Malone, and Bill Field—were among the best. Consequently, Beverly and Louis won many competitions. The March 1983 issue of *Saddle & Bridle* reported the following in an article titled, "Denver National Western Horse Show":

Denver area exhibitors presented fine horses. Most outstanding of all the stables was the Pendletons' Shamrock Ranch. Trainer Bill Field had nothing but blues on display in the barn aisle, where all exhibitors were welcome to stop, visit, and admire the winning horses. National Champion Zeberdee made his debut with Louis Pendleton to win the over 15.2 class and then the grand championship. Zeberdee is an absolutely amazing horse to watch, and Louis teams him perfectly. Pert and pretty Bev Pendleton has been responsible for winning the five-gaited championship here the past two years, aboard Beau Peavine Commander. This year she won the amateur with Beau, but brought back her new gelding, Making Waves, with a powerhouse performance to win the

championship. Bev has always been the crowd's favorite, and again this year generated ear-splitting cheering and whistling with Making Waves as he racked in top form at top speed. What a pair!

A partial collection of the ribbons Beverly and Louis won were given to the Wismers and are on display in the Wismers' ranch history room. They are shown here and on the following page, in 2008.

The following article by Dorothy Eberhard, which ran in the April 1983 issue of *Saddle & Bridle*, gives an idea of the scope and success of the Pendleton's Shamrock Ranch equestrian operation:

Pendleton's Shamrock Ranch

It's Kentucky style all the way at Bev and Ed Pendletons' Shamrock Ranch near Colorado Springs. Situated among towering Ponderosa pine trees on 6,000 acres, the entrance sign proclaims, "Shamrock Ranch Saddlebreds." Fences separate pastures "just like in Kentucky" and the show barn interior is designed just like the fabulous Pendleton barn in Lexington. The navy blue and kelly green stable colors are used throughout, starting with the Cavalier hitching post outside the stable office. This Cavalier is a replica of the Pendletons' Lexington Executive Airport statue. The Pendletons' weekend home (they live in Littleton, Colo. during the week) is apart from the stable area, amid more Ponderosas. There are more homes, including that of

trainer Bill Field, his wife Chris, and young son Zach. Outdoor facilities include show and work rings, paddocks, pastures, and equipment buildings. The show barn includes 13 huge box stalls, and an adjacent large indoor arena. All are insulated and heated, and a joy to visit even in winter.

Ed and Bev Pendleton, and son Louis and wife Julie, are gracious hosts, complementing the hospitality of Bill Field, showing visitors the horses and the beautiful ranch. The Pendletons are true Saddlebred lovers, and their breeding program features the bay five-gaited stallion Titleist, four-times World Champion, that stands at their Kentucky farm. Most recently they produced the amazing Shannon Run Sale that will be long remembered.

At Shamrock Ranch during a late winter visit, Bill jogged the exciting World Champion three-gaited gelding, Zeberdee, that had recently won the Denver National Western's Over 15.2 and Championship classes with Louis Pendleton, and then swept the Phoenix A-Z's Amateur Division again with Louis. Louis is understandably excited with his thrilling new horse. Another World Champion is Stutz Bearcat, five-gaited gelding shown so successfully by Bev. He's a big baby at home, and loves attention, especially when Bev rubs him under the jaw!

Making Waves, chestnut powerhouse gaited gelding, is popular at the Ranch. He was debuted in Colorado by Bev to win the Grand Championship at the Denver National Western, and then went on to continued top successes with Bev at the A-Z. They'll be hard to beat this season in the ladies division.

MAKING WAVES
and Bev Pendleton

DENVER'S GRAND CHAMPION FIVE-GAITED

A Colorado debut by a most outstanding gaited horse and his dynamic rider. Bev Pendleton was outstanding with her 1983 crowd-thrilling Five-Gaited Championship performance and victory.

**PENDLETON'S
SHAMROCK RANCH STABLES**
Colorado Springs, Colorado
Bill Field, Trainer
(303) 495-2157

Beverly Pendleton and the Pendleton's horse Making Waves, as pictured in the April 1983 issue of *Saddle & Bridle*.

Louis Pendleton and the Pendleton's horse Zeberdee, as pictured in the April 1983 issue of *Saddle & Bridle*.

Pendleton's So Rare, the elegant five-gaited daughter of Oman's Desdemona Denmark and out of a Genius Better Bourbon mare, was raised by Pendleton. In her first show in Colorado with Louis, they won the Open Class at Denver National Western. Pro Staff, talented bay walk-trot gelding by Titleist also debuted in Colorado at the National Western with Louis, winning the Amateur Three-Gaited Stake. The Pendleton entry for the Rocky Mountain Shows Road Horse Division is Expressway, almost-black Standardbred Speedster. At National Western, Louis rode and drove to win both the under saddle and bike classes.

Pidgeon Forge, pretty dark chestnut four-year-old gaited contender, will be debuted by Bill Field. Bill states, "I believe he's a great one." Another Pendleton-raised Titleist son, Profit Time, is being readied by Bill for the three-year-old UPHA Classics. Bill is excited about two full sisters by Courageous Admiral and out of Midnight Express (by Status Symbol). Queen City Kitty is a bay three-year-old gaited filly and Colorado Coal is a fine black two-year-old prospect. Both fillies show a lot of talent. Another promising two-year-old in the barn is a big-eyed gelding by Wild Chance and out of a Grand Command mare. He's already racking well for Bill.

A special pleasure horse that is consistently a favorite with show audiences as well as visitors to the Ranch is Denver Bronco. A winner both under saddle and in harness, he's been shown by Bev, Louis, Julie and good friend Ramon Martinez. The World Champion pleasure gelding Britannia and Bev will debut in Colorado and show on the Rocky Mountain circuit.

The two yearlings in the pasture love visitors, too. Typhoon is a chestnut colt by Titleist and out of Calypso Rose. Double Stuff is a classy spotted filly with a sensational set of ears. She's by Bounty Hunter and out of Midnight Express.

Stutz Bearcat and Zeberdee went on to win even more awards. The list for Stutz Bearcat as printed in the December 1983 edition of *Saddle & Bridle* includes:
• Kentucky State Fair Horse Show—World's Amateur Five-Gaited Grand Champion
• Tulsa Charity Horse Show—Amateur Five-Gaited Stallion/Gelding and Amateur Five-Gaited Champion
• North Carolina State Championship Horse Show—Amateur Five-Gaited Stallion/Gelding and Amateur Five-Gaited Champion

Zeberdee's award list from the same magazine reads as follows—
• Kentucky State Fair Horse Show—Amateur Three-Gaited Over 15.2 and World's Amateur Three-Gaited Grand Champion
• National Western Stock Show—Amateur Three-Gaited Over 15.2 and Three-Gaited Grand Champion
• Aid to Zoo National Horse Show—Amateur Three-Gaited Over 15.2 and Amateur Three-Gaited Grand Champion
• Pin Oak Charity Horse Show—Amateur Three-Gaited Over 15.2
• Santa Barbara National Horse Show—Three-Gaited Over 15.2
• North Carolina State Championship Horse Show—Amateur Three-Gaited Over 15.2 and Amateur Three-Gaited Champion

(Notes: "Over 15.2" refers to horses that are more than 15 hands and 2 fingers tall. Also, the only difference between Amateur and Professional classes is that a rider doesn't get paid to ride in the Amateur class.)

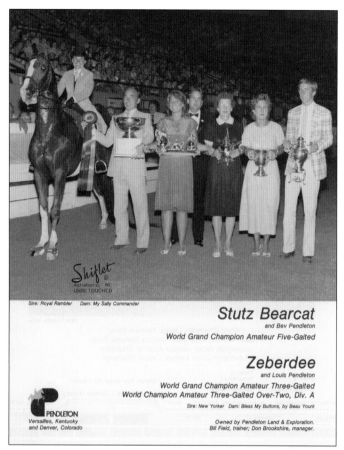

Beverly Pendleton and the Pendleton's horse Stutz Bearcat, as pictured in the September 1983 issue of *Saddle & Bridle*.

Louis Pendleton and the Pendleton's horse Zeberdee, as pictured in the September 1983 issue of *Saddle & Bridle*.

According to Jeannette, Bobby trained horses so that *he* could win riding them. As a result, they were too strong and powerful for most amateur riders, who ride for love of the sport rather than for a profession. Beverly often struggled with these horses—especially Stutz Bearcat, who was accustomed to Bobby's strength. So Ed brought Stutz to Colorado where Beverly could ride him more often. Then he hired Bill Field to calm the gelding and make him more controllable—so everyone could relax.

This worked well at the ranch, but whenever Stutz heard the crowds and saw the lights of a show, he instantly resumed his true nature as a champion show horse—making it difficult for Beverly to control him. Jeannette's job was to catch Stutz coming out of the ring

so he didn't get away from Beverly, who struggled with fear that someday he would.

Bill was the trainer who took Beverly and Stutz to the top during 1983 and 1984. He never got mad when Beverly had a bad ride, and he always encouraged her to smile and have fun. No wonder Ed and Beverly thought a lot of Bill!

Bill Field (left) with Stutz Bearcat and Beverly and Ed Pendleton (1983).

The show horse lifestyle is expensive and egocentric. Since a first place ribbon in the 1980s earned no more than $100, competing wasn't about prize money for the Pendletons. Rather, Beverly competed because she enjoyed it—until the pressures of competing and the behaviors she saw in other competitors finally got to her.

As Jeannette put it, "The horse show business is dominated by people who are driven to win—one could say they live for the glory of winning. Beverly, on the other hand, was a very strong believer in the Lord and lived for eternal values. It disturbed her to be around the culture of winning at all cost. She was torn between enjoying and despising the business."

In late 1984 or early 1985, Ed shut down the show horse operation at Shamrock Ranch. Financial pressure contributed to this decision as well, for he was spending $20,000 a month to keep it going! While the horse breeding businesses at both ranches helped to offset some of these expenses, Ed never broke even.

First he let most of his trainers go, including Bill Field and Bobby Gatlin—Terry Malone was already gone by then. Although he and Beverly were very fond of Bill, who was responsible for Beverly's extraordinary success in the ring, they had to let him go with their blessing because of financial woes. Then they shipped all their show horses back to Pendleton in Kentucky, where they could be sold at another Shannon Run Sale. Stutz Bearcat was the drawing card for this sale—the nine-year-old gelding sold for more than $250,000! Lastly, Ed sold the Pendleton operation to the last trainer he had employed in Kentucky.

The photograph here shows a blackboard hanging on the wall of the Shamrock Ranch forge room with specifications for the farrier

Blackboard with farrier specifications in the forge room at the Shamrock Ranch (2008).

about how the front and hind shoes should be made. Note the detail specifying shoe size and hoof angle for the following horses—Making Waves, Stutz Bearcat, Beau P. Command, Royal Title, Denver Bronco, Fashion's Carina, Broadway Hoofer, Miss Waterford, Helacious, Scooter, Britannia, and Casual Elegance—all stabled at the Shamrock Ranch.

Prior to purchasing the Shamrock Ranch, Ed ran a small ranch in Elizabeth where he raised red Angus—the only breed of cattle originally bred exclusively for beef. Kevin Loftus worked on this ranch. When Ed bought the Shamrock, he asked Kevin to move to the Bar X Ranch (the Bar X was included in the purchase,

Red Angus heifer

Ed Pendleton showed his cattle at live-stock shows all over the country—including the National Western Stock Show—thus maintaining the virtually continuous Shamrock Ranch tradition that Benjamin C. Allen started in the first decade of the 1900s!

Then, in 1985, he leased the lands of Shamrock Ranch to Wade Zimmerman for summertime cattle grazing. Next he promoted Jeannette to Shamrock Ranch Manager and invited her to move into the house that Bill Field had just vacated. She still had a few horses under her care, but they were trail horses used mainly for recreational riding.

see page 168) and manage the cattle there. Kevin ran between fifty and seventy-five head for Ed. He kept them on the Bar X most of the time, but allowed them to graze on the Shamrock each year before the pine needles began to fall. According to Jeannette, Kevin was a good manager with a very low percentage of loss. Later on, Jake White took over the cattle business for Ed.

Like Mac McLaughlin, Ed loved to entertain when his oil business supported it. He and Beverly held numerous parties at Shamrock Ranch, which Jeannette and Opal Reese attended. Their guests, like so many before them, always enjoyed the spectacular beauty of this pristine ranch.

Shamrock Ranch and Pikes Peak (2007).

Ed also sponsored several golf tournaments for his friends at the prestigious Woodmoor Pines Golf and Country Club in Monument, Colorado. About thirty guests came to each tournament to enjoy golf, dinner, and an evening of entertainment. Sometimes Ed hired local entertainers Robert Sennert and Danny Newton from the Edelweiss Restaurant in town to provide entertainment in the form of mirthful German music. Jeannette remembers keeping Beverly company at those lively dinners.

Gazebo on Shamrock Ranch where Julie and Louis Pendleton were married (2008).

When Louis married his first wife, Julie, they were wed on Shamrock Ranch in the picturesque gazebo that Howard Battista built. What a setting!

It seemed like Ed and Beverly were destined to live happily ever after. But tribulation has a habit of forcing its way into life—and it granted the Pendletons no exception. In 1988, Ed's primary lender, Silverado Savings and Loan Association of Denver, failed. This eventually caused Ed to default on his payments to Mark McLaughlin for the Shamrock Ranch.

When Ed defaulted on his Shamrock Ranch payments, Mark McLaughlin hired a Colorado attorney to foreclose on the property. After the foreclosure took place, Ed was given six months to redeem the ranch.

Determined to redeem it, he made a deal with A.J. Miller, a shrewd Denver investor who was Executive Vice President, Chief Financial Officer, and Treasurer of Hamilton Oil Corporation at the time. Ed knew Mr. Miller through his own oil business, the Pendleton Land and Exploration Company. The deal provided Ed with the $2.42 million he needed to redeem the Shamrock Ranch from Mark

Woodmoor Pines Golf and Country Club. *Courtesy Woodmoor Pines Golf and Country Club.*

The Silverado Savings and Loan Association of Denver and the United States Savings and Loan Crisis

Prior to its demise in December of 1988, Silverado Savings and Loan Association was one of the largest financial institutions in Colorado. While it was only one of several savings and loan associations that contributed to the United States Savings and Loan Crisis of the 1980s and 1990s, it was one of the most visible. That's because Neil Bush, son of President George H. W. Bush and brother of President George W. Bush, was one of its directors.

The U.S. Savings and Loan Crisis ultimately cost the country about $160 billion, of which $124 billion was paid for by the U.S. government.[6] Author John Kenneth Galbraith called it "the largest and costliest venture in public misfeasance, malfeasance and larceny of all time."[7] The failure of Silverado alone cost the federal government $1 billion.

There were many causes that led to this crisis, but the practice of making high-risk loans was key. Sadly, fraud and insider transaction abuses also contributed. The taxpayer-funded bailout that resulted from this crisis may have encouraged lenders to make similar high-risk loans that resulted in the 2007/2008 subprime mortgage financial crisis.[8]

The Silverado failure was in the public spotlight because the involvement of Neil Bush on the board "brought congressional scrutiny to a savings and loan that was said to have paid its officials excessive salaries, padded its capital by requiring borrowers to buy certain classes of Silverado stock, and used phony appraisals to prop up illegal land investments."[9]

The Office of Thrift Supervision ruled that Mr. Bush had engaged in conflicts of interest as an outside director from 1985 to 1988 after the Federal Deposit Insurance Corporation sued Silverado directors and officers for negligence. The FDIC sought $200 million from Mr. Bush and ten other directors.

The case was closed with a $49.5 million settlement. On March 11, 1990, the *Houston Post* printed, "A failed Colorado savings and loan whose board of directors included a son of President Bush was part of an intricate web of federally insured financial institutions that had business links to organized crime figures and CIA operatives."

Needless to say, the Silverado scandal gave both the Bush family and the State of Colorado a black eye in the public's view. Unfortunately, it seems that not all the lessons to be learned from it have been embraced by modern financial institutions.

McLaughlin, but it also required him to pay A. J. $5 million one year later. If he defaulted on this future payment, then A. J. Miller would own the Shamrock Ranch. But if he paid the $5 million on time, A. J. would make 100 percent profit. Either way, A. J. couldn't lose!

Before the deal was struck, A. J. and his wife came to the Shamrock to check it out. The first time Ed and Beverly were with them,

but they came another time by themselves. Jeannette hosted both visits. She remembers that A. J. and his wife were quite "insistent" about what they wanted her to do with Ed's horses for their grandchildren. Fortunately for her, A. J. Miller did not get the ranch, as will be explained in the next chapter.

Ed and Beverly Pendleton eventually moved to a condominium in Columbine,

Colorado, not far from the home they once owned in Littleton. Their sons Alan and Louis followed in their father's footsteps by forming an oil exploration and production company called PENSA, Inc., that is still in operation today.

OPAL REESE, housekeeper for Mac and Claire McLaughlin (see page 197ff), in effect came with the Shamrock Ranch when Ed Pendleton purchased it. That's because Mark McLaughlin had put a condition on the sale that Opal be allowed to live in her room at the ranch until she either retired or passed away. Beverly and Ed graciously took her under their wing, as did Jeannette.

Since Beverly liked to dine out, she and Ed made it a routine to take both Jeannette and Opal out to dinner whenever they came to the ranch. Before long, the four of them had visited every good restaurant in town. They had some wonderful times together. According to Jeannette, "Mrs. Reese was a very neat little lady!"

A picture of Opal and Jeannette in a pleasure buggy pulled by one of the Pendleton saddlebreds is shown below. Pleasure buggies are used in horse shows for the pleasure driving show class. Sabaka, the German shepherd in the photograph, belonged to Jeannette, who has always owned German shepherds and collies. The buggy is in front of the main ranch house.

The Pendletons had several dogs. One was an Italian greyhound named Tulip. Another was a Chihuahua called Spanky. Bell was the third, but no picture of her is available.

Whenever the Pendletons traveled, Opal took care of all three dogs. She always had them cleaned and groomed at a pet salon before the Pendletons returned. She thoroughly enjoyed the opportunity to care for them.

Opal Reese and Jeannette Billings in a pleasure buggy with Jeanette's German shepherd Sabaka watching (1986). *Courtesy Doreene (Reese) Wiley.*

Tulip. *Courtesy Doreene (Reese) Wiley.*

Spanky. *Courtesy Doreene (Reese) Wiley.*

In her spare time, Opal did quilting. She also played cards with her friends. Opal's grandson Jerry called them "the gambling ladies."

When gasoline reached a price of 99.9 cents per gallon in the 1980s, Opal wrote to her daughter Doreene that she would have to limit her driving. Doreene could only laugh at her frugality!

In the late 1980s, Opal invited her daughters and their spouses to the ranch for dinner. Ed Pendleton was kind enough to let her use the main ranch house to entertain them. He made an appearance during the evening to meet all of them. Opal's daughter Doreene remembers that "he was a very nice person."

From 1985 to 1990, Opal and Jeannette, two remarkable women, took care of the Shamrock Ranch and its houses by themselves. Opal retired and left the ranch in 1990, but Jeannette still runs the ranch today. Their stories will be continued in the next chapter.

The Wismer Era

Like General Palmer, Benjamin C. Allen, Maria Allen, and Mac McLaughlin—all former owners of Shamrock Ranch—David Arthur Wismer Jr. and his wife, Mary Anne, have roots in Pennsylvania. As a matter of fact, many important Americans and Coloradans have been associated with this historic state, including Declaration of Independence signer Thomas McKean, founding father Benjamin Franklin, Quaker William Penn (for whom the

Pennsylvania farm

state is named—Pennsylvania means "Penn's Woods"), William Jackson Palmer, Sam Stout, Spencer Penrose, and others. As with all these notable Pennsylvanians, David and Mary Anne Wismer have generously shared the bounty of their lives' harvest to help make the world a better place.

David's roots in Pennsylvania go back seven generations, to Jacob Wismer, patriarch of the Wismers in Pennsylvania. Jacob was born in Germany in about 1684. Because of religious persecution there, he was driven from his home on the Rhine. In 1710, he emigrated to America along with his father, Jacob Sr.; his mother, Maria Friedt (or Fretz); and an older sister whose name is unknown. They were joined by a hundred or so other German families. After landing in the British colony of North Carolina, these families founded the town of New Bern at the confluence of the Neuse and Trent Rivers.

The *Wismer Family History,* written by A.J. Fretz before his death in 1893, enlightens us with the following analysis of why so many Europeans came to America during the early 1700s:

> *The motive that impelled the Wismer ancestor to these shores is not known, but undoubtedly was on account of religious persecution which raged in the father-land, and which was the chief cause of the emigration in those early days of so many of the pioneer fathers to the New World where no cruel persecution was waged against the devout worshipers of God. Here was a refuge for the oppressed people of God, of other nations, and hither they came by the thousands where they might worship God under the bright sun of religious freedom, untrammeled and unoppressed.*

Sadly, around this time the Tuscarora War began, and on October 2, 1711, a party of Tuscarora Indians attacked this German settlement and murdered a hundred and thirty people. Jacob's sister was among those killed. Young Jacob would also have lost his life if he hadn't held out some tobacco as a peace offering. This enabled him to escape. Legend has it that he walked and ran 90 miles in a single day to get away from the war, which lasted until 1715. Traveling north, he covered a total distance of at least 350 miles, ending up in Philadelphia County, Province of Pennsylvania.[1]

In 1726, Jacob moved to Bucks County, another 50 or so miles north of Philadelphia County. According to legend, the party who brought the Wismers to Bucks County unloaded them and their belongings under a big tree in the woods and then left with this tart advice: "Now Wismer work or die."

Jacob rented a 375-acre tract from John Leech and was the first white man to settle there. William Penn, Proprietor and Governor of the Province of Pennsylvania, had originally granted and conveyed the tract by indenture to John Alcok, an emigrant from England, in 1691. By 1749, Jacob was able to purchase the 210 southwestern acres of this land for the sum of "£100 lawful money."

Toward the end of his life, Jacob worked as a wheelwright, but he probably farmed as well. He is believed to have been married three times. He married his last wife after he arrived in Philadelphia County. Her name was Nanny and she was the mother of all eleven of his children.

Jacob and Nanny were married for sixty-seven years. She was eighty-four when he died in 1787 at the remarkable age of one hundred and three.

Excerpts in this chapter are from "A Life Well Lived—Autobiography of David A. Wismer," unpublished manuscript, 2007.

The final words that A.J. Fretz wrote about Jacob and Nanny Wismer are, "The remains of himself and wife were no doubt laid to rest in the grave-yard of the Old Mennonite church at Deep Run, the scene of their zeal for God's cause, and where for many years they worshiped the God of their fathers, and left to their numerous posterity an undying example, to 'go and do likewise.' And so shall they remain until that day when the great angel shall descend from heaven with a shout, and swear with a solemn oath, that 'time was, time is and time shall be no more,' when God shall again quicken the bones, and bid the sleepers come forth. Then may it be their great joy to see their numerous posterity safely sheltered in the fold of the great Shepherd, and together join in the triumphant shout of the redeemed."

Clearly, David Wismer has been blessed with a humble yet inspiring spiritual heritage!

Born in Easton, Pennsylvania—less than 50 miles from Jacob Wismer's homestead in Deep Run—on January 6, 1938, David was the only child of David Arthur Wismer Sr. and Pearl Celesta Schaffer. Although born in Penn-

View from Mount Pocono

sylvania, he was raised in Phillipsburg, New Jersey, which is just across the Delaware River from Easton. His father was a longtime employee of Metropolitan Edison Company and his mother was a schoolteacher and keen reader. Even so, David remembers modestly that he was only an average-to-good student, but was skilled with his hands, building models and crafts of all sorts.

He was also an accomplished musician. In high school, he played tenor saxophone in a twelve-piece dance band called the Rhythm Kings. They were a very good Glenn Miller–style band, and played at both local dances and those held in the Pocono Mountains of northeastern Pennsylvania—a popular outdoor recreation spot. Two of the band's most popular numbers were Glenn Miller's *Moonlight Serenade* and *In The Mood*. As a sax player, David was central to the band's success.

He was also an athlete in high school and college, competing in the high jump. By the time he stopped competing, he could clear a 6-foot high bar.

The house in Phillipsburg where David Wismer was raised (1988).

David became active in politics at a very early age. In 1952, when he was only fourteen, David, his girlfriend, and some other friends formed the Teenage Republican Club of Warren County, New Jersey. Dwight D. Eisenhower was running for president of the United States that year, and Richard Nixon was his choice for vice president. The club was very active in distributing flyers for the Eisenhower/Nixon campaign. When Ike won the election, David and his club were rewarded with a trip to Washington D.C. and a meeting with Vice President Nixon.

Eisenhower and Nixon campaigning (circa 1952).

The club campaigned for Eisenhower and Nixon again in 1956. When Ike won a second term, they were invited once again to Washington D.C. to be thanked and recognized—but this time they were given the privilege of meeting with the president himself. The meeting was held in the Rose Garden of the White House. During that meeting, club members proudly presented Ike with a red, white, and blue Warren County Teenage Republican Club beanie and pennant. To David's amazement, the beanie and pennant were on display years later when he visited the Eisenhower Museum at Ike's boyhood home in Abilene, Kansas!

David's mother had a huge impact on him during his youth. She always encouraged him to "give it a try." This inspiring challenge has motivated him throughout his life to attempt many things that he probably wouldn't have otherwise. One of his first successes that resulted from her direct encouragement was playing the lead male role in the play *You Can't Take It With You* during his senior year in high school.

David's mother also brought reading and culture into his life. The public library was over a mile away, yet she walked to it at least weekly and took David along with her. Before he was old enough to walk on his own, she pulled him in a wagon or sled.

When David was a high school student, she took him to New York City during his Easter vacations. They always stayed at the

Poster for the original Broadway production of *The King and I*. Yul Brynner starred as the king. (1951)

Astor Hotel in Times Square, and would spend their time taking in Broadway plays, vaudeville at the RKO Palace, and various shows at Radio City Music Hall. David got to see many famous performers, such as Danny Kaye and Betty Hutton, on these wonderful and memorable trips, and he learned to love the great and beloved musicals of Rodgers and Hammerstein, Lerner and Loewe, and the like. Today, his enduring love for Broadway musicals has been passed on to his children and grandchildren.

Lehigh University Alumni Building

David's mother also encouraged him to worship God. As a child, he attended the nearest Episcopal Church and became an acolyte there. Later on, the family attended the Wesley Methodist Church together. When David was a freshman in college, the church's pastor, Reverend Virgil Mabry, asked him if he wanted to become a pastor. He chose engineering instead.

David attended Lehigh University in Bethlehem, Pennsylvania, where he enrolled in a five-year curriculum that led to two undergraduate degrees: a bachelor of science in mechanical engineering and a bachelor of arts in applied mathematics. At his mother's recommendation, he also took English courses, which prepared him to write two books and numerous papers later on.

Throughout his time at Lehigh, David lived in the freshman dormitory and worked first as a dormitory counselor, then as the resident director of counselors. Utilizing his developing leadership abilities, he helped to found the Gryphon Society and was its first secretary.

A gryphon is a legendary creature with the body of a lion and the head and wings of an eagle. The name Gryphon Society was selected because one of the definitions of a gryphon denotes a counselor. The house newsletter was called the *Pricked Ear*. With encouragement from his mother, David ran for president of this society and was elected the very next year. The Gryphon Society gave Lehigh dormitory counselors a fraternity-like experience and still thrives today at Lehigh.

Gryphon

Battelle Memorial Institute

While he was a student at Lehigh, David worked for a summer at the Battelle Memorial Institute in Columbus, Ohio. This non-profit research institute located near the Ohio State University campus developed the xerography process, which Xerox copiers later made famous—after IBM rejected the technology! David's work-study project was to design a "guided knife" for a surgeon at Ohio State University Medical Center. The prototype he developed minimized the amount of tissue that had to be removed during cancerous breast removal and was actually used by the requesting surgeon.

David was the Middle Atlantic States Épée Champion during his senior year at Lehigh University (1959).

Remarkably, David found time to play his saxophone in Lehigh's fast-stepping marching band and participate in the school's fencing team. His weapon of choice was the épée, the modern derivative of the original dueling sword, the rapier, used in sport fencing. Épée is the French word for "sword." While modern sport fencing has three events, each using a different weapon (the foil, épée, and sabre), épée, is the only one in which the entire body is a valid target area. Épée is the heaviest of all sport fencing weapons. Electronic machines score touches during matches. During his senior year, David was not only the team's captain, but also the Middle Atlantic States Épée Champion.

It was through a fencing honorary society called Cut and Thrust that David met his future wife, Mary Anne Winkelmann. She was working in nearby Allentown, Pennsylvania, for Prudential Insurance Company. One of David's fencing friends at Lehigh, Paul Huska, and his girlfriend, Patti Davco, who worked at Prudential with Mary Anne, arranged a blind date for the two for a club picnic. Even though the picnic was cancelled because of rain, David decided to take Mary Anne dancing another day. It's a good thing he did . . . because they've been happily married now for more than forty-eight years!

Mary Anne grew up in Ridgefield Park, New Jersey, where her father was a Lutheran pastor. After graduating from high school, she moved to Allentown, where she was living when she met David.

David married Mary Anne soon after he graduated from Lehigh University. On February 6, 1960, they said their vows in Christ Lutheran Church in Allentown, Pennsylvania. Upon their return from a honeymoon in Mexico City and Acapulco, they moved to Cleveland Heights, Ohio. David had obtained employment with the General Electric Company and was about to start graduate school at Case Institute of Technology. His goal was to obtain a master of science degree in instrumentation engineering. Surprisingly, at the time neither Lehigh nor Case was coed.

Cleveland's Severance Hall

General Electric logo

While they were living in Cleveland Heights, Mary Anne, who has a beautiful lyric soprano voice, successfully auditioned for the Cleveland Symphony Orchestra Chorus, which was under the direction of the famed Robert Shaw. She performed several times in historic Severance Hall, where both Robert Shaw and legendary conductor George Szell led the glorious music. She also shared her talent, which has inspired all who have heard her, with the Bethlehem Bach Choir and her church choir. Photographs of George Szell and Severance Hall are provided here. Following is a letter written by a member of Robert Shaw's Cleveland chorus that appeared in the *Cleveland Plain Dealer* in January 1999. Mary Anne remarked that she feels the same way about Robert Shaw as the writer of this letter does.

Legendary conductor George Szell (1897–1970)

At Case Institute of Technology (now Case Western Reserve University), David worked as a research assistant in a relatively new group called the Systems Research Center. The team was devoted to the automation of in-

Famous conductor more than music genius

With the death of conductor Robert Shaw on Monday after a stroke in New Haven, Conn., we have lost a truly great person and a transcendent asset to the cultural well-being of our county ("Conductor dies," Life, Tuesday).

Shaw was the pre-eminent choral conductor of all time, here and abroad. His original Robert Shaw Chorale's Christmas album was RCA Victor Red Seal's best seller in any category during the 1950s.

He was a hero to many of us when he signed with the Cleveland Orchestra in 1956. We who sang in the incomparable 200-voice chorus he developed here have never been quite the same.

Robert Shaw (1916–1999)

It was not only Shaw's music-making; he was a philosopher whose weekly letters to chorus members seemed worthy of being bound into a volume to benefit the ages for their wisdom about many aspects of life, in addition to music.

Yes, he won 14 Grammy Awards, Kennedy Center honors and recognition around the world. His Christmas program telecast by PBS a month ago was remarkable for its beauty and continuity: This 82-year-old genius conducted without pause a seamless 90 minutes of gorgeous music performed by three choirs, the Atlanta Symphony, soloists and Shaw himself reading Scripture and other appropriate words.

I remember most the American-born kid next door who used examples from pop songs and sports metaphors to help demonstrate what he wanted when we sang Beethoven, Bach or Stravinsky with the renowned Cleveland Orchestra. Oh, the sonorities, the sounds he enabled us to produce.

Shaw is irreplaceable in the choral-music world. I was changed forever by my association with him 40 years ago.

Now it is difficult to accept that he is gone. If the angelic choruses think they're great now, wait till they hear how they sound after Robert Shaw puts them through a few of his rehearsals.

— Olney Dekker, Chagrin Falls, Ohio

Tribute to famed choral conductor Robert Shaw, written in January 1999. *Photo credit: Courtesy Singers.com*

Case Western Reserve University campus

dustrial processes using both analog and digital computers. Both types of computers were used because it was not known at that time which would ultimately prevail in the world of industrial automation (today, digital computers are preferred).

David's master's thesis was titled *Dynamic Control of a Continuous Strip Process*. It guided development of a control system for industrial processes that use continuous strip devices, such as papermaking machines and steel and aluminum rolling mills. The mathematics behind his research required the use of partial differential equations, which became of particular in-

terest to him and led to further work on a Ph.D. dissertation. His education in mathematics and engineering provided a problem-solving basis that allowed him to eventually make a livelihood in computers and financial software, even though he took no classes in either subject.

To supplement David's income as a research assistant at Case, Mary Anne worked once again for the Prudential Insurance Company. Later on, she worked for the Western Reserve Historical Society.

It was during this time that David submitted a paper for a competition sponsored by the Cleveland Chapter of the Instrument Society of America. He won the contest. A photograph of him accepting the award is shown here. His mentor, Professor Donald Eckman—who led the Case Systems Research Center—is standing to his left.

David wrote another technical paper during his last year at Case and submitted it for the Joint Automatic Control Conference that was to be held in Boulder, Colorado. This was the second of many such papers he wrote and presented. The paper was accepted, so he traveled to Boulder and spoke at the conference. While there, some other attendees invited him to attend an opera in Central City with them. During dinner before the show, they engaged in a discussion about David's paper, and he began scribbling mathematical equations on his napkin. As the party prepared to leave, the maître d´ scooped up the napkins and declared that he was going to frame them and place them in his collection of mementos, which he had garnered from special guests!

When David graduated from Case, he took employment with TRW Computers in Canoga Park, California. His parents encouraged him to take this job over offers from

David accepting an award for a paper he wrote for the Cleveland Chapter of the Instrument Society of America (1961).

General Electric, Honeywell, and Corning Glass because they felt it was in California that "all the new things are happening." Although it meant they would undoubtedly see less of him and Mary Anne, they were unselfish enough to guide him to the best opportunity.

So, in April of 1962 David and Mary Anne packed up their belongings and traveled along historic Route 66 in their blue 1955 Chevy 210—a gift from David's father—to Canoga Park. After renting a house, David started a new career that was based on the topic of his master's

degree thesis. He worked on digital computer control applications to automate a polymer plant in Texas, a papermaking machine in Georgia, and other industrial processes.

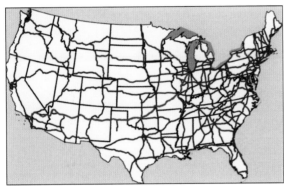

Historic Route 66 (shown in red)

Fourteen months after they arrived in Canoga Park, Mary Anne gave birth to their first child—Susan Elizabeth. Soon after, they bought their first house—for $20,000. It was located in Woodland Hills.

When TRW sold its Computer Division to General Electric, it meant that David would need to move to Phoenix to stay with his job. He had an important decision to make. Rather than move his family to Arizona, he decided to return to school full time and pursue a Ph.D. degree in control systems engineering at the University of California, Los Angeles (UCLA).

Los Angeles Memorial Coliseum, aka The Grand Old Lady

David and Mary Anne relished cheering at UCLA football games that were played in the Los Angeles Memorial Coliseum ("The Grand Old Lady")—site of the 1984 Summer Olympics.[2] They also enjoyed attending basketball games where the legendary John Wooden was coaching for UCLA. Wooden was the first person to be honored by the Basketball Hall of Fame as both a player and a coach, and his coaching record of ten NCAA National Championships (1964–1975) has never been matched. Wooden is shown here on his ninety-sixth birthday at a ceremony in the office of California Congressman Brad Sherman.

John Wooden (2006)

While David was working on his Ph.D., Mary Anne gave birth to David Arthur III, their second child and only son. Upon graduating in 1966, David took an assistant professor position in the UCLA

Engineering School's new department of engineering systems. His salary was $9,600 a year for a nine month appointment. With their growing family, the Wismers moved into a larger house in West Hills.

To supplement this salary, David developed and taught some short courses that were offered through UCLA Extension during the summer months. Since his Ph.D. work had involved computers, control systems, and operations research, he developed five different courses in industrial control, utilizing many well-known guest lecturers. These courses provided enough additional income that Mary Anne didn't have to work outside the home.

During this time, David achieved the status of professional industrial engineer and was registered as such by the State of California. Earlier he was elected to the prestigious engineering honor society Tau Beta Pi. This association was founded at Lehigh University in 1885 "to mark in a fitting manner those who have conferred honor upon their Alma Mater by distinguished scholarship and exemplary character as students in engineering, or by their attainments as alumni in the field of engineering, and to foster a spirit of liberal culture in engineering colleges."

As a professor at UCLA, David taught eight different courses and conducted research in the theory and applications of control systems, systems engineering, mathematical programming, optimization, and operations research.

David's Ph.D. dissertation was titled *Optimal Control of Distributed Parameter Systems Using Multilevel Techniques*. This title indicates that David had mastered the difficult partial differential equations upon which this science is founded. He later authored a chapter in the book *Optimization Methods for Large-Scale Systems with Applications* that was titled "Distributed Multilevel Systems." He also edited the entire book, which was published by McGraw-Hill in 1971. The back cover is shown here. Subsequently, he wrote

Back cover of *Optimal Control of Distributed Parameter Systems Using Multilevel Techniques,* which David edited and helped write (1971).

Royce Hall, UCLA

Linear and Nonlinear Programming, with R. Chattergy, which was published by Elsevier Publishing Company in 1978.

In order to stay at UCLA and succeed with an academic career, David needed to obtain tenure. This required an extensive vita, or academic résumé, which highlighted his research, teaching, and community service activities. His community service needed to include public speaking engagements as well as other forms of extracurricular activities. David worked hard in all three areas and was awarded tenure at the age of thirty-three, after just four years as an assistant professor. His vita included four doctoral and nine masters' students who had done their research with David, as well as four book chapters, six research reports, and eighteen published papers. In addition, he served as the chairman of the department's Ph.D. field committee in large-scale engineering systems.

The promotion actually came through in 1971 while David was working for a year on a research project off campus! In 1970 David had requested a leave without pay from UCLA in order to join a new startup company called Systems Control, Inc. (SCI), located in Palo Alto, California. He was named manager of the operations research division and was one of the company's early employees.

While there, he helped write proposals that led to several groundbreaking projects and a substantial organization for the company. One such project was a joint venture with the Nolte Engineering firm of San Jose, California, that was sponsored by the U.S. Department of Housing and Urban Development (HUD). It demonstrated that computers and mathematical models could be used to design and implement automated applica-tions for public utilities, such as waste disposal and water distribution. Another was a computer-controlled sewage treatment plant for the city of Palo Alto.

Immersing himself in this exciting, fast-paced startup environment, David was bitten by the entrepreneurial bug. So when his leave was about to end, he contacted the head of the department of engineering systems at UCLA and requested an extension for a second year, which was denied. So David had a major decision to make—either return to UCLA or resign from his tenured position there.

Besides enjoying the startup environment at SCI, David was not especially happy as a professor, since the challenge had disappeared for him once he obtained tenure. Furthermore, UCLA was a very liberal environment and had been the scene of great disruption and contention because of protest demonstrations over the Vietnam War and sit-ins over the Free Speech Movement. A photograph

Mario Savio at UC Berkeley in 1966.

of Mario Savio leading such a protest at UC Berkeley is shown on the previous page. For these reasons and others, David made the decision to resign from his professorship at UCLA.

Ironically, many years later, while he and Mary Anne were traveling in Vienna, Austria, David met a professor from his department at UCLA who told him that, since he had tenure, he could not have been fired, even if he had failed to return during the year after the unpaid leave ended. David believes the Lord guided him in making the decision to leave UCLA.

But all was not rosy after he made the decision. Executive management at SCI had promised him significant stock options and future advancement, but he soon found that they intended to renege on their commitments. As David still asserts, "Trust, once lost, is very difficult to restore."

Consequently, he resigned from SCI within a year of leaving UCLA. He then took a position with another industrial control company in Los Gatos, California, but only worked there a short time.

David's leaving of three promising careers, all within the period of a year, put tremendous pressure on the Wismer family. David remembers feeling the cruel and disturbingly sharp edge of panic for the first time. By then Jennifer Anne had been born, so he had a family of five to house and support.

Believing his best opportunities were in Southern California, he took his family back to their home in West Hills, which had just come off lease. Unfortunately, the house had sustained considerable damage while it had been rented, so David and Mary Anne incurred significant costs to get it back in shape. Things were looking very bleak for them at the time.

The Wismer house in West Hills, California (2006).

Not one to panic, David worked diligently to renew relationships he had formed in earlier days while teaching and working at TRW. His first manager at TRW, Dr. Thomas Stout, had formed a company in Woodland Hills called Profimatics, Inc. Dr. Stout was pleased to hire David as a consultant for a project underway with Standard Oil of Ohio. Then he rented some office space and a telephone to David, and encouraged him to form a business of his own. At the same time, a former student found David some teaching opportunities at Computer Sciences Corporation (CSC) in Richland, Washington—also called "Atomic City" because of the atomic energy work that was going on there.

Eventually David's contacts led to an opportunity in Anaheim, California (not far from Disneyland and less than fifty miles from his house) that changed everything for the Wismers. It came during the mid–1970s—when the distressing Arab oil embargo was causing fuel prices to soar and long lines to form at fuel pumps. The scarcity of fuel had prompted Bridgford Foods, Inc. to find a way to deliver products while driving fewer miles.

Bill Bridgford, right, and the Bridgford Foods management team (1962).

Bridgford Foods had pioneered the manufacture and sale of frozen bread dough to restaurants and supermarkets. Bill Bridgford, owner of the family business and an entrepreneur in his own right, approached CSC for a solution.

Management at CSC had no idea how to even approach the problem, but they knew David Wismer might. So they introduced David to Bill with the stipulation that he use CSC computer resources if he won the business.

Two other companies also offered their services to Bill—IBM and Homes & Narver, a large engineering firm in Orange County, California. How on earth could David compete with such formidable competitors?

Although he didn't know it at the time, David can now see God's hand in the outcome. He proposed a contest . . . between IBM, Homes & Narver, and himself.

The contest rules were formulated to give each contestant the bare necessities he needed to compete:

- details about the Bridgford Foods fleet of trucks
- a copy of one week's worth of orders to be delivered
- $1,000 to cover expenses (Note: Even though neither IBM nor Homes & Narver needed the money, *David did!*)

During his days at UCLA, David had become acquainted with a little-known math tool called the Chinese Postman Algorithm. It was directly applicable to Bridgford Foods' optimization problem.

Needless to say, the Chinese Postman and David came through with flying colors! David won the competition and got the order.

Reflecting on this experience, David reported, "It was Mr. Bridgford who taught me one of my life's greatest business lessons. He said, 'David, you've got to ask for the order!' He would send his own boys out to get new accounts and tell them not to come home until they had at least one new order each day."

The computer program David developed for Bridgford Foods became a product labeled *Econofuel* and was marketed in Southern California by David and CSC. Although it was a technical success, it was not a marketing success "largely because most trucking companies could not be convinced that a computer could improve on their years of experience."

Nevertheless, *Econofuel* was the launch pad for David's phenomenal success with

Cover of Econofuel sales brochure

computer software. It wasn't long before CSC introduced him to Bob Citron, county treasurer of Orange County, California. Like Bill Bridgford, Bob was looking for an optimization solution—only the thing he wanted to optimize was the county's return on fixed income investments.

Once again, David had to overcome skepticism that a one-man company could handle such a significant challenge. And once again he came up with a creative solution to this sales objection. He proposed a system of four modules and stipulated that the county would not have to pay for any module until he delivered it and they accepted it. He also offered to give the county joint ownership if employees would help with testimonials and allow marketing visits from prospective buyers.

His strategy worked. Over the next three years, he developed *Moneymax*, which had the following modules:

- Fixed Income Portfolio Accounting
- Cash Flow Forecasting
- Linear Optimization of Strategic Investment Decisions
- Bond Swaps and Trades

In order to do the programming, David needed to understand the accounting involved. Ray Wells, Bob's assistant, was gracious enough to spend time with him to transfer this knowledge. According to David, "Ray was in many ways the brains behind the portfolio accounting portion of *Moneymax*." He and David are good friends to this day.

Moneymax was extremely beneficial for Bob Citron. Its success was due to precise accounting and an innovative feature that enabled Bob to predetermine profitable bond swaps. He often told prospective buyers that Orange County had realized a total bond swap profit of more than $3 million in the first year alone!

Bob was a natural marketeer. He wrote lots of press releases, gave numerous testimo-

---

FOR ORANGE COUNTY TREASURY

'Money Machine' May Make $3.8 Million

By SANDI MOSLEY
Register Staff Writer

SANTA ANA — County Tax Collector-Treasurer Robert Citron has a machine he says makes money. Legally.

He claims that this year it will produce as much as $3.8 million the county might not otherwise have earned.

It goes by the trade name of Moneymax, but Citron fondly calls it his "new kind of money tree."

In its first week at work, Moneymax raised $39,050 in unexpected funds.

During August, the "money machine" added $112,815 to the county's treasury.

Moneymax is a fortune-telling computer system, capable of telling county officials how much money to invest, what to invest it in and the best time of the year to invest it.

Moneymax went into full operation May 12, and already financial officers from California, Arizona and the city and county of San Francisco have come here to look over its figures.

Moneymax will be for sale as soon as negotiations settle

how much the county will get for it. But in an article touting the system in a national financial magazine, Citron advises no one to get too interested unless he has $25 million to invest.

That's because Moneymax, programed into a time-sharing computer in chicago, costs $1,500-a-month to operate Citron said.

But Moneymax is worth the cost, he added. His office, the third largest treasurer's office in the state, has an average of $445 million in taxpayers' money invested in various programs at all times.

In the past, county officials —like county officials everywhere—have had only calculators to help them decide the best investment policies for the county, local school districts and various special taxing districts.

"I decided there must be a better way of deciding how much to invest than the system we were using," Citron said.

"The investment officer, no matter how competent and professional that person is,

might be slightly on the conservative side in making investments to make sure the money is available when it's needed."

About two years ago, he sold county supervisors on the idea of designing a computerized investment system, which he said at the time would earn at least $91,000 a year over current investments.

"What it will do, simply, is allow us to invest more money for a longer time," he explained.

Supervisors gave him $44,300 to begin working with Dr. David A. Wismer, a Woodland Hills comptuer consultant, to devise the system.

They came up with Moneymax, which, in simple terms, keeps track of how much is invested, what kind of investments are made and the

The Register
THE REGISTER Sunday, September 21, 1975 E1

amount they will earn on maturity.

Then, from information programed into it, the system gives printouts showing the dates money will be needed to pay expected bills.

It also shows how much revenue will be available each two-week period during the year; how much of it to invest and in which future two-week period it should mature, based on expected cash flow needs and short-term interest rates.

Citron had programmers add a "swaps and trades" capability to the computer to analyze the county's current investments and compare them with other available investments.

He said the computer will show if there is a gain to be made by getting out of one investment program and into another.

If individuals had calculated that, Citron explained, they would have made investments in July to mature in March so funds would be available to cover that period, even though they'd know leav-

If Citron's assistants decide to try one of the trades, they can test the recommendations against the current day's interest in three minutes with another part of Moneymax called "playback."

In its first run, Moneymax's "swaps and trades" recommendations "made" $39,050 in eight trades. Its average weekly - increase is about $34,016, Citron said, and during August, 13 trades amounting to $73.5 million added $112,815 to the treasury.

Knowing exactly how long to invest is important, Citron added, because $1 million is capable of earning $200 a day under current interest rates.

Moneymax is programmed to show the longest possible investment time. One day in July it's printout showed the county would be spending more money next March than it will take in.

ing the funds invested for a full year would bring a better interest rate.

"Moneymax told us that even though we had a $19 million negative cash flow between March 3 and March 13, we had large cash flow revenues in December that could be used to cover that March period," he added.

"Before Moneymax, we would have had to be more conservative."

Citron added the job of county treasurer to his tax collecting duties two years ago and won praise from supervisors for reducing the budgets for the combined departments both years.

Citron, whose secretaries sometimes answer his phone with "Bob Citron, your friendly tax collector," has even tried to win over county taxpayers by sending out tax notices with poems on them.

In his article lauding Moneymax, Citron admits it could sound like just another "suede shoe scheme," but in the best of used car salesmen manners, added in jest:

"Have I got a deal for you!"

nials, and he and David made many presentations together. One such joint presentation took place in 1975 at the annual meeting of the California Association of County Treasurers. This presentation was the turning point for David's company—Wismer Associates, Inc. (WAI)—for sales took off immediately after it.

One sales experience that resulted is worth retelling.

When David met with Joseph Alioto, mayor of San Francisco, Mr. Alioto only had one question for him. "Dr. Wismer, will you *guarantee* that the city will make an additional $1 million next year if we buy your product?"

David gulped. He realized that the future of *Moneymax,* and perhaps WAI, depended on his answer.

Out of nowhere, the answer suddenly came to him, clear and concise. "Mr. Mayor, while I can't guarantee that you will make an additional $1 million with *Moneymax* next year, I *can* guarantee that, if you don't, you won't owe me a cent. I have only one condition—that we share 50/50 the profits you make over and above $1 million."

There was no further conversation. David was promptly escorted from the office.

The next day, Tom Scanlon, San Francisco city treasurer, called David to tell him that the money for *Moneymax* was in the budget and

that the mayor had just ordered an audit of the results at year-end. Evidently, Mayor Alioto did not want to share the profits—because he paid for the product up front!

Moneymax passed the year-end audit with flying colors and San Francisco management became a very satisfied customer, providing helpful references for many years.

As WAI continued to grow, David transitioned from worker/manager to executive and focused on hiring good people. One of his first and most loyal employees was Sujit Pal, who was from London by way of New York City. Here is Sujit's own account of his interview with David:

The year was 1979. One year after getting my bachelor's in physics and computer science, I was ready to conquer the world of astrophysics. After having just moved to Southern California from New York City, I decided to take a temporary job departing from my field of study—say for just about two weeks—with a recently formed financial software company providing investment accounting to portfolio managers.

Remember, this was the '70s and such automated, computerized solutions were almost unheard of back then. This was a state-of-the-art company, utilizing state-of-the-art technology and talent. Besides this, the office also happened to be immediately behind my apartment. What more could I ask for?

The interview is one for the books. The position was for a FORTRAN programmer. That I could do quite well. The subject of the programming was investments and their related financial calculations. To call my understanding of this subject back then

Home of Wismer Associates, Inc. (circa 1986).

as 'clueless' would be overstating my knowledge in the area.

Inevitably, during the first interview which was with the founder of the company, Dr. David A. Wismer, author of Introduction to Non-Linear Optimization and a former UCLA professor in the field, I was asked, "What do you know about bonds?"

Believing I had already impressed him with my technical programming knowledge, I didn't want to disappoint him in the area of investments. Before I could offer a somewhat plausible, effective answer consisting of coupon rates and maturity date facts, I heard myself blurt out, "I think Sean Connery was the best!"

Surely having never heard such a response before, Dr. Wismer laughed . . . however, with a slight wincing of the eyebrows that said, "Did he just say that?"

I quickly followed up my Freudian slip with a full admission of my lack of knowledge in the area of investments. Needless to say, the manager of the development area, who was looking to fill the open programmer position, gave me a thumbs down due to my investments knowledge, or lack thereof. Dr. Wismer, however, decided to take a chance with me and hired me anyway.

And here's the punch line—my temporary, two-week job turned into a 24-year career ending with my eventually taking on Dr. Wismer's role as the head of the company years after his retirement!"

The success of Moneymax led to substantial growth for WAI. They developed three other products for different market niches:

Tradermax was developed for Merrill Lynch Management Services, and was also sold to other prestigious investment bond firms such as Scudder, Stevens & Clark, and Payden & Rygel.

Cashmax was developed for Standard Oil of Ohio, and later sold to Newmont Mining Company and other such companies.

Pensionmax, a pension fund management system, was sold to states and counties,

including Arizona, West Virginia, and Orange County.

Moneymax was by far the most successful of all the products. It became the company's growth engine and was installed in many city, county, and state treasuries throughout the United States. Initially, it was leased to customers with access via a timeshared computer

at CSC. With this arrangement, WAI became CSC's largest customer. This was a wise strategy, as it sustained WAI cash flow during periods of slow sales.

Wismer Series 2 was the last product developed by WAI. It was the firm's most sophisticated investment management product and was successfully marketed to the savings and loan industry long before the industry's well-publicized problems in the late 1980s and 1990s.

David eventually transferred all data processing from CSC to a new WAI computer center in Canoga Park. His father, who had invested David's mother's teaching paychecks in blue-chip stocks throughout the years, loaned him the money to purchase the required computer equipment. Later, the loan was forgiven—along with a second six-figure loan that had enabled David and Mary Anne to buy their house in the Palo Alto area.

Regarding his father, David wrote, "I was always deeply appreciative of Dad's generosity and have tried to adopt his mindset as my own in dealing with family and friends."

With so many customers, David started a user group called the Wismer Investment Systems (WISE) Users Group. His good friend Ray Wells became president of this organization, which helped instill the value of WAI software in municipalities and corporations throughout America.

By 1985, a decade after founding WAI, David could see that the market was changing. New business was harder to obtain and was often less profitable. More customization was required, yet customers usually couldn't provide clear specifications for the costly changes they wanted. Consequently, David began to think about selling his company—even though he was only forty-seven years old and had no interest in retiring.

news

A Computer System For Maximizing Return From Investment Decisions

August 1977

FIRST ISSUE

With this issue of the MONEYMAX Newsletter, we are beginning a series to be published periodically for clients and other money-market portfolio managers. The Newsletter will contain new developments, plans for new enhancements, new client profiles, occasional case studies, and other items of current interest. Through this means we hope to keep you informed and also solicit your constructive comments and ideas.

PROGRAM TO DATE

MONEYMAX was originally developed over a 2½ year period by Wismer Associates, Inc., in conjunction with the Treasurer's Office in Orange County, California. Bob Citron, dynamic Orange County Tax Collector-Treasurer, manages a treasury portfolio of over $470 million in short term investments. This initial development was completed in May 1975 and MONEYMAX was first introduced for general use at the California County Treasurers' Association annual meeting in Anaheim, California in June 1975.

During the first year three additional MONEYMAX systems were installed in California County Treasuries. These Treasuries were:

San Francisco City/County, California
Thomas C. Scanlon, Treasurer
Installed: December 1975: $350 million Average Daily Balance

Ventura County, California
Robert G. Branch, Treasurer-Tax Collector
Installed: January 1976: $100 million Average Daily Balance

San Diego County, California
Delavan J. Dickson, County Treasurer
Installed: April 1976: $300 million Average Daily Balance

These early users represent a total of over 6½ years of operation with the system.

More recently, a burst of additional installations has taken place. These are characterized by expansion of the application to State Treasuries, City Treasuries, and smaller County Treasuries including:

State of Arizona
Bartlett S. Fleming, State Treasurer
$200 million ADB
Installed: November, 1976

Sonoma County, California
Mabel Strong, Treas.-Tax Coll.
$45 million ADB
Installed: January, 1977

City of Los Angeles, California
Robert M. Odell Jr., City Treasurer
$400 million ADB
Installed: March, 1977

Santa Cruz County, California
William P. Murphy, Treas.-Tax Coll.
$35 million ADB
Installed: March, 1977

City of San Diego, California
Eunice E. Winston, City Treasurer
$120 million ADB

Marin County, California
Stanley J. Fontez, Treas.-Tax Coll.
$45 million ADB
Installed: January, 1977

Montgomery County, Maryland
Albert W. Gault, Dir. of Finance
$100 million ADB
Installed: February, 1977

Monterey County, California
Orville N. Molmen, Treas.-Tax Coll.
$60 million ADB
Installed: March, 1977

State of Michigan
Allison Green, State Treasurer
$400 million ADB
Installed: May, 1977

State of Washington
Robert S. O'Brien, State Treasurer
$500 million ADB

About this same time, Broadview Associates, a firm that brokered acquisitions of financial management companies, approached him. With the help of this firm, he became acquainted with a British company called SCI (not the SCI in Palo Alto that had previously employed him). After reviewing all the books, SCI offered to buy WAI for cash. David gladly accepted the offer.

During the contract signing meeting that was held in a Broadview Associates office in Fort Lee, New Jersey, the principals of SCI reneged on their previous offer and proposed a new, lower price. Their justification for this last minute change was that, since WAI used the cash accounting method rather than the more common accrual method, they could not accurately size already-accrued expenses.

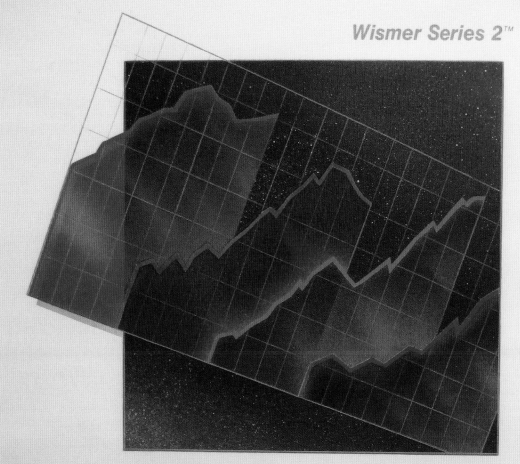

Their cruel bait-and-switch ploy left David feeling shocked and betrayed. SCI had been aware of WAI's accounting method for weeks! He refused to sell at the lower price, so the meeting with SCI was a short one.

Fortunately, Bernie Goldstein, the owner and founder of Broadview Associates, rescued David when he picked up the telephone and called his good friend Jim Mann—President, Chairman, and CEO of SunGard Data Systems. These men knew each other from previous employment at IBM.

After Bernie explained the situation, Jim drove from his office in Wayne, Pennsylvania, that very afternoon—a distance of more than 100 miles. About an hour after midnight, Jim and David concluded negotiations to have SunGard acquire WAI. The deal called for cash and stock up front, plus a bonus to be paid if certain growth milestones were met after three years. To celebrate the agreement, they both ate the tuna salad sandwiches that had been brought in earlier for the SCI deal!

As it turned out, WAI was the first of more than 100 acquisitions SunGard has executed since 1986. David became the SunGard spokesman for promoting such acquisitions, and the Wismer contract became the model for many subsequent acquisitions.

Eventually, David was asked to become CEO of SunGard Financial Systems—a SunGard company comprising WAI and four other acquisitions. His new company had 450 employees, a $100 million revenue stream, and required a totally different management style. David found this work to be much more stressful and less enjoyable than it had been when he was building WAI. Furthermore, he felt guilty that he could not spend more time with his former coworkers.

From left to right: Ralph Wong, manager of Wismer Computer Center; Jim Mann, CEO of SunGard Data Systems; David Wismer; Sujit Pal (circa 1990).

Securities Processing and Investment Support Systems.

Providing Tomorrow's Solutions... Today.

SUNGARD
FINANCIAL SYSTEMS

Nevertheless, David worked hard in his new position and grew the business. After developing several new products and acquiring several more companies, he believed he was at the very apex of his career.

But in October of 1993, he had a surprise meeting with Jim Mann that abruptly ended his career at SunGard. They met at the United Airlines Red Carpet Club in the Los Angeles Airport, where Jim claimed that David was spending too much time on outside interests and fired him. He had already hired David's replacement.

To this day, David is not sure of the real reason why Jim let him go—the excuse given was plainly not true. Sadly, such things occur all too often in corporate America because of personalities and politics.

But at least David was treated well during the transition period that followed. He was given a part-time position for thirty months, paid a significant salary, and permitted to keep his office in a building that he still owned but leased to SunGard. His new assignment was to assist with the transition. Even after he left SunGard for good on October 1, 1996, he was still invited to attend the annual President's Club event that recognized top sales executives. Remarkably, David does not harbor any bad feelings or grudges about his time with SunGard.

Still, this was a traumatic event in David's life. His family, his friends, and the people he had worked with were there to help him though. A letter David received from his son and one he received from a long-time friend and employee are shown on the next two pages.

With many tribulations in life, when a door closes, the Lord opens another one. With God's help, a humble man can turn an apparent failure into a golden opportunity for achievement and growth. After leaving Sun-Gard, David volunteered to act as vice president of advancement at The Master's College[3]—where his daughter Jennifer was a student. He was on the school's board of directors at the time. While in this position, he increased enrollment by a hundred students, which significantly helped the college financially. He also implemented an innovative work-study program that allowed students to work up to twenty hours a week in jobs on campus or in the community of Santa Clarita, California. This program is an important part of student recruiting and financial aid to this day. David did all this without pay.

David also got involved in a tragic situation affecting his mother. After David's father died in 1987, she had moved to Thousand Oaks, California, to be closer to David. She paid $100,000 to stay in a retirement home called La Serena. The second year she was there, the owner of La Serena—Pacific Homes—declared bankruptcy, so La Serena was taken over by Security Pacific Bank. The bank planned to evict all the residents and put the facility up for sale at an auction.

David stepped in and was able to delay the eviction while he attempted to solicit friendly buyers willing to retain the home as a retirement community. After gaining the cooperation of the residents to cut expenses, he helped facilitate sale of the property to an automobile dealer named Paul Rusnak, who renamed the home Castle Hill Retirement Village and made many improvements.

October 26, 1993

Dear Dad:

I can only imagine how you are feeling right now. When you told me about your circumstances at Wismer, I began to think about the years that it took to build that. At first I was angry. The more I thought about it, the more I understood that God tests us to see whether we will trust Him. I am very excited for you. SunGard is a mere glimpse of eternity. I know the transition will be bittersweet and I don't want to trivialize that. I will continue to pray for you and will always be here for you should you ever need anything.

You have always encouraged me. I hope now I can encourage you. I am encouraged about what the Lord has in store for you. Because of your wisdom and insight, I am confident that God will use you in a mighty way to glorify Him. I am also confident that as He reveals what it is that He wants you to do, that you will find more joy in it than you could possibly have at SunGard. It is sort of funny as I think about the things that mom said in Colorado (and continues to say) about you and your future. We all laughed, but she had a view of the "big picture." We all have great confidence in you. I simply cannot believe that this has all transpired at random. I know God did this for a reason. That reason remains to be seen, but He has chosen you for something.

I am so proud of you dad. I thank you for your constant support, love, provision and care. I can never repay that. You probably can relate to that as you think about your relationship to grandma and grandpa. I love you because of who you are. You mirror the humility, strength in uncertainty, love, gentleness, and integrity that Christ represents in His word.

Love always,
Dave

October 26, 1993

Dear Dr. Wismer

Just wanted to drop you a note to express my appreciation for your leadership over the last 20 years, 12 of which I have benefited from tremendously. Sad and uneasy as we are by the turn of events in the last few days, we do have much to be thankful for. Those with whom I have spoken, and all would agree, think of you as a friend and mentor as well as a great leader, and in our minds you will always be the father of the company.

It was your entrepreneurship that brought us employment and the many benefits we enjoy, of course, but beyond that I've always respected your personal integrity and character. Honesty in compensation to employees has been above reproach, and a high standard of professionalism and decorum has been both engendered and demonstrated under your leadership. Beyond that, your good common sense, keen judgment, and exceptional tact and diplomacy in facing a wide variety of difficult situations has been remarkable. You always seem to know what to say, in a way that puts everyone at ease.

I appreciate also the personal warmth and respect you have shown to your subordinates, never acting high and mighty or dictatorial, but instead being friendly and genuinely interested in each of us. You've never seemed too busy to talk to any of us, and I think you set a great example as a conversationalist, both as a good listener and communicator, keeping even (rare) disagreements on a positive, respectful note. I've appreciated also your gift of visualizing achievement in others and looking for opportunities to maximize their potential.

These are traits that may not necessarily advance the bottom line, but are extremely valuable personal qualities that have commanded the respect and admiration of all us who have had the privilege of working under you. It may seem now according to the proverb that "virtue is its own punishment," but I hope instead that the coming days will provide new avenues of personal satisfaction for you, maybe in ways only God knows. In the meantime, thank you again, sincerely, for all you have done for us in both deed and example these may years.

Gratefully,
David F. Coppedge

From the website of Castle Hill Retirement Village (2008).

Years later, the California Department of Social Services successfully sued Pacific Homes and refunded the remaining deposits owed to all the residents. By keeping the residents together and delaying eviction, David was directly responsible for this happy ending to an otherwise tragic event. David's mother continued to live there until her death in 2003 at age 103.

In January of 1992, David and Mary Anne were invited to accompany their son David and his wife Jill to Colorado Springs for a job interview. Young David had developed a great fondness for Pikes Peak Country during an earlier vacation and wanted his parents to see it. After the interview, the four took a tour of the area with a real estate broker to get a feeling for the residential communities that might be suitable for David and Jill.

When they finished, David asked the broker if there were any vacant lots available on which to build a retirement home for him and Mary Anne in case the kids decided to move. He had something like five acres in mind—which was a huge step up from his quarter-acre lot in California! The broker did not deal in undeveloped real estate, so she asked another broker, John Cassiani, to call David the next morning.

John took the party to see Turkey Creek Ranch, located south of Colorado Springs near Fort Carson, and Shamrock Ranch—all

2,970 acres of it! The asking price for Shamrock Ranch was a mere $10 million!

The Wismer party laughed all the way home over the humor of the incident. But young David was not offered the job, so they all stopped thinking about Colorado Springs.

Later that same year—in November—John Cassiani called David to see if he would be interested in joining a land development venture. The land involved was the Shamrock Ranch. Ed Pendleton was about to lose it to A.J. Miller, who had bailed him out with a $2.42 million loan when Mark McLaughlin had foreclosed on the ranch nearly 18 months earlier. Ed needed to pay Mr. Miller $5 million in order to pay off his note so he could keep the ranch. Because he was so highly leveraged, he could not come up with the cash himself— so he formed a land development venture that would generate the $5 million and maintain his ownership, at least partially. The sales brochure developed for the sale of both the Shamrock Ranch and the Bar-X Ranch is shown on the next five pages.

Since David had visited the ranch only ten months earlier, he knew the $5 million price tag was reasonable. So he decided to join the venture. Besides Ed Pendleton, Jack Vickers III was also involved. David's brief encounters with Jack left him with the impression that the man could be trusted, so Jack eventually became the general partner of Shamrock Investments, LLC, established in January of 1993.

According to the deal they struck, the partners would put up the $5 million. After two years they would be paid regular interest payments, and then they would receive a portion of the proceeds when the land was developed. Jack found other financing for the Bar-X, so David was not involved in that transaction.

Featuring

4810 Acres • Six Bedroom Estate Home • Guest Cottage • Estate Manager's Residence • Equestrian Center • Indoor Arena

Shamrock Estate

BLACK FOREST, COLORADO

Shamrock Estate

A 4,810 acre alpine estate & equestrian center located between Denver & Colorado Springs

Nestled in the foothills

against the base of the Rocky Mountains is a massive forest land. . . so densely green with towering native pine, spruce and fir, that it is called the Black Forest. At 7,500 feet above sea level, Black Forest is nearly a thousand feet above nearby Colorado Springs.

Broad meadows cut wide emerald swathes through the deeper greens of the forest. . . in fall, groves of Aspen, willow and cottonwood take on the vivid colors of the season. Wild strawberries, Bluebells, Columbine, Indian paintbrush and dozens more varieties of native vegetation carpet the landscape from early spring to autumn. A winter snow transforms Black Forest into a sparkling wonderland.

Water is plentiful here, fed by abundant underground aquifers that assure the land an ample supply for years to come.

Wildlife abounds . . . deer and elk . . . foxes, raccoons and squirrels share the Shamrock's thousand-acre forests with eagles, owls, quail and pheasant. Spring-fed ponds are a fisherman's paradise, full of trophy-size mountain trout.

Above: Among the towering pines, the country elegance of the Estate Home.

A historic haven

Since the turn of the century, The Shamrock has been a Black Forest landmark. The Allens of Pittsburgh, then publishers of the Saturday Evening Post, were the first to enjoy the beauty of the Shamrock. They built the original estate home in 1904.

Later owned by a prominent Texas oil baron, the Shamrock has a distinguished history as a retreat for Presidents and movie stars alike. Both President Eisenhower and President Johnson were overnight guests at the Shamrock.

Snow scene . . . Shamrock in winter.

in the Black Forest of

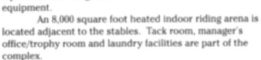

Among the finest equestrian centers in Colorado

Shamrock Estate has been home to World Champion American Saddlebreds. Its Equestrian Center ranks as one of the finest in the state. The thirteen-stall stable is paneled in natural knotty pine, fastidiously maintained by a resident stable manager. The complex is fully equipped with the most modern equestrian handling facilities and equipment.

An 8,000 square foot heated indoor riding arena is located adjacent to the stables. Tack room, manager's office/trophy room and laundry facilities are part of the complex.

All 4,810 acres of the Shamrock are fully fenced, offering expansive pasture land for grazing and exercise area.

Adjoining the Equestrian Center is the two-story, three-bedroom Estate Manager's residence-- ideal as the Stable Master's home or spacious guest accommodations.

Attention to detail and meticulous care have made the Equestrian Complex a crowning jewel to the Shamrock.

The estate home

Just over a knoll, to the west of the Equestrian Center, lies the stately country elegance of the Estate Home. The main residence features six bedrooms, most with private bath. Majestic Pikes Peak is framed by the French-paned windows in the sun room of the master suite. Each bedroom suite features its own private entrance to the forest outside, inviting guests to slip away for an early morning walk and perhaps pause to quietly enjoy the beauty of a white tailed deer at sunrise.

The Great Room of the home is dominated by a massive stone fireplace. Gleaming wooden beams accent the high stucco ceiling . . . finely crafted bay windows and built-in sideboards add warmth and country style to the main living area.

A large, sunny country kitchen opens to a redwood patio, an ideal spot to entertain among the pines. A winding walkway leads to the intimate luxury of the private guest cottage.

The Great Room (above) features a massive stone fireplace and beamed ceilings.

The sunroom of the master suite (left) offers breathtaking views of the Rockies.

Colorado Springs

Unlimited potential for development . . .

To help envision the vast potential of the site, a concept plan has been designed. This concept plan explores the options for development of The Shamrock as a multi-use resort complex.

The meadows that wind through the forest form an ideal setting for an 18-hole championship golf course. Complementing the golf course are a number of other recreational uses such as a golf and country club, hiking and riding trails, a gun club and retail shops. The existing Equestrian Center could be expanded and offered as a unique amenity.

Scenic sites bordering the golf course offer single and multi-family residential development opportunity. With some of the Pikes Peak Region's most affluent and fastest growing neighborhoods within close proximity to Shamrock Estate, the expansion on this luxury homesite theme would seem to be ideal.

...or the ultimate private retreat

For the individual, company or organization seeking a place to escape to the clean air and casual western pace of Colorado, Shamrock Estate represents a retreat . . . a high country haven. The home and grounds are impeccably maintained and ready to enjoy today. The Shamrock is easily accessed from anywhere in the country via the Colorado Springs Municipal Airport (just 15 minutes south) or Denver's Stapleton Airport (45 minutes north via Interstate 25).

Concept Plan

The concept plan shown here has been developed to explore potential resort development.

1 New Equestrian Center
2 Gun Club
3 Golf Club
4 Driving Range
5 Retail Shops
6 Townhomes
7 One-third to one-half acre
   housing clusters
8 Five acre ranch housing

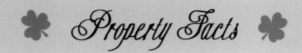

Property Facts

Ten minutes north of Colorado Springs, forty minutes south of Denver

Land & Grounds
- Three individual parcels comprise the Shamrock Estate:
  Shamrock West ....2,280 acres
  Shamrock East ....690 acres
  Bar X Ranch ....1,840 acres
- All parcels are fully fenced
- The Colorado Division of Forestry provides land management support to Shamrock Estate, including forest care and the annual planting of 3,000 new trees
- Forested by Ponderosa Pines, Douglas Fir, Colorado Blue Spruce, willows and aspen
- Wildlife on the forest grounds include deer, elk, fox, eagles, hawks, raccoons, turkeys, pheasants and quail
- Plant life includes wild strawberries and asparagus, chokecherries, apple and crabapple trees, native grasses, oak and kinnikinick
- Wildflowers are abundant; Indian Paintbrush, Bluebells and Columbine are native to the region
- Spring-fed ponds yield trophy-caliber brown, rainbow and cut throat trout

Grounds

Estate Home
- Original structure built in 1904, major renovations in 1980
- 4,300 square feet
- Six bedrooms, recently renovated
- Master suite features sun room, French-paned windows, private entrance and over-sized shower and bathroom
- Fireplaces and separate outside entrances are featured in several of the bedroom suites
- Country kitchen with butler's closet
- Maid's quarters adjoin kitchen
- Outdoor entertaining area with redwood patio
- Massive native stone fireplace in Great Room
- Built-in natural wood sideboards and bay windows
- Beamed ceilings

Estate Home

Guest Cottage
- Two bedrooms, one bath
- Close-by privacy for guests

Estate Manager's Residence
- Two-story, 2,000 square feet
- Three bedrooms, two baths
- Fireplace
- Adjoins Equestrian Center, ideal Stable Master's home
- Fully modern

Estate Manager's Residence

Equestrian Center
- Home of World Champion American Saddlebreds
- Thirteen-stall, knotty-pine paneled stable
- Heated, indoor riding area - 40' x 200'
- Tack room
- Office/trophy room

Stable and Barns

Equestrian Center, Indoor Arena

As it turned out, Jack was unable to attract either investment capital or buyers for any of the land, even though he and his father, who was owner and chairman of the Vickers Oil Company, had previously started development of the prestigious Castle Pines Golf Community just 35 miles north of Shamrock Ranch. After two years, Jack was unable to meet the commitment to pay the interest payments, so Shamrock Investments broke up in 1995. The southern 350 acres of the ranch, which host the houses and barns, were deeded to the Wismers, but the rest of the land was in dispute.

Rather than take the matter to court, David engaged Peacemakers, a Christian legal firm from Billings, Montana, to mediate a settlement.

The settlement bought Ed Pendleton out for cash and divided the rest of the ranch between David and Jack. Jack received 1,000 acres at the corner of Highway 83 and Hodgen Road. David received the remaining 1,946 acres, plus the lease on section 36—the school section. Later on, Jack sold his portion to Classic Communities, who developed it into the prestigious High Forest Ranch subdivision (see map on page 269).

When Shamrock Investments was in force, each of the partners had the opportunity to visit the ranch and stay in the main house. David and Mary Anne did this several times, inviting their children to join them. They came to love and appreciate the beauty, grandeur, and tranquility of the ranch. By the time the settlement was concluded, they had warmed to the idea of actually living there.

When David left SunGard in October of 1996, he and Mary Anne sold their office building in Canoga Park as well as their vacation home in Twin Peaks, California, and headed to their ranch in the Black Forest. Mary Anne was especially anxious to make the move. She was looking for a better lifestyle and also saw the potential for new Christian service opportunities.

When they arrived, they did extensive remodeling of the ranch's main house. During the thirteen-month remodeling period, they lived in the two-room guesthouse just behind the main house. This small house, shown on page 14, was initially built as a playhouse for Maria McKean Allen's daughter, Hope.

While contractors remodeled the house, David engaged in a remodeling project of his own. He converted the chapel—originally built as an icehouse—into a hobby room where he built an extensive HO scale-model railroad. The layout represents the Front Range of the Rocky Mountains along with Shamrock Ranch and the Black Forest during the mid 1900s. Even working ten-hour days, six days a week, the project took him a year and a half to complete. It's operated by direct digital computer control.

Another project that took place soon after the Wismers arrived was the renovation of the older barn (the Allen's Barn No. 2). David noticed that it was literally falling down, so he hired a historic structures renovator named Chuck Murphy to check it out. Chuck told David that the cement blocks that were used to construct the walls of the barn were lacking in binding cement and were therefore disintegrating prematurely. But he also told David that he could fix the barn by using steel beams and supports inside, then removing the north-facing wall, pouring a new footing, and rebuilding the wall block by block. David agreed to have this done, but ended up keeping the steel support structure in place once the barn was fixed in order to prolong the life of this historic structure.

During this remodeling time, all the Wismer children and their families moved to Colorado Springs in rapid succession. David had participated in Southface, a second land development project in Colorado Springs, at the same time he was in the Shamrock Investments partnership, and David III built a house on one of these parcels. He, his wife Jill, and their children live there today. Jennifer and her three girls reside where the Hardestys' Pleasant View Hereford Ranch was once located. Susan and her two children now live in Brentwood, Tennessee.

In 1998, David and Mary Anne Wismer completed full ownership of the Shamrock Ranch when they purchased the school section in the middle of the ranch from the State of Colorado. At last, Shamrock Ranch had a single owner! The large area to the right of the school section is a 700-acre pasture known as the Antelope Pasture because of the resident herd of pronghorn antelope there. This herd can be seen in the photo on page 20.

In 1994, Mrs. Opal Pauline Reese and her daughter Doreene visited the Shamrock. Opal, who retired at the age of ninety, wanted to see the ranch one more time. David and Mary Anne were pleased to receive her and were

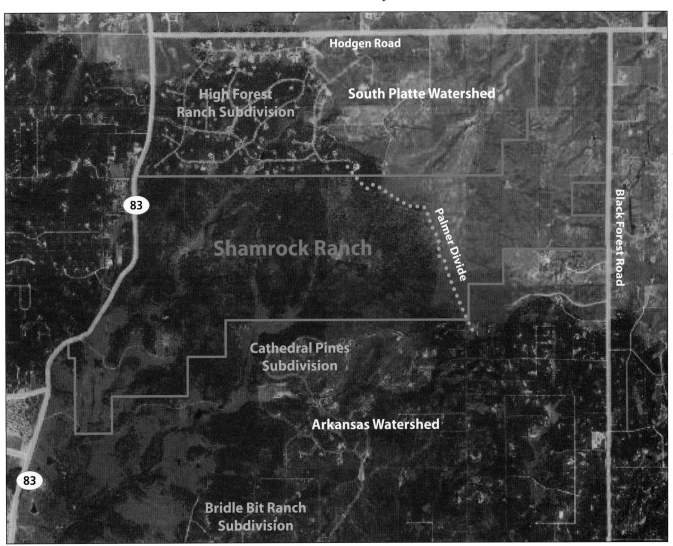

The school section became part of the Shamrock Ranch in 1998.

Pronghorn Antelope

Mrs. Opal Reese in her old room at the Shamrock Ranch with David and Mary Anne Wismer (1994).

delighted to meet the lady who had cared for their house from 1969 to 1990.

While there, Opal reflected on the history of the ranch. One thing she shared is that the main house's southeast-facing bedroom was once set up as a schoolroom for the McLaughlin grandchildren. Before the house was remodeled, the Wismers referred to the room where Opal stayed as "Mrs. Reese's room."

Although David did not grow up on a farm, he became acquainted with horses when he bought each of his daughters a quarter horse. Later on, he bought himself one and took riding lessons. He and his daughter Jennifer rode the trails of San Fernando Valley

The Shamrock Ranch logo adorns the ranch's entrance gate today (2008).

together before they moved to Colorado. Jennifer's mare, Lottiee, made the move to Shamrock Ranch, and David later bought a gelding named Bucky and a mare called Linny for himself and Mary Anne. Lottie has since died, but Bucky and Linny are still around. David also purchased a two-gaited Standardbred driving horse named Traveller to pull a four-wheel surrey made by Amish craftsmen in Indiana.

When Ed Pendleton owned the Shamrock Ranch, he leased the grass on it to Wade Zimmerman, a Colorado cattleman who lived nearby. Wade's cattle grazed on the Shamrock pastures each year from May to October. Upon acquiring the ranch, David continued to lease the grass to Wade. He wanted to learn the cattle business, so Wade allowed him to participate in the operation. Before long, David had learned to help buy and sell, brand

David Wismer riding Linny (2003).

David Wismer driving his Amish-made surrey, pulled by Traveller. Also in the surrey are David Wismer III and Sandy Williams, Traveller's former owner. Note the sleigh bells fastened to Traveller's harness (circa 2000).

Wade Zimmerman rounding up cattle for shipment (2004).

and doctor, hedge on the commodities board, roundup, count and ship, do proper accounting, and repair barbed wire fence. David even programmed some software to help manage the herd. You can probably guess what he called it—*Cattlemax!*

David and Wade became good friends as well as business partners in the cattle business. Eventually Wade moved away, and David had to pull back from day-to-day cattle operations. But he still has cattle on the ranch from May to October each year. The animals that graze here gain up to two pounds a day on the lush, nutritious Shamrock grasses, which include Grama, Buffalo, Wheatgrass, Brome, and others. Thus David has continued the tradition of raising cattle on the Shamrock Ranch, which first started with Calvin Husted and has continued virtually uninterrupted for more than 120 years!

Ultimately, the prediction that Thomas Fitzpatrick made in 1853 (see page 30) has literally been fulfilled here on the Shamrock Ranch: "On the high table lands a . . . nutritious grass affords excellent grazing, and will cause this country to be someday much prized for pastoral purposes."[4]

The cattle business is complex and subject to many variables, such as the cost of fuel for transportation, the cost of corn for the feed lot, and the weather, which affects the amount of grass for grazing. During its life, a steer or heifer can be transported over many miles. The record-high costs of diesel fuel and corn—driven up by ethanol production—in 2008 will undoubtedly have a direct impact on the price of beef in 2009.

The Wismers have also been good stewards of the Shamrock Ranch's forests, which are subject to four types of pests—mountain pine beetles, ips beetles, dwarf mistletoe, and porcupines.

Mountain pine beetles infect the cambium layer of the tree under the bark and transmit a blue-stain fungus that prohibits nutrients from moving upward. Thus the tree fades from the top down and eventually dies. Ips beetles, also known as "engraver beetles," develop under the bark of ponderosa pines, tunneling egg galleries that can kill the trees, causing them to fade from the bottom up. Both beetles normally only attack trees in decline from stress conditions, such as drought. The only remedy is to cut and remove the infected trees. Under severe conditions, such as extended droughts, these beetles can destroy entire forests, as has happened in Winter Park, Colorado, and Lake Arrowhead, California. In order to prevent a beetle infestation, David has a forester survey all the woodlands of Shamrock Ranch every year and remove the infected trees.

Dwarf mistletoe is a parasitic, flowering plant that lodges in the bark of the trees. Each year, its seeds become engorged and explode, shooting new seeds up to fifty feet away where they can attack other trees. The parasite is identifiable when yellow, green, or brownish-green shoots, which form two or three years

New herd of cattle being delivered to the Shamrock Ranch (May, 2008)

Wade Zimmerman, right, with his ranch-hand Jay Peterson (2008).

Notice the Wismer brand—a shamrock over double quarter circles.

Most of these cattle were born in eastern Oregon or Idaho.

after infection, protrude from the infected part of the tree. By the time it's discovered, it's too late to do anything about it except remove the tree. However, it can take up to fifty years before the tree dies, although it can become severely deformed in the process. Infected limbs that become deformed are called "witch's brooms."

Porcupines, which prefer smaller, younger trees, actually eat the bark of ponderosa pines. If they girdle a tree, everything above that point dies from lack of nutrients. Since they usually feed at night, porcupines are difficult to spot and control.

In 2007, David hired a local firm to thin and beautify the forests on Shamrock Ranch. Because this massive project is labor-intensive and expensive, it will take many years to complete the job. However, for the sake of wildfire prevention and the enjoyment of future generations, David considers this money well spent.

Working in the timber of Shamrock Ranch, as many have done for over a hundred

John Psensky, owner of Treemasters, displays a rusted, two-man crosscut saw blade that his crew found while doing forestry work on the Shamrock Ranch (2008).

years, provides the opportunity to find old tools, bottles, and other artifacts. Here is a photograph of John Psensky, owner of Treemasters, with an old, rusted, two-man crosscut saw blade that his crew recently found in the forest.

Another recurring problem that requires attention on Shamrock Ranch is noxious weeds—especially knap weed, mullen, leafy spurge, and various types of thistle. To keep these under control, the Wismers have each pasture sprayed annually.

Management of the ranch is a full-time job—and even more so during the summer months when most of the work needs to be done. Therefore, David was pleased when Jeannette Billings agreed to stay on as Ranch Manager when he formed Wismer Enterprises, Inc. Not only does she take excellent care of the horses and the ranch, she also helps David and Mary Anne in too many ways to count.

With Jeannette's help and Mary Anne's support, David has been able to spend time in various pursuits that benefit many others. Currently he serves in the following positions:

• *Secretary of the Board of Directors of The Master's College and Seminary*
With the motto "For Christ & Scripture," the mission of this college is to empower students for a life of enduring commitment to Christ, biblical fidelity, moral integrity, intellectual growth, and lasting contribution to the Kingdom of God. The Master's Seminary prepares men for the ministry.
• *Member of the Board of Directors of the Master's Academy International*
The Master's Academy International is dedicated to providing resources, services, and materials to training centers in

(currently) 15 countries where seminary graduates are training men to effectively proclaim the Word of God in their own languages.

- *Cofounder (along with Mary Anne, Jennifer, and David III) of the Shamrock Foundation* This foundation is aimed exclusively at funding Christian outreach and Christian educational endeavors.
- *Chairman of the Board of Directors of the Institute for Creation Research (ICR)* ICR is the premier educational and research institution that equips individuals with scientific evidences of the Bible's accuracy and authority regarding creation and the Creator. The evidences that have been uncovered to date, through contemporary scientific methods, cast convincing doubt on the widely-held theories of evolution and an earth that is millions or even billions of years old. ICR scientists have published numerous scholarly papers that support their research. Under David's leadership, ICR has flourished and is presently moving its facilities from California to Dallas, Texas. In 2007, ICR hosted a successful conference called "Back to Genesis" in Colorado Springs that was attended by over 700 people. In July 2008, David helped sponsor an even larger conference called "The Beginning and the End of the Universe," which attracted over 1,500 people and was held in the Colorado Springs' Pikes Peak Center.

The desire of David and Mary Anne Wismer is to use their resources in the service of the Lord. What better way can anyone share the bounties of his or her life's harvest?

David and Mary Anne with the "boys" (right to left)—Titus, Timothy, and Theophilus (Theo) (2006).

EPILOGUE

Like the land, character is prized for the bounty of its harvest.

THEY LOVED THE LAND! Without exception, all those who ever lived on this ranch have loved the land!

Whether labeled as the Evergreen Ranch, the Husted Ranch, the Divide Ranch, the Allen Ranch, or the Shamrock Ranch, this land has been universally treasured as a gem of bounty, beauty, and grandeur. As the most picturesque and pristine ranch in all of Pikes Peak Country, it has become a natural sanctuary of peace, tranquility, and inspiration. To those who have lovingly worked and cared for it, the land has always returned a bounteous harvest. Despite arduous conditions imposed by weather, Native Americans, and the sheer toil of living, the character of these stouthearted inhabitants shines through their inspiring stories of life here on the Shamrock Ranch.

Situated at the very edge of the bustling city General Palmer founded more than a hundred and thirty years ago, and only a short jaunt from the vast and unsullied Air Force Academy woodland that Charles Lindbergh personally championed, Shamrock Ranch is today a refreshing, uplifting, and unique place in Colorado.

Unlike most other ranches, Shamrock Ranch is two-thirds wooded, yet it is virtually adjacent to a modern urban setting. The forest is made up of rustic ponderosa pines with a smattering of rustling aspens and majestic Douglas firs. Dominated by stately Pikes Peak and the beckoning Front Range of the Rocky Mountains, the vistas are stunning from almost anywhere you might be. And there's always serenity, order, and repose to be found in abundance once you enter this secluded refuge—where the only sounds may be the chirping of birds, the howling of coyotes, the bugling of elk, or the rustling of a soothing breeze through the towering trees.

As a working ranch, the land produced some of America's finest cattle for more than ten decades, beginning in the late 1800s. At one time it was used to breed and train an elite collection of champion gaited show horses. Today it's still a working ranch, yet it's also home to a marvelous ecosystem of native wildlife that is protected from the relentless ravishes of modern progress.

But for all its history, beauty, and grandeur, the thing that impressed the authors most when writing this book was the enthusiastic love expressed by all for the land. As one descendant put it, *"You can't take the land out of my blood!"*

For many, life was not easy on the land that is now Shamrock Ranch. Native Americans lost their lives defending it. Homesteaders shed blood, sweat, and tears to own it. Others grew old and weary trying to farm it. In those early days, before electricity and motorized implements were available, ranch life was harsh—like the winter weather that often batters and blankets the lofty Palmer Divide.

But still they came and lived here. Though the ranch was remote and often lonely, they didn't complain. They brought children into the world and mourned the loss of loved ones while faithfully working the land. By persevering and willingly helping each other, they carved out a way of life that is exemplary for us today: *"Back then, it was all about being good neighbors."*

They danced and quilted, cooked and sewed, played pinochle and taught Sunday School, attended church whenever possible, and raised money for a Community Center that still serves the Black Forest. Plowing the land with crude implements pulled by horse teams, they raised some of the finest potatoes

and hay to be found anywhere. They reaped some amazing harvests of timber, crops and livestock, and shared many personal traits and ambitions—including hard work, appreciation for nature and beauty, and a desire to help others. In many ways, they may have actually achieved the inspired vision of Psalm 133: *"Behold, how good and how pleasant it is for brethren to dwell together in unity!"*

During the summer of 1893, Katharine Lee Bates, a poet and professor of English literature from Wellesley College in Massachusetts, visited Pikes Peak Country. It is not known if she ever roamed the Shamrock Ranch land, but it is certain that she looked upon it as she stood atop the summit of Pikes Peak and viewed the breathtaking panorama below her. Remembering her ascent to that famous mountaintop, she later wrote: *"Near the top we had to leave the wagon and go the rest of the way on mules. I was very tired. But when I saw the view, I felt great joy. All the wonder of America seemed displayed there, with the sea-like expanse."* [1]

After descending from that lofty view, she hastily jotted down the draft of a poem in her notebook. Then, in conjunction with teaching at Colorado College that summer, she continued to work on the verse. It was first published on Independence Day 1895 in *The Congregationalist*, a weekly journal. A revised version was printed in the November 19, 1904, edition of the *Boston Evening Transcript*. Then, in 1913, she finally perfected her poem.[2] It conveys, perhaps better than any other literary work, what *character and love of the land* really mean.

O beautiful for spacious skies,
For amber waves of grain,
For purple mountain majesties
Above the fruited plain!
America! America!
God shed His grace on thee,
And crown thy good with brotherhood
From sea to shining sea!

O beautiful for pilgrim feet,
Whose stern impassioned stress
A thoroughfare for freedom beat
Across the wilderness!
America! America!
God mend thine every flaw,
Confirm thy soul in self-control,
Thy liberty in law!

O beautiful for heroes proved
In liberating strife,
Who more than self their country loved,
And mercy more than life!
America! America!
May God thy gold refine,
Till all success be nobleness,
And every gain divine!

O beautiful for patriot dream
That sees beyond the years
Thine alabaster cities gleam,
Undimmed by human tears!
America! America!
God shed His grace on thee,
And crown thy good with brotherhood
From sea to shining sea!

What a fitting prayer Katharine Lee Bates penned for lovers of freedom and the land that supports it! She lived from 1859 to 1929 and was only thirty-four years old when she stood atop Pikes Peak and admired the view of "purple mountain majesties and amber waves of grain . . ." words that have become one of our country's most beloved patriotic songs—"America the Beautiful"—set to music by Samuel A. Ward.

Looking at this beautiful prayer a bit closer, note that the first four lines of each stanza address a different characteristic of this great county, America.

The land—
O beautiful for spacious skies,
    For amber waves of grain,
For purple mountain majesties
    Above the fruited plain!

The people—
O beautiful for pilgrim feet,
    Whose stern impassioned stress
A thoroughfare for freedom beat
    Across the wilderness!

The patriots—
O beautiful for heroes proved
    In liberating strife,
Who more than self their country loved,
    And mercy more than life!

The future dream—
O beautiful for patriot dream
    That sees beyond the years
Thine alabaster cities gleam,
    Undimmed by human tears!

And then, the beseeching prayers for America and her people . . . despite all their flaws, still the last, best hope for mankind—

America! America! God shed His grace on thee,
and crown thy good with brotherhood from sea
to shining sea!
God mend thine every flaw, confirm thy soul in
self-control, thy liberty in law!
May God thy gold refine, till all success be no-
bleness, and every gain divine!

In this book, we have described *the land* with all its beauty and nuances of forests and plains, peaks and valleys, wildlife and flowers.

We have also tried to convey something of the character and fortitude of *the people* who lived and worked in Pikes Peak Country—Native Americans, soldiers, trappers, explorers, gold seekers, farmers, miners, ranchers, cowboys, philanthropists, and businessmen . . . all possessing an abundant love of the land and, as far as we can tell, an appreciation for the freedom they were afforded here.

But what of the patriots? It would be remiss not to acknowledge the part that the military has played in the development of this region. Hosting four major military facilities, including the United States Air Force Academy—one of only four service academies in America—Pikes Peak Country is home for many of those liberty-defending heroes about whom Katharine Lee Bates wrote so long ago.

And what of the future dream—that sees beyond the years thine alabaster cities gleam, undimmed by human tears? This dream may seem extremely remote as we write from our vantage point in the early part of the twenty-first century. But with God all things are possible, and we can pray for a revival in the land that will renew faith in our Creator, increase love and support for human life, and rebuild strong families.

Although life may be easier physically in Pikes Peak Country today because of technology, some modern challenges are just as daunting. In the name of progress, we've lost much of the charm, neighborliness, and refinement of bygone days—all for a more materialistic lifestyle and an ever-coarsening culture. In the name of freedom, we've lost much of the *self-control, nobleness, and brotherhood* for which Katharine Lee Bates prayed—all for a more self-indulgent way of life. As a nation, we're moving farther and farther from the timeless commandments and associated blessings of God. *But we can change—and change we must!*

We close with some memorable words about Shamrock Ranch from one who lived, worked, and worshipped here . . .

"It was and is a ranch that inspires one to give thanks to God for living in America."
—Alvin Eden, Shamrock Ranch Manager*

. . . and also, with a bold prayer of confidence,
"I don't know what the future holds, but I know Who holds the future."
—Anonymous

*As we go to press with this book, Al Eden has gone to his Heavenly home above. We dedicate this chapter, which we think he would have liked, to his memory.

Endnotes

Introduction

1. Judy von Ahlefeldt. *Thunder, Sun and Snow: The History of Colorado's Black Forest.* Colorado Springs: Century One Press, 1979.

2. von Ahlefeldt. *Thunder, Sun and Snow.*

3. von Ahlefeldt. *Thunder, Sun and Snow.*

4. von Ahlefeldt. *Thunder, Sun and Snow.*

5. von Ahlefeldt. *Thunder, Sun and Snow.*

Beginnings

1. *Wikipedia: The Free Encyclopedia* (www.wikipedia.com).

2. Judy von Ahlefeldt. *Thunder, Sun and Snow: The History of Colorado's Black Forest.* Colorado Springs: Century One Press, 1979.

3. von Ahlefeldt. *Thunder, Sun and Snow.*

4. von Ahlefeldt. *Thunder, Sun and Snow.*

5. *Wikipedia.*

6. von Ahlefeldt. *Thunder, Sun and Snow.*

7. *Colorado Springs Gazette* April 6, 2008.

8. *Colorado Springs Gazette* March 30, 2008.

9. *The World Book Encyclopedia* Volume 15. World Book, Childcraft International, Inc., 1979.

10. End of the Oregon Trail Interpretive Center (http://www.endoftheoregontrail.org/wagons.html).

11. *The World Book Encyclopedia* Volume 15.

12. *The World Book Encyclopedia* Volume 15.

13. *Colorado Springs Gazette* March 23, 2008.

14. *The World Book Encyclopedia* Volume 15.

15. *The World Book Encyclopedia* Volume 15.

16. *The World Book Encyclopedia* Volume 15.

17. von Ahlefeldt. *Thunder, Sun and Snow.*

18. *Wikipedia.*

19. von Ahlefeldt. *Thunder, Sun and Snow.*

20. *Wikipedia.*

21. Wayne C. Lee and Howard C. Raynesford. *Trails of the Smoky Hill.* Caldwell, Idaho: The Caxton Printers, LTD., 1980.

22. Lee and Raynesford. *Trails of the Smoky Hill.*

23. Lee and Raynesford. *Trails of the Smoky Hill.*

24. Lee and Raynesford. *Trails of the Smoky Hill.*

25. Lee and Raynesford. *Trails of the Smoky Hill.*

26. Lee and. Raynesford. *Trails of the Smoky Hill.*

27. *Wikipedia.*

28. Margaret Long. *The Smoky Hill Trail.* Denver, Colorado: The W. H. Kistler Stationery Company, 1947.

29. Margaret Long. *The Smoky Hill Trail.*

30. Long. *The Smoky Hill Trail.*

31. Long. *The Smoky Hill Trail.*

32. Lee and Raynesford. *Trails of the Smoky Hill.*

33. Lee and Raynesford. *Trails of the Smoky Hill.*

34. Lee and Raynesford. *Trails of the Smoky Hill.*

35. Lee and Raynesford. *Trails of the Smoky Hill.*

36. Lee and Raynesford. *Trails of the Smoky Hill.*

37. *Wikipedia.*

38. The Homestead Act of 1862 by Richard Pence (http://users.rcn.com/deeds/homestead.htm).

39. Teaching with Documents: The Homestead Act of 1862—from The National Archives (http://www.archives.gov/education/lessons/homestead-act/).

40. *Colorado Springs Gazette* March 30, 2008.

41. Judy von Ahlefeldt. *Thunder, Sun and Snow.*

42. *Wikipedia.*

43. *Wikipedia.*

44. von Ahlefeldt. *Thunder, Sun and Snow.*

The Original Patentees

1. NationalAtlas.gov (http://nationalatlas.gov/articles/boundaries/a_plss.html#top).

2. NationalAtlas.gov.

3. *The Weekly Gazette* September 21, 1878 (see Appendix A).

4. Margaret Long. *The Smoky Hill Trail.* Denver, Colorado: The W. H. Kistler Stationery Company, 1947.

The Colorado Pinery Trust Era

1. *Colorado Springs Gazette* May 29, 2001.

2. *Wikipedia: The Free Encyclopedia* (www.wikipedia.com).

3. *Wikipedia.*

4. *Wikipedia.*

5. *Wikipedia.*

6. *Wikipedia.*

7. Colorado History and Heritage, General William Jackson Palmer by Tom Stockman (http://www.coloradovacation.com/history/colorado-springs-william-palmer.html).

8. *Wikipedia.*

9. *Wikipedia.*

10. Colorado History and Heritage.

11. *Wikipedia.*

12. Colorado History and Heritage.

13. *Wikipedia.*

14. Colorado History and Heritage.

15. Colorado History and Heritage.

16. *Colorado Springs Gazette* May 29, 2001.

17. *Colorado Springs Gazette* May 29, 2001.

18. Judy von Ahlefeldt. *Thunder, Sun and Snow: The History of Colorado's Black Forest.* Colorado Springs: Century One Press, 1979.

19. El Paso County, Colorado Biographies (http://www.co-files.biofiles.us/ElPaso.444-476.html).

20. Pikes Peak Library District Archives, Colorado Springs Company (http://library.ppld.org/specialcollections/manuscriptcollections/mss0073.asp).

21. von Ahlefeldt. *Thunder, Sun and Snow.*

22. von Ahlefeldt. *Thunder, Sun and Snow.*

23. Famous Mineral Localities: The Cripple Creek Mining District: Colorado (http://find-articles.com/p/articles/mi_qa3672/is_200503/ai_n13485990/pg_3).

24. von Ahlefeldt. *Thunder, Sun and Snow.*

The Husted Era

1. *Colorado Springs Gazette* October 5, 1908.

2. El Paso County, Colorado Biographies (http://www.co-files.biofiles.us/ElPaso.444-476.html).

3. El Paso County, Colorado Biographies.

4. El Paso County, Colorado Biographies.

5. El Paso County, Colorado Biographies.

6. *Colorado Springs Sunday Gazette and Telegraph* March 23, 1930.

7. El Paso County, Colorado Biographies.

8. *Colorado Springs Gazette* October 5, 1908.

9. El Paso County, Colorado Biographies.

10. *Colorado Springs Gazette* October 5, 1908.

11. *Colorado Springs Sunday Gazette and Telegraph* March 23, 1930.

12. *Colorado Springs Sunday Gazette and Telegraph* March 23, 1930.

13. *Colorado Springs Sunday Gazette and Telegraph* March 23, 1930.

14. *Colorado Springs Sunday Gazette and Telegraph* March 23, 1930.

15. *Colorado Springs Gazette Telegraph* March 27, 1949.

16. *Colorado Springs Gazette* October 5, 1908.

17. *Colorado Springs Sunday Gazette and Telegraph* March 23, 1930.

18. *Colorado Springs Gazette Telegraph* March 27, 1949.

19. *Colorado Springs Sunday Gazette and Telegraph* March 23, 1930.

20. *Colorado Springs Gazette* October 5, 1908.

21. Famous Mineral Localities: The Cripple Creek Mining District: Colorado (http://find-articles. com/p/articles/mi_qa3672/is_200503/ai_n13485990/pg_3).

22. *Wikipedia: The Free Encyclopedia* (www.wikipedia.com).

23. "Robert 'Bob' Womack of Colorado," by Joyce and Linda Wommack (www.womacknet.com/features/bobwomack.html).

24. The Gold Belt Tour—Byway History (http://www.goldbeltbyway.com/history.htm).

25. *Wikipedia.*

26. "Robert 'Bob' Womack," by Wommack.

27. *Wikipedia.*

28. *Wikipedia.*

29. *Wikipedia.*

30. The Gold Belt Tour—Byway History.

31. The Cripple Creek Gold Boom, from *The Westside: An Introduction to its History and Architecture.* A publication by the City of Colorado Springs (http://www.springsgov. com/units/ planning/Historic/Docs/Westside/part3.pdf).

32. Margaret Long. *The Smoky Hill Trail.* Denver, Colorado: The W. H. Kistler Stationery Company, 1947.

33. *Colorado Springs Gazette Telegraph* March 27, 1949.

34. *Colorado Springs Gazette* October 5, 1908.

35. Postcard from The Husted House Bed and Breakfast.

36. *Colorado Springs Gazette* October 5, 1908.

37. *Colorado Springs Gazette* October 5, 1908.

The Benjamin C. Allen Era

1. George Mifflin Wharton (http://www. wharton.freeservers.com/georgemifflin.html).

2. *Wikipedia: The Free Encyclopedia* (www.wikipedia.com).

3. *Wikipedia.*

4. *Wikipedia.*

5. *Wikipedia.*

6. *Wikipedia.*

7. *Wikipedia.*

8. *Wikipedia.*

9. Dr. James W. Hilty. *Talamore at Oak Terrace.*

10. *Wikipedia.*

11. Hilty. *Talamore at Oak Terrace.*

12. *Wikipedia.*

13. www.modern-woodmen.org/Public/ AboutUs/History/

14. Marshall Sprague. *El Paso Club—A Century of Friendship—1877-1977.* Colorado Springs, 1976.

15. Sprague. *El Paso Club.*

16. Sprague. *El Paso Club.*

17. Sprague. *El Paso Club.*

18. Sprague. *El Paso Club.*

19. Elena Bertozzi-Villa. *Broadmoor Memories: The History of the Broadmoor.* Pictorial Histories Publishing Company, Inc., 2003.

20. Bertozzi-Villa. *Broadmoor Memories.*

21. Bertozzi-Villa. *Broadmoor Memories.*

22. Bertozzi-Villa. *Broadmoor Memories.*

23. Bertozzi-Villa. *Broadmoor Memories.*

24. Bertozzi-Villa. *Broadmoor Memories.*

25. Bertozzi-Villa. *Broadmoor Memories.*

26. Famous Mineral Localities: The Cripple Creek Mining District: Colorado (http:// findarticles. com/p/articles/mi_qa3672/is_ 200503/ai_n13485990/pg_3).

27. Bertozzi-Villa. *Broadmoor Memories.*

28. Elaine Freed and David Barber. *Historic Sites & Structures: El Paso County, Colorado.* Colorado Springs, 1977.

29. Jenny Karber "Every brick, shingle in Chapel of our Savior was once part of 80-room mansion on property." *The Cheyenne Edition.* Colorado Springs, Colorado: November 11, 2005.

30. Hilty. *Talamore at Oak Terrace.*

31. Hilty. *Talamore at Oak Terrace.*

32. Hilty. *Talamore at Oak Terrace.*

33. Hilty. *Talamore at Oak Terrace.*

34. Hilty. *Talamore at Oak Terrace.*

35. Bertozzi-Villa. *Broadmoor Memories.*

36. Susan Shipman. *Tutt & Penrose: A Golden Partnership* (http://www.cripplecreekhistory. com/tutt_penrose_bio.htm).

37. "Spencer Penrose." Gilpin County News Online Edition (http://www.gilpincountynews. com/ 20070628/spencer_penrose.htm).

38. Kennecott Utah Copper website (http://www.kennecott.com/).

39. Shipman. *Tutt & Penrose.*

40. "Spencer Penrose." Gilpin County News.

41. The Broadmoor Hotel and Resort website (http://www.broadmoor.com/five-star-hotel.php).

42. *Wikipedia.*

43. Thomas J. Noel. *Riding High: Colorado Ranchers and 100 Years of the National Western Stock Show.* Golden, Colorado: Fulcrum Publishing, 1979.

44. History of the American Field Service in France, Appendix J (http://net.lib.byu.edu/estu/wwi/memoir/AFShist/AFS3j.htm).

45. Hilty. *Talamore at Oak Terrace.*

46. *Wikipedia.*

The Maria McKean Allen Era

1. Penn Biographies (www.archives.upenn.edu/histy/people/1800s/mcgoodwin_robt.html).

2. Jenny Karber "Every brick, shingle in Chapel of our Savior was once part of 80-room mansion on property." *The Cheyenne Edition.* Colorado Springs, Colorado: November 11, 2005.

3. Elaine Freed and David Barber. *Historic Sites & Structures: El Paso County, Colorado.* Colorado Springs, 1977.

4. Karber. "Every brick, shingle."

5. Karber. "Every brick, shingle."

6. Karber. "Every brick, shingle."

7. Karber. "Every brick, shingle."

8. Pennsylvania Academy for the Fine Arts website (http://www.pafa.org/paintingsPreview.jsp?id=8875&currentCount=4).

9. Karber. "Every brick, shingle."

10. El Pomar Foundation website (http://www.elpomar.org/ page.asp?pageid=0|5&id=0|about_el_pomar).

11. *Wikipedia: The Free Encyclopedia* (www.wikipedia.com).

12. Karber. "Every brick, shingle."

The Wharton Allen Era

1. Marshall Sprague. *El Paso Club—A Century of Friendship—1877-1977.* Colorado Springs, 1976.

2. Sprague. *El Paso Club.*

3. Sprague. *El Paso Club.*

4. Sprague. *El Paso Club.*

5. *Wikipedia: The Free Encyclopedia* (www.wikipedia.com).

Allen Ranch Employees and Tenants

1. *Wikipedia, The Free Encyclopedia* (www.wikipedia.com)

2. Juanita L. and John P. Breckenridge. *El Paso County Heritage.* Dallas, Texas: Curtis Media Corporation, 1985.

3. Lewis-Palmer School District #38 (http://lewispalmer.org/).

4. Claire Walter. "The Broadmoor at 90." Edible Front Range/Spring 2008 website on *Wikipedia.*

The McLaughlin Era

1. The Handbook of Texas Online (www.tshaonline.org/handbook/online/).

2. The Handbook of Texas Online.

3. The Handbook of Texas Online.

4. The Handbook of Texas Online.

5. The Handbook of Texas Online.

6. *Wikipedia: The Free Encyclopedia* (www.wikipedia.com).

7. The Handbook of Texas Online.

8. *Snyder Daily News* February 19, 2004.

9. *Snyder Daily News* February 19, 2004.

10. *Wikipedia.*

11. The Handbook of Texas Online.

12. *Wikipedia.*

13. *Wikipedia.*

14. *Wikipedia.*

15. George V. Fagan. *Air Force Academy Heritage: The Early Years.* Golden, Colorado: Fulcrum Publishing, 2006.

16. *Wikipedia.*

17. Fagan. *Air Force Academy Heritage.*

18. Fagan. *Air Force Academy Heritage.*

19. Fagan. *Air Force Academy Heritage.*

20. Fagan. *Air Force Academy Heritage.*

21. Fagan. *Air Force Academy Heritage.*

22. *Wikipedia.*

23. Fagan. *Air Force Academy Heritage.*

24. Fagan. *Air Force Academy Heritage.*

25. Fagan. *Air Force Academy Heritage.*

26. *Wikipedia.*

27. *Colorado Springs Sun* July 30, 1975.

28. *Colorado Springs Sun* 1973.

29. ZoomInfo website (http://www.zoominfo.com/Search/PersonDetail.aspx?PersonID=169403228).

30. El Pomar Foundation (http://www.elpomar.org/page.asp?pageid=0|4|138&id=0|ackerman_fund).

31. Edd Hayes website (http://www.eddhayes.com/jasper_ackerman.html).

32. *Wikipedia.*

33. *Wikipedia.*

34. The Internet Movie Database (http://www.imdb.com/title/tt0040370/awards)

35. *Colorado Springs Sun* July 30, 1975.

36. *Snyder Daily News* February 19, 2004.

McLaughlin's Employees and Neighbors

1. *The Free Press* – Colorado Springs' Own Newspaper.

2. *Wikipedia: The Free Encyclopedia* (www.wikipedia.com).

3. John F. Kennedy Presidential Library and Museum—Historical Resources (www.jfklibrary.org).

4. *Wikipedia.*

5. *Colorado Springs Gazette* July 3, 2006.

6. *Colorado Springs Gazette* July 3, 2006.

7. *Colorado Springs Gazette* July 3, 2006.

8. www.roundupforautism.com/robert_norris_bio.htm.

9. *Wikipedia.*

10. *Wikipedia.*

11. *Wikipedia.*

12. *Wikipedia.*

13. Marc Eliot. *Jimmy Stewart: A Biography.* New York: Harmony Books, 2006.

14. Eliot. *Jimmy Stewart.*

15. Eliot. *Jimmy Stewart.*

16. www.starsummary.com.

17. Vernon E. Snow. "John Ben Snow" (http://web.syr.edu/~snowshoe/johnbensnow.htm).

The Pendleton Equestrian Era

1. http://ftp.rootsweb.com/pub/usgenweb/ks/sedgwick/bios/wichpion.txt.

2. *Wikipedia: The Free Encyclopedia* (www.wikipedia.com).

3. Robert L. Hilten. *The Hiwassee Story.* 1970.

4. *Wikipedia.*

5. *Wikipedia.*

6. *Wikipedia.*

7. John Kenneth Galbraith. *The Culture of Contentment.* Houghton Mifflin, 1992.

8. *Wikipedia.*

9. *The New York Times* June 19, 1991.

The Wismer Era

1. *Wikipedia: The Free Encyclopedia* (www.wikipedia.com).

2. *Wikipedia.*

3. The Master's College website (http://www.masters.edu/).

4. Judy von Ahlefeldt. *Thunder, Sun and Snow: The History of Colorado's Black Forest.* Colorado Springs: Century One Press, 1979.

Epilogue

1. *Wikipedia: The Free Encyclopedia* (www.wikipedia.com).

2. *Wikipedia.*

"On The Divide"

from *The Weekly Gazette* (Colorado Springs)

September 1878
The Lumber Districts—Lumber Mills—Agriculture—Stock Raising—
Old Settlers—Indian Reminiscences

It was past 3 o'clock, on Monday afternoon last, before we started from Colorado Springs, but striking out as boldly as did Franklin when in search of the North Pole, we took the same direction, but with the Divide as our objective point. The afternoon was decidedly a cold one. One of Colorado's northern zephyrs pierced our very inmost anatomy, causing our teeth to rattle like a castanet and imparting to our nose, ears and hands, a color bordering on sky blue. Of course we had left our gloes at home and were therefore entirely at the mercy of Old Boreas. We pressed on, however, and finally at eight o'clock p.m. reached Husted and Sloan's saw mills, instead of Commissioner Husted's residence, of which we were in search. Upon finding that the afore3said gentleman lived some two miles from the mill and that the road lading to his house was through the timber we were only too glad to accept the invitation of Mr. Slan to spend the night at the mill. While our supper was being prepared we "thawed out" over a 12x15 box stove, finishing the process soon after with a cup of coffee.

A good night's rest put us in excellent order, and after breakfast we took a look at the mill and its surroundings. It is situated six miles east of Husted's station, in the midst of the timber. A portable engine and boiler of 20 horse power furnishes the power by which it is run. The machinery now in use consists of a single saw, an edger and a planer. The capacity of the mill is 8,000 feet per day, and the force necessary to run it is ten men about the mill and six loggers. Fifteen yoke of cattle are used in hauling the logs, and four four-horse teams in carrying the lumber to the railroad. The firm are at present at work on contracts for the Denver and Rio Grande Railway. There is a good demand for the lumber at the mill at $14 per 1,000. Mr. Sloan, to whom we are indebted for courteous attentions, superintends in person the workings of the establishment.

Taking a trail through the timber we made our way to the residence of C.R. Husted, Esq., whose reception tended in every way to make us feel at home. After a short rest, in company with Mr. Husted, we took a ride of some ten miles or more and were surprised and pleased at the flourishing appearance the country presented on every side. It seemed almost impossible to credit the statement that within ten years past the ground over which we were riding had been the scene of struggles with the Indians. We were shown the exact spot where ten years ago, the 4th of this month, two men, Jos. Talbot and Ed. Avis, were killed by the redskins. This occurred at the time of the Indian troubles of '68. Many of the old settlers will recall the "powwow" held that year at Fort Russell, between chiefs of the Cheyennes and Arapahoes and the United States Commissioners. The Indians were all furnished with papers, signed by the peace commissioners, stating that they were peaceable, etc., etc. With these passports they were free to go unmolested, anywhere their inclination led them. At the close of the "powwow" they divided into small bands and scattered themselves throughout the country. With their proverbial curiosity they would walk into a man's house, examine his guns, etc., thence into his corral, where they would take an inventory of his live stock, and were he so much as to remonstrate with them, they would flaunt a dirty paper into his face, signed by the so-called peace commissioner, and stating that they were known to be peaceable and law abiding Indians. This continued until the 1st of September, 1868. Then, as if by a preconcerted arrangement, from Cheyenne on the North to the Raton mountains on the South; from the rocky mountains on the West to Kansas on the East, there was a general uprising of the Indians. They confined themselves principally to "running off" stock, but many a poor settler was short down by the wretches, while bravely attempting to defend his family and property. And these same Indians are the acknowledged pets of the United States Government, caressed by the "powers what be," and immortalized by poets. But enough on this score.

During our ride we passed the home of Mr. S.C. Stout, Superintendent of the Colorado Pinery Trust Company's lands. He has several hundred acres of fine farm and pasture lands. But owing to his absence from home we were uynable to gwet any particulars regarding his crops, &c. Continuing our ride for about a mile, we came to the ranch owned by Robert Donnelly, a former sheriff of El Paso county. This ranch is situated on the site of the old Bassett mill. Lying, as it does, within a valley, for agricultural purposes it is admirable. He has 320 acres of land—all enclosed. From thirty acres he has cut over forty tons of excellent hay. Five acres are devoted to oats, and over twenty-five to potatoes. Notwithstanding the fact that the flood last spring inundated the meadows and fields, and leaving thereon great quantities of debris, the grain crop is considered excellent. He also owns eight head of American cattle, besides fifteen milch cows. He makes on an average seventy-five pounds of butter per month.

Leaving the Donnelly ranch we took a trail, leading through the timber, for Mr. Husted's place. On the way we passed the supposed wintering quarters of Lieut. Pike and party—used by them at the time of their first expedition to Colorado. Two miles further on we come to the house where dinner awaits us. After dinner we re-saddle our horses and start for the northern side of the divide. Here we come upon G.W. Phillips' ranch—adjoining Mr. Husten's place. He has 160 acres; thirty acres enclosed. He has raised ten acres of potatoes, and fifteen of oats. These last will probably average forty-five bushels to the acre. He has been in the ranch business for three years, and is at present engaged in building a new house.

A short distance to the east we come to T.J. Jesse's place. This contains 160 acres—thirty-five enclosed. He has raised twenty acres of potatoes and four acres of oats. He owns forty-five head of cattle.

Michael McQuade, a rollicking, good-natured representative of the "Ould Sod," owns a ranch some three-quarters of a mile west of Phillips'. This contains 160 acres—100 enclosed. He has twelve acres devoted to oats and twelve to potatoes In the line of stock he has

100 head of cattle, four head of American horses and a span of mules.

I.H. Parker is located within a mile of the summit. He has 160 acres—all enclosed; will have fifteen acres of oats and twenty-five of potatoes. He has seventy-five head of cattle and eight head of horses.

J.W. Crowley has 160 acres—sixty enclosed; will raise this year five acres of oats and twenty of potatoes.

G.W. Copeland adjoins Crowley on the east. He has 160 acres, fifty enclosed. Has seven acres in wheat, oats and rye; fifteen acres of potatoes. Good house and barn.

R.H. Harris has 160 acres, seventy enclosed. He planted twelve acres of oats and rye and twenty of potatoes. His herd consists of fifty head of cattle.

Wm. Mulhern is located two miles north of the divide. He has 160 acres, 100 being enclosed; had ten acres of oats and forty of potatoes and owns a few head of cattle.

M. Griffiths has 160 acres, fifty enclosed, twelve acres of wheat and oats, fifteen acres of potatoes, and some twenty head of cattle.

Finishing our tour among the ranches we "struck across" for Blakeley's Mill. Upon reaching the mill we found it to be in full operation. It is at present under the superintendence of Mr. E.F. Thomas.

We first visited the boiler room which we found to contain two 2-flue boilers, forty-two inches in diameter and eighteen feet long. An engine of sixty-five horse power furnished the motive power. In the cutting room we found a large circular saw, a Stearns head block and carriage; one of Stearns' improved gang edgers, a lath machine and a shingle machine.

The capacity of the mill is 18,000 feet per day. Thirty-five men are employed here, fourteen about the mill. Six teams are used in logging. The lumber is hauled to Greenland station, some thirteen miles. There is a fair demand for it in Denver markets at $20.00 per 1,000 feet.

Leaving the mill we returned to Mr. Husted's residence, which we have not yet described. It is situated on the old Denver and Santa Fe stage road, some sixteen miles north of Colorado Springs, and includes 700 acres of land, 500 of which are enclosed. The house is one of the finest on the divide and is furnished in a most comfortable manner. Within a few rods of the house are commodious outbuildings and corrals for the accommodation of live stock. He as 110 head of cattle, including twenty milch cows, and twelve horses. He put up this season 100 tons of hay and will harvest seven acres of oats. Three and a half acres are devoted to the raising of potatoes and other vegetables.

Mr. Husted is looked upon as one of the oldest and leading lumber men of this county. In 1866 he bought what was known as the Squirrel creek saw mill, at that time the only mill in the county. The firm name was Perrenoud, Husted & Co., and for two years the business was carried on at this place. In 1868 they moved the mill some six miles west, and within three miles of the present town of Monument. Since that time the mill has be moved to different points throughout the timber.

TENDERFOOT

September 21, 1878

[Note: Edward H. Talbert's name is spelled Talbot in the article—misspelling of names was common at the time.]

Our next visit was to the ranch of Mr. E.H. Talbot, which adjoins that of Commissioner Husten on the south. This place is known to old settlers as "Buzzard's roose," on account of being owned and occupied, some years ago, by one, William Buzzard. It was famous at that time for being the only place where liquors could be obtained between Colorado City and Russelville. It was the rendezvous of all the "characters" of the country, and has been the scene of many a pugilistic encounter. But with the lapse of time, this has passed away and a more respectable or well conducted ranch cannot be found on the divide. Of the 160 acres which composes it 110 are enclosed. Fifteen acres of this are devoted to wheat growing, and the same number to oats. It is at present occupied and carried on by Mr. John Burnside. At the time of our visit, the grain had been harvested, and stood in "shocks," awaiting transportation to the thresher. At the home ranch, about a mile northeast of this place, Mr. Talbot resides. Here he has 200 acres, only 60 being enclosed. His acreage in grain and millet is eleven acres. Of stock he owns thirty head of cattle, fourteen milch cows, and six horses. He will cut this year about sixty tons of hay. The place is well watered by springs and creeks, and in this way the irrigation is made excellent. He expects to harvest forty bushels of wheat to the acre.

TENDERFOOT

February 19, 1956 *Colorado Springs Gazette and Telegraph*

Husted, Now 'Ghost Town,' Soon to Disappear Entirely

Day in, day out, more than 6,000 cars and trucks speed along U.S. Highway 85-87 thru Husted, Colo.

They go thru. They don't stop. There's no reason to stop.

The Branding Iron Café has a "no trespassing" sign. Jones General Store has a few boxes of Wheaties, some Certo; a couple of cans of sauer kraut still on the shelves, but the store is closed. The empty gas pump at Allison's Service reads: this sale, $0.00.

Tourists and truckers speeding thru Husted don't know that in the window of the store there's a plaid calico camel. It's been tossed aside. It gathers dust. It's unwanted. But once upon a time some child hugged that plaid calico camel with tender love.

Husted, once an important stop on the Santa Fe and Rio Grande Railroad, once a bustling center of ranchers and lumbermen, is a dead town—sacrificed on the altar of progress.

Just north will be the main entrance to the Air Force Academy. Here will be a national monument, one of the finest service schools ever conceived by man. Thousands of future officers in the United States Air Force will get their training here. They won't know about Husted, and they won't care. Anymore than they care about Ramona, Glasstown, Frog Hollow, Piedmont, Lihue, Montclar—other towns swallowed up by progress in the Pikes Peak region.

A dozen or so buildings make up Husted today. The Branding Iron Café still has its pan-

eled knotty pine walls, its coffee counter, its sink. Picturesque symbolic menus boasting "we sell soups in pints and quarts" are scattered over the floor. A year ago you could get minced ham and scrambled eggs with toast for 48 cents. The ubiquitous tumble weeds in the back room tell you a different story today.

Scattered along the highway, and down the hollow toward the railroad tracks, are the remnants of Husted—homes, shacks, pigpens, a train station. The telephone instrument is still in at the filling station, but it doesn't ring anymore. Nobody's there.

This was great country. This was Indian country, cattle rustling country, potato country. It didn't appeal to one historian who wrote, with cruel candor, that the land immediately east of Pikes Peak had no charm then and it has no charm now.

Mr. and Mrs. J.C. Kinner will argue that point.

The Kinners are typical pioneer stock. They are bright, lively folks, friendly—and in love with the land which is now being transformed into the U.S,. Air Force Academy. They sold their home at Husted to make way for the academy, and now live in Colorado Springs at 9 S. 8th St.

They're not sorry they had to move, in a sense, yet nostalgia is obvious in their every recollection of the land they love. Their version of the history of Husted is pretty much a series of anecdotes—of the time a girl kidnapped by Indians managed to find her way home by following a scrap paper trail left by her mother, of the 18-inch stone walls of the old fort on the Teachout Ranch, formerly the "old Welty place."

They tell of the time young Clark raced for help on a buckskin pony owned by D. Simpson, and of the later murder of he same Clark by vigilantes, of the picnics held by Ben and Henry Walker, Henry Guise, Dave and Dick Roberts, of the time a prankster put a skull from Dead Man's Canon under the picnic table cloth.

They feel that the Air Force Academy will be a great institution of learning, and that Colorado Springs should be proud of it. Yet, in their reveries, they look back wistfully upon the days when they roamed the wooded mountains west of Husted.

And Husted.

It was never a great city, not even much of a town, according to Mr. and Mrs. Kinney, but it was a likeable place. It once had a grammar school, until the days of consolidated schools made it obsolete. It had a saloon which became a store which became a postoffice, which in turn became a church. Finally the same frame was used to make the present forlorn Branding Iron Café.

Husted, was named after Calvin R, Husted, a prominent pioneer and former county commissioner of el Paso County. In the early days he operated a sawmill in the Black Forest, Many Colorado Springs buildings were constructed from the lumber hauled from the Husted sawmill, hauled with oxen from the Black Forest.

He was a generous man, according to the Kinners. He'd give anyone a grubstake. He fed and clothed passing tramps. And he died in a Colorado Springs poorhouse. His son, Walter E. Husted, died in 1950 at the age of 79.

Kinner's father moved to Denver in 1859. He hauled provisions over Colorado, Wyoming, and New Mexico. Kinner's mother was a second cousin to the famous poet, Eugene Field.

Mrs. Kinner's parents settled in the Monument area in 1864, near Dirty Woman's gulch. The name, they say, came from just that, "a dirty woman, who made butter by tramping the cream with her bare feet."

Kettle Creek, another landmark of the area, got its name from a huge black kettle which either soldiers or early settlers left there. It became a community cooking kettle, and was used by an passing wagon train.

The Kinners at one time owned a portion of what is now the Cathedral Rock Ranch, the heart of the future Air Force Academy. This ranch was first settled by a man named Barnard, and the picturesque rock was a favorite picnic spot for the pioneers.

They had windstorms in those days, too, Mrs. Kinner recalls. In fact, she says one wind blew an entire railroad train off the track near Husted.

Mr. and Mrs. Kinner had three children. A son, John, was a teacher in the Monument school, and died at the age of 37 of polio. Another son, Jerome, teaches in the Colorado Springs schools, and a daughter, Alice, is employed by Shepard's Citations.

The Air Force Academy Construction Agency is planning an orderly and economical program for removal of structures which will not be required for the Air Gore Academy. Headed by Col. James A. Barnett, operations chief, a board will decide which buildings will be retained. It has already been decided that Husted will go.

One of these days demolition crews will begin tearing down the buildings. But they can't tear down memories—like the plaid calico camel in the window.

Acknowledgments

This history could never have been written without the generous assistance, support, and cooperation of numerous people and organizations. Some have shared memories and historical facts; others have provided photographs, articles, sketches, permissions, and guidance. Most importantly, all have donated significant time and encouragement.

The authors wish to extend special thanks to the following for their invaluable contributions:

Adam P. Merilson, General Manager, El Paso Club

All those who contributed relevant information and images in *Wikipedia, the Free Encyclopedia*

Allen Steppler, descendant of the Lou Steppler and William Clark Brown

Alvin Eden, C.T. McLaughlin ranch manager

Amy Brooks, Special Collections Coordinator, Tutt Library, Colorado College

Barbara Katus, Rights and Reproductions, Pennsylvania Academy of the Fine Arts

Beth Bullinger, Director, Wyeth Hurd Gallery

Bill Bridgford, Bridgford Foods, Inc.

Bob Knect, Kansas Historical Society

Bonnie (Hubbell) Devore, daughter of Peggy (Romick) Hubbell

Bonnie Linder, Music Director, Chapel of Our Savior

Connie Jones Pillsbury, descendent of Wm. Henry and Mary Peters McBroom

David A. Wismer, III, son of David and Mary Anne Wismer

David F. Coppedge, former employee, Wismer Associates, Inc.

Debbie and Bob at Tri-Lakes Advertising

Don Whitmore, Chief Title Officer, LandAmerica

Doreene Wiley, daughter of Mrs. Opal (Pauline) Reese

Doris and Tom Baker, Filter Press

Dr. James W. Hilty, Professor of History and Dean of Ambler College at Temple University

Dr. Mary Elizabeth Ruwell, Chief of Archives and Special Collections, United States Air Force Academy McDermott Library, Special Collections

Edd Hayes, Official Texas State Sculptor

Erin J. Edwards, Special Collections Librarian for Acquisitions, Western History and Genealogy, Denver Public Library

Eurelle Eden, wife of C. T. McLaughlin ranch manager

F. W. (Willy) Moreland, C. T. McLaughlin employee

Father Dayle Casey, Rector, Chapel of Our Saviour

Gail Ann Levis, Historian, Modern Woodmen of America Archives

Gaye White, Lion Oil Company

George Nelson Allen Jr., grandson of Benjamin and Maria Allen

Gertrude (Trudy) Pollok, Archive Technician, United States Air Force Academy

Greg Thatcher, member, Cheyenne Mountain Country Club

Howard Battista, contractor who built the Shamrock Ranch horse stables

Iola Geiger, wife of C. T. McLaughlin employee

J. Mark McLaughlin, son of C. T. McLaughlin

J. Ruthven Ryan Jr., grandson of Benjamin and Maria Allen

James Carlson, Assistant Librarian, University of Minnesota, Crookston

Jeanette Billings, Shamrock Ranch Manager

Jeffrey A. Thompson, Publisher, *Saddle & Bridle* Magazine

Jenny Karber, author of a prior article on the Allen Mansion

Jill Lain Weaver, Manager of Public Relations, Modern Woodmen of America

Jim Carnahan, General Manager, Talamore Country Club

John Psensky, owner of Treemasters

Judy von Ahlefeldt, author of *Thunder, Sun and Snow—the History of Colorado's Black Forest*

Kathy Burns, Circulation Manager, *Saddle & Bridle* Magazine

Kati Anderson, Media and Public Relations Manager, National Western Stock Show Association

Kelly Murphy, Research Coordinator, Starsmore Center for Local History, Colorado Springs Pioneers Museum

Louis Pendleton, son of Ed and Beverly Pendleton

Martha Kay Shaw, provider of Village Inn postcard

Marya Allen, granddaughter of Benjamin and Maria Allen

McDermott Library, Special Collections

Meryl Leskovitch, Castle Hill Retirement Village

Mike Betzer, Assistant Vice President and Title Operations Manager, Central Bancorp

Molly Ingram, Director of Communications, St. Mark's School

Nancy R. Miller, The University Archives and Records Center, University of Pennsylvania

Oleta Goodrich, friend of George and Stella Hardesty

Peggy Hubbell, daughter of Joe Romick, an Allen Ranch manager

Peter de la Fuente, grandson of Peter Hurd

Phyllis Bonser, The Lucretia Vaile Museum

R. Thayer Tutt, President, Cheyenne Mountain Country Club

Robert Cheesman, son of Milton C. Cheesman, an Allen Ranch manager

Robin Adair, Community Relations Manager, Lewis-Palmer School District #38

Sam Cheesman, son of Milton C. Cheesman, an Allen Ranch manager

Samuel C. Tease, son of Cameron M. Tease, Maria Allen's chauffeur

Scott Gipson, Vice President and Publisher, Caxton Press/Caxton Printers Ltd.

Sharon DeBartolo Carmack, author and Certified Genealogist

Sujit Pal, former employee, Wismer Associates, Inc.

Susan Koch, descendant of the Lou Steppler and William Clark Brown

Terry Stokka, member of the Black Forest Land Use Committee

The *Colorado Springs Gazette*

The National Park Service

Thomas Barron, son of Archibald and Gloria Barron, C. T. McLaughlin's neighbors

Thomas Joerger, Parish Administrator, Chapel of Our Saviour

Tim Blevins (manager) and the kind and extremely helpful staff of Penrose Public Library, Special Collections, Pikes Peak Library District

Vernon and Georgia Dayhoff, friends of George and Stella Hardesty

Virgil Dean, Kansas Historical Society

Wade Zimmerman, David Wismer's cattle business partner

Willard Miller, C. T. McLaughlin ranch manager

William M. Kurtz, President, El Paso Club

William McCullough, son of Mayor James McCullough

Special thanks to the extremely friendly, competent, and helpful staff of Johnson Books, especially Mira Perrizo, publisher.

And finally, the authors wish to thank their respective wives, Mary Anne Wismer and Sharon Rae Wright, for their enduring patience, constant encouragement, and selfless support.

References

Wikipedia Licenses and Fair Use Rationale

Certain reproductions of photographs, copies of paintings, etc. used in this book were obtained from the English *Wikipedia* website (*Wikipedia, The Free Encyclopedia* at www.wikipedia.com). They are identified below in the order they appear. Credit for authors is given where authors are known. Some reproductions are licensed under the *GNU Free Documentation License* and/or the *Creative Commons Attribution-Share-Alike License*. Others are in the public domain and are taken from the *Wikimedia Commons* (see http://commons.wikimedia.org/wiki/Main_Page).

Any of the images licensed under the *GNU Free Documentation License* and/or the *Creative Commons Attribution-ShareAlike License* may be reproduced under the conditions of their respective licenses, which are documented in the web addresses given below—

For the *GNU Free Documentation License,* see http://en.wikipedia.org/wiki/Wikipedia:Text_of_the_GNU_Free_Documentation_License For the *Creative Commons Attribution-ShareAlike License,* see http://creativecommons.org/licenses/by-sa/3.0/

Beginnings

Digital elevation model relief map of Colorado by the United States Geological Survey, an agency of the United States Department of Interior *(in the public domain)*

The Original Patentees

Map of Louisiana Purchase from an edition of the National Atlas of the United States, a work of the United States Federal Government *(in the public domain)*

Painting of Thomas Jefferson by Charles Willson Peale *(in the public domain)*

Portrait of Henry Dodge from Biographical Directory of the United States Congress *(in the public domain)*

Photograph of John C. Fremont by Mathew Brady *(in the public domain)*

Map of Santa Fe Trail by National Park Service *(in the public domain)*

Photograph of replica of Bent's Old Fort by Sally Pearce of Colorado Department of Transportation *(in the public domain)*

Map of Oregon Trail from *The Ox Team or the Old Oregon Trail 1852-1906* by Ezra Meeker (Fourth Edition 1907), courtesy of the University of Texas Libraries, the University of Texas at Austin *(in the public domain)*

Photograph of prairie schooner replica by B.D.'s World from Monroe, Washington, *licensed under the Creative Commons Attribution ShareAlike 2.0 License*

Engraving of Stephen W. Kearny by Y.B. Welch, expressly for Graham's Magazine; photograph by Peter A. Juley & Son *(in the public domain)*

Photograph of Pikes Peak Gold Seekers from Alpenrose Press *(in the public domain)*

Photograph of American bison by Jack Dykinga, U.S. Department of Agriculture *(in the public domain)*

Map of Kansas Territory from *Cyclopedia of American Government,* Andrew Cunningham McLaughlin and Albert Bushnell Hart, published in 1914 by D. Appleton and Company *(in the public domain)*

Photograph of James Buchanan by Mathew Brady *(in the public domain)*

Photograph of Abraham Lincoln by Alexander Gardner *(in the public domain)*

Photograph of ceremony for driving the golden spike at Promontory Summit, Utah on May 10, 1869 to complete the first transcontinental railroad by Andrew J. Russell *(in the public domain)*

The Colorado Pinerty Trust Era

Photograph of Ulysses S. Grant by Mathew Brady or Levin C. Handy) *(in the public domain)*

The Husted Era

Photograph of Medal of Honor from years 1862 to 1895 a work of the United States Federal Government *(in the public domain)*

Fair use rationale for photograph of General Palmer Statue, modified from the Palmer High School website for *Wikipedia—its primary use is for informational and educational purposes it is a low resolution image no free equivalent is available or could be created that would adequately give the same information reproduction of the image is not believed to limit the copyright owners' rights or profit in any way*

Painting of the *Mayflower in Plymouth Harbor* by William Halsall *(in the public domain)*

The Benjamin C. Allen Era

Photograph of covered wagon by Larry D. Moore, *licensed under the Creative Commons Attribution ShareAlike 2.5 License*

Photograph of Winfield Scott Stratton from the collection of the Western History Department of the Denver Public Library *(in the public domain)*

Photograph of Grover Cleveland from the United States Library of Congress Prints and Photographs Division *(in the public domain)*

Photograph of narrow gauge steam locomotive by Dennis Adams, Federal Highway Administration *(in the public domain)*

The Maria McKean Allen Era

Drawing of British Stamp by Thomas J. Scharf *(in the public domain)*

Painting of Thomas McKean by C. W Schreyleer *(in the public domain)*

Image of Governor Thomas McKean courtesy of The Pennsylvania State Archives *(in the public domain)*

Photograph of Cheyenne Mountain by Fish Cop *(in the public domain)*

Image of Red Cross emblem by unknown author *(in the public domain)*

Declaration of War from the German Empire in 1914 by Wilhelm II (Friedrich Wilhelm Albert Victor von Preußen) *(in the public domain)*

Photograph of World War I trenches from Bishop Museum *(in the public domain)*

The Wharton Allen Era

Fair use rationale for U.S. postage stamp commemorating the cartoon strip *Bringing Up Father*—*its primary use is for informational and educational purposes it is used the illustrate the stamp itself no free equivalent is available or could be created that would adequately give the same information reproduction of the image is not believed to limit the copyright owners' rights or profit in any way*

Allen Ranch Employees and Tenants

Photograph of Major General Emmett "Rosie" O'Donnell by unknown author *(in the public domain)*

Photograph of polo ponies by Rkurrat, *licensed under the GNU Free Documentation License*

Photograph of John F. Kennedy by White House Press Office *(in the public domain)*

The Hardesty/McCullough Era

Photograph of Model A Ford by Douglas Wilkinson for www.RemarkableCars.com *(unrestricted use given)*

Photograph of 1926 Packard Series 243 Touring Car by Lars-Goran Lindgren, *licensed under the GNU Free Documentation License*

Photograph of wild columbine by Ragesoss, *licensed under the GNU Free Documentation License*

Photograph of kerosene lantern by Gnangarra, *licensed under the GNU Free Documentation License*

The McLaughlin Era

Photograph of Hereford bull by Robert Merkel, U.S. Department of Agriculture *(in the public domain)*

Photograph of Harry S. Truman by U.S. Army Signal Corps *(in the public domain)*

Photograph of mixed Angus herd by Poster, *licensed under the Creative Commons Attribution Share-Alike 3.0 License*

Fair use rationale for image of Village Inn logo—*its primary use is for informational and educational purposes it is a low resolution image no free equivalent is available or could be created that would adequately give the same information reproduction of the image is not believed to limit the copyright owners' rights or profit in any way*

McLaughlin's Employees and Neighbors

Photograph of Burkburnett, Texas oilfield by unknown author *(in the public domain)*

Photograph of Rambouillet ram by Cgoodwin, *licensed under the GNU Free Documentation License*

Lion Oil Company logo used by permission of the Lion Oil Company

Map of Colorado Plateau by unknown author *(in the public domain)*

Photograph of Lyndon B. Johnson by Yoichi R. Okamoto, White House Press Office *(in the public domain)*

Photograph of Women Airforce Service Pilots (WASP) with Jackie Cochran in the center by unknown author *(in the public domain)*

Photograph of Angus cow and calf by Dukemeiser *(in the public domain)*

Photograph of Hereford calf by John O'Neill, *licensed under the GNU Free Documentation License*

Photograph of belted Galloway cow by Dirk Ingo Franke, *licensed under the Creative Commons Attribution ShareAlike 2.0 License*

Photograph of Robin Olds from U.S. Air Force *(in the public domain)*

Photograph of Earle E. Partridge from U.S. Air Force *(in the public domain)*

Photograph of Fred Korth from U.S. Navy Historical Center *(in the public domain)*

Photograph of U.S. Air Force Academy cadets from U.S. Air Force *(in the public domain)*

Emblem of U.S. Air Force Academy from U.S. Air Force *(in the public domain)*

Fair use rationale for photograph of George Szell by Carl Van Vechten, available from the U.S. Library of Congress—*its primary use is for informational and educational purposes it is a low resolution image no free equivalent is available or could be created that would adequately give the same information reproduction of the image is not believed to limit the copyright owners' rights or profit in any way*

Photograph of Severance Hall by Einar Einarsson Kvaran, a.k.a. Carptrash, *licensed under the GNU Free Documentation License*

Photograph of Case Western Reserve University campus by Rick Dikeman, *licensed under the GNU Free Documentation License*

Image of U.S. Route 66 sign by SPUI *(in the public domain)*

Map of U.S. Route 66 by English Wikipedia, *licensed under the GNU Free Documentation License*

Photograph of John Wooden by Congressman Brad Sherman's office *(in the public domain)*

Photograph of Los Angeles Memorial Coliseum by upeslases, *licensed under the Creative Commons Attribution ShareAlike 2.0 License*

Photograph of Royce Hall, UCLA by Satyriconi, *licensed under the GNU Free Documentation License*

Photograph of Mario Savio at UC Berkeley in 1966 by unknown photographer, *licensed under the GNU Free Documentation License*

In addition, David A. Wismer gives the following Fair Use Rationale under the principles of copyright law for certain other images reproduced in this book—

The primary use of this book is for informational and educational purposes.

The images reproduced are low resolution images.

No free equivalents are known to be available or could be created with reasonable effort and resources to adequately provide the same information.

Reproduction of these images is not believed to limit the respective copyright owners' rights or profits in any way.

The images that apply to this Fair Use Rationale include—

Earth map of Shamrock Ranch from Google Maps

Map of the Cherokee Trail from *The Smoky Hill Trail* by Margaret Long

Photograph of Packard touring car from *The Making of Modern Michigan* website

Photograph of Model T Ford pickup truck from Motormint Vintage Cars Diecast Collectibles website

Photograph of Lewis Consolidated School

Image of Victrola from the Victor-Victrola Page website

Photograph of Abert's squirrel from the presentation "A Comparison of Abert squirrels, pine squirrels and fox squirrels with respect to life in the cold" by Justina Thorsen

Photograph of Bob Norris from Roundup for Autism website

Photograph of John Ben Snow

Photograph of American Saddlebred horse

United States Equestrian Federation logo

Photographs from *The Hiwassee Story* by Robert L. Hilten

All newspaper articles and images

Index

Abert, John James, 196

Academy Site Selection Board, 175, 176

Ackerman, Jasper, 205

Ackerman, Joseph, 183, 184

Adams, John, 71

Aeron (dog), 104; photo of, 104

Air Force Academy Construction Agency, 181, 291

Air Force Academy Foundation, 180–181

Air Force Historical Art Museum, 184

Air Gardens, photo of, 179

Alcok, John, 240

Alioto, Joseph, 253

Allen, Benjamin Curtis, 66, 69, 71–72, 73, 76–77, 80, 90, 91, 92, 96, 100, 101, 104, 106, 118, 121, 122, 124, 127, 131, 133–136, 156, 200, 204, 234, 239; country club bill of, 78; death of, 93–94; marriage of, 93; photo of, 69, 73, 77, 78, 90, 92, 94; Romicks and, 143; Shober and, 76; tuberculosis for, 75, 76, 78, 88

Allen, Bonnie, 117, 123

Allen, Charles Schwartz, 103

Allen, Curtis, 75, 91, 94, 101, 124; photo of, 73, 92, 101, 124

Allen, Dorothy Fox, 94, 101; photo of, 94

Allen, Edith Allison Leavens, 102; photo of, 102

Allen, Emma Louise Schwartz, 100, 101

Allen, George Nelson, 69, 71, 75, 102, 122, 124; autobiography of, 72; photo of, 73, 92, 102

Allen, George Nelson, Jr., 102, 103, 109, 138, 187; on Curtis, 124; photo of, 103; Wharton and, 117, 123, 124

Allen, Maria Wharton McKean, 69, 71, 72–73, 75, 76, 79, 80, 82, 91, 100, 101–102, 104–109, 113, 121, 124, 127, 135, 137–139, 146, 152, 199, 200; Cheyenne Court and, 92, 95; death of, 110, 111, 122, 148, 159; divorce of, 92, 93, 96; grave plot of, 110 (photo), 111 (photo); photo of, 70, 73, 92, 95, 100, 104, 112; ranch house of, 103 (photo), 110 (photo)

Allen, Mary Ridg, 71

Allen, Marya, 101, 109

Allen, McKean, 100–101, 103, 107, 108, 118; children of, 101; photo of, 92, 101

Allen, Rosalie Cameron, 92–93, 94, 95, 100; photo of, 94

Allen, Samuel, 71

Allen, Sonia, 101, 103

Allen, Thomas McKean, 75; photo of, 73

Allen, Thomas McKean, Jr., 101, 103, 107, 108

Allen, Wharton, 75, 78, 91, 96, 110, 111, 117, 130, 133, 134, 137, 138, 146, 178, 205; Davidson and, 147; death of, 122, 123; El Paso Club and, 115–116; grave plot of, 110 (photo), 123 (photo); photo of, 73, 92, 100, 115, 118, 119, 124, 134; Romick and, 142, 148; shorthorns and, 118, 119, 120, 121, 135, 140; South Ranch and, 93; will of, 124

Allen, William B., 71, 72

Allen Cattle Company, 88, 90, 120, 121, 146; Auction Sale/photo of, 120, 121

Allen Ranch, 33, 88, 91, 95, 96, 100, 103–107, 118, 122, 127, 128–130, 132–135, 140, 142, 144, 145, 148, 178, 189; described, 41; layout of, 137 (illus.); map of, 106, 123, 132, 153; photo of, 87, 89, 105, 107, 108, 135, 137; sale of, 113, 152, 154, 156, 158; summer house at, 100 (photo), 105 (illus.)

"America the Beautiful" (Bates), 279, 280

American Horseman, 205

American saddlebreds, 16, 208, 209, 224, 228, 237; gait of, 225–226; photo of, 225

American Shorthorn Breeders' Association, 118, 119

Anderson, Merton S., 160

Anemones, 195; photo of, 195

Angus cattle, 157, 172, 173, 199, 233; photo of, 157, 172, 234

Annual Report of the Pinery Trust, 51–52

Antelope, 195; photo of, 20, 270

Atkinson, Henry M., 43

Avis, Edward, 286

"Back to Genesis" (conference), 275

Bant, Billy, 158

Bar-X Ranch, 167, 194, 233, 234, 262; map of, 168

Barns, 88, 137, 268; burning of, 195; photo of, 16, 41, 105, 137

Barnett, James A., 291

Barron, Archibald, 183, 205

Barron, Gloria, 183, 205

Barron, Thomas, 205

Bates, Katharine Lee, 278, 279, 280

Battelle Memorial Institute, 244; photo of, 244

Battista, Howard, 222, 223–224, 235; horse stalls by, 223 (photo); photo of, 223

"Beginning and the End of the Universe, The" (conference), 275

Bell, John R., 26

Bell, William A., 48

Belted Galloways, 173, 194; photo of, 172

Bend, George H., 40, 48, 49, 54, 156

Benjamin Franklin (1706–1790) (Martin), 108 (illus.)

Bent, Charles, 29

Bent, William, 28, 29, 37

Benton, Jessie, 27

Bent's Old Fort, 26, 27, 29, 32, 37; photo of, 28

Billings, Barbara Jeannette, 220–222, 224, 232–238, 274; photo of, 14, 237

Black Forest, 2, 19, 24, 26, 28, 30, 34, 35, 38, 39, 44, 48, 49; fire in, 195; map of, 21; naming, 21–22; natural gas/phone services for, 167; Shamrock Ranch and, 3, 18

Black Forest Community Center, 131, 144, 146, 153, 278; photo of, 145

Blunt, Harry, 161; photo of, 169

Blunt, Mrs. Harry: photo of, 169

Bonbright, George, 75; Stanley Steamer of, 75 (photo)

Bond, Dwight, 108

Bond, Gay Eloise, 108

Boone, Daniel, 27

Boone, Nathan, 27

Boudreau, Arthur E., 175

Brands: Cross-Bar-P, 128, 128 (illus.), 199; Diamond M, 186; McCullough, 158 (illus.); McLaughlin, 166 (illus.), 173 (illus.); Steppler, 128, 128 (illus.); Wismer, 280 (photo)

Breeder's Gazette, 134

Bridgford, Bill, 251, 252; photo of, 251

Bridgford Foods, Inc., 250, 251; photo of, 251

Briggs, James E., 180

Bringing Up Father (postage stamp), 104 (illus.)

Broadmoor Casino, 79

Broadmoor City, 78

Broadmoor Dairy, 78, 80

Broadmoor Golf Club, 111, 117

Broadmoor Hotel, 79, 80, 111, 181, 194, 204

Broadmoor Invitational, 117

Broadmoor mesa, 79; photo of, 79

Broadmoor Tavern, 117, 124

Brookshire, Don, 209, 217

Brown, Adaline Straight, 66, 131; photo of, 66

Brown, Allie, 66, 132

Brown, Beulah Rae, 66, 131–133; photo of, 66, 132

Brown, Sarah Fannie, 66, 133

Brown, William Clark, 66, 126, 131–133; photo of, 66, 132

Brown, William Lester "Billie," 66, 132, 133, 134, 147

Brunner, Elizabeth Key, 221

Brunner, John Hamilton, 221; photo of, 221

Bryce, Henry, 165

Buchanan, James, 36, 69, 70; illustration of, 36

Buffalo, 26; photo of, 34

Buffy (dog), 197; photo of, 198

Bungalow, 100; photo of, 87, 88

Burkburnett, Texas, 163, 164; photo of, 164

Burnett, Lawrence E., 100

Burnside, John, 289

Bush, George H. W., 236

Bush, George W., 236

Bush, Neil, 236

Buzzard, William M., 41, 44, 289

Buzzard's Roost, 41, 44, 56, 57, 64, 106, 289

C. T. and Claire McLaughlin Arbor and Memorial Garden, 185, 186

Cadet Chapel, 179; photo of, 179

Cahill, George, 115

Cameron, Rhoda, 92

Camp Bird Gold Mine, 202

Camp Carson, 133, 148, 175

Carlson, Sam, 107

Carnegie, Andrew, 45

Carson, Kit, 28, 29

Case Institute of Technology, Wismer at, 245

Case steam tractor, 130–131; photo of, 130

Case Systems Research Center, 246

Case Western Reserve University, 245; photo of, 246

Casey (horse), photo of, 223

Cashmax, 254; brochure for, 254 (illus.)

Cassiani, John, 262

Castle Hill Retirement Village, 259; photo of, 262

Cattlemax, 272

Certificate of Appreciation, photo of, 91

Chapel of Our Saviour, 80, 96, 111, 112, 123, 124; photo of, 112

Chattergy, R., 249

Chauffeur's house, illustration of, 105

Cheesman, Milton C., 123, 124, 133, 147; photo of, 123, 133

Cheesman, Robert, 103, 122, 124; photo of, 122

Cheesman, Sam, 88, 96, 103, 117, 118, 119, 120, 121, 122, 124, 147, 148; photo of, 122

Cheesman, Wharton Allen, 124

Cherokee Trail, 32, 33, 34, 41, 64; map of, 32, 33

Chevalier, Maurice, 184

Cheyenne Court, 80, 82; photo of, 80, 81, 82; tearing down, 92, 95, 121

Cheyenne House, 100, 101, 103, 104, 107, 108, 110, 112, 116, 117, 123, 146, 159; described, 95–96; photo of, 96, 97, 98, 99, 109; sale of, 111

Cheyenne Lake, Land, and Improvement Company, 78

Cheyenne Mountain, 78, 147, 167; photo of, 79

Cheyenne Mountain Country Club, 76, 77, 78, 79; photo of, 76, 79

Chicken Bill, 62

Chicken houses, 136; photo of, 136

Chisholm, Tina, 80

Cimarron Route, map of, 27

Citron, Bob, 252

Cleveland, Grover, 63; photo of, 63

Cochran, Jacqueline, 170; photo of, 170

Coleman, John, 71

Colorado and Southern Railroad, 23

Colorado City, 40, 41, 47, 52, 55, 57, 58, 60, 63, 66, 67

Colorado Coal and Iron Company (CC&I), 47, 49

Colorado College, 48, 124, 133, 182, 278

Colorado Fuel and Iron Company, 47

Colorado Pinery and Land Company, 52, 54, 57, 156; trust holdings of, 49 (map)

Colorado Pinery Trust, 48, 49, 51, 52, 54, 56, 287

Colorado Plateau, uranium mining on, 168, 168 (map)

Colorado School for the Deaf and Blind, 48

Colorado Springs: Air Force Academy and, 175, 176, 177, 180, 181–183, 185–187; Palmer and, 46, 47, 48, 49; photo of, 182; promoting, 61

Colorado Springs and Cripple Creek District Railway, 63

Colorado Springs Chamber of Commerce, 175, 176

Colorado Springs Gazette and Telegraph, 52, 57, 60, 67, 101, 133, 146, 155; Allen and, 93; article from, 290–291

Columbine, 195; photo of, 139, 195

Columbus, Christopher, 25

Computer Sciences Corporation (CSC), 250, 251, 252, 255

Conger, Bill, 128–129, 142; home of, 128 (photo)

Conger, Lewis, 128, 129

Conger, Marie Steppler, 127, 128, 129, 131; photo of, 127

Connally, John Bowden, 196

Connery, Sean, 254

Connors, Shorty, 157

Cooper, George, 164

Copeland, G. W., 288

Coppedge, David F.: letter from, 261

Cornwallis, General Lord, 70

Cowboy and His Elephant, The (MacPherson), 202

Cowboy Hall of Fame, 183, 185

Coyotes, 138, 195; photo of, 198

Creel, Howard, 111, 112, 123

Creel Foundation, 112

Cricket (dog), photo of, 14

Cripple Creek, 61, 62, 63, 76, 79

Cripple Creek Gold Rush, 63, 64, 79

Crowley, J. W., 288

Cummings, Harry F., 44

Curtis, Elizabeth J., 69

Curtis, Leonard, 134

D-4 Caterpillar, 199, 200; photo of, 199

D-6 Caterpillar, 200

Darlow, Albert, 118

Davco, Patti, 244

Davidson, Walter, 147; photo of, 119

Davis, Edward, 60

Davis, Katherene, 103, 108

Davis, Narrye, 116

DC-3 airplane, 172, 194; photo of, 172

Declaration of Independence, 69, 70, 71, 239

Declaration of War by the German Empire, 90 (illus.)

Delaware and Raritan Canal, 72

DeMille, Cecil B., 179, 184

Denver and Rio Grande Western Railroad, 21, 46, 48, 49, 57, 60, 63, 126, 178, 286

Denver and Santa Fe stage road, 64, 288

Diamond M Foundation, 171, 185

Diamond M Museum, 171

Diamond M Ranch, 165, 166, 168, 170, 171, 173, 185, 191

"Distributed Multilevel Systems" (Wismer), 248

Divide Chancellor (bull), 120
Divide Goldpiece (bull), 120; photo of, 119, 120
Divide Pure Bred Registered Short Horn Herd, The:
    cover of, 87 (illus.)
Divide Ranch, 120, 137, 277
Dodge, Henry, 26, 27; illustration of, 27
Donaldson, Agnes, 116
Donnelly, Robert, 287
Downs, Phebe Warren McKean, 82, 108, 109
Dynamic Control of a Continuous Strip Process
    (Wismer), 246

Eberhard, Dorothy, 228
Eckman, Donald, 246
Econofuel, 251–252; sales brochure for, 251 (illus.)
Eden, Alvin "Al," 154, 191–192, 193; photo of, 192;
    quote of, 280
Eden, Bret, 192
Eden, Eurelle, 154, 192; photo of, 192
Eden, Leah, 192
Eden, Mark, 192
Eden, Paul, 192
Eisenhower, Dwight D., 204, 242; Air Force Academy
    and, 174, 175, 180; photo of, 175, 180, 242
Eisenhower Museum, 204, 242
El Paso Club, 75, 76, 77, 115–116, 205; photo of, 77
El Paso County, 21, 36, 48, 57, 60, 64, 67, 80;
    map of, 106
El Pomar, 80, 111
El Pomar Foundation, 111, 184
El Pomar Investment Company, 111
Elk, photo of, 12
Ellis, Charles, 72
Ellis, Mary, 72
English riding, 225–226
Equipment annex, photo of, 137
Evergreen Cemetery, 110; photo of, 110, 111, 123
Evergreen Ranch, 57, 59, 61, 66, 126, 277

Falcons, 180; photo of, 179
Farmer, Addie, 144
Farmer, Frank, 143, 144
Farnsworth, Edith, 78
Father Struck It Rich (McLean), 202
Federal Deposit Insurance Corporation (FDIC), 236

Field, Bill, 224, 227, 228, 231, 232, 233, 234;
    photo of, 232
Field, Chris, 228
Field, Eugene, 291
Field, Zach, 228
Fitzpatrick, Thomas, 30, 36, 272
Folger, Ed, 222, 223; horse stalls by, 223, 223 (photo)
Fordyce, H. T.: photo of, 169
Fordyce, Mrs. H. T.: photo of, 169
Forrestal, James, 175
Fort Carson, 133, 184, 262
4-H, 193; emblem of, 193 (illus.)
Foxes, 138; photo of, 138
Franklin, Benjamin, 70, 239; painting of, 108
Fremont, John Charles, 27–28, 29, 30; photo of, 27
Fretz, A. J., 240, 241
Furness, Frank, 82–83

Gaits, 225–226; photo of, 225
Galbraith, John Kenneth, 236
Garden, photo of, 88
Garden of the Gods, 47, 48, 159; photo of, 47
Gatlin, Bobby, 209, 222, 224, 227, 232, 233
Gazebo, photo of, 235
Geiger, Iola, 189, 190, 198; photo of, 190
Geiger, Richard, 189–191, 198; photo of, 190
General Electric Company, 245, 247; logo of,
    245 (illus.)
George IV, 203
George Washington (Peale), 109 (illus.)
Gibson, M. W., 220
Glen Eyrie, 47, 133, 147
Goldstein, Bernie, 258
Goodrich, Max, 150
Goodrich, Oleta Hamilton, 150, 152, 153, 154
Goodwin, Philip R., 170
Grace/St. Stephen's Episcopal Church, 75, 111,
    124, 159
Gramlich, H. J.: photo of, 119
Grandma tree/grandpa tree, 50, 51; photo of, 50
Grant, Ulysses S., 42; photo of, 42
Grasses, 272; photo of, 17
Great Depression, 142, 145, 148, 164, 170, 208
Great Plains, 18, 28, 29, 30, 55
Great Smoky Mountains, 220; photo of, 220
Great Snow of 1913, 23

Griffiths, M., 288

Grizzlies, 76–77; photo of, 77

Gryphon, 243; illustration of, 243

Gryphon Society, 243

Guest house, photo of, 14, 88

Guire, Jacob, 38

Guise, Henry, 291

Hamilton, Ross, 150

Hancher, Virgil M., 176, 177

Hanlon, A. J., 174

Hardesty, Althea, 152

Hardesty, George E., 113, 149, 150, 151, 152,
    153, 156, 157; death of, 154; photo of, 151;
    pond stocked by, 150 (photo)

Hardesty, Stella Venus Starr, 113, 149, 150, 151, 152,
    153, 154, 156, 157; photo of, 151

Hardesty Hall, 154

Hardesty Ranch, 151, 153; map of, 152, 157;
    photo of, 150

Harmon, Hubert R., 175; photo of, 176

Harris, R. H., 288

Hartley, Frank, 148, 189

Haughton, Marian Shaw McKean, 92

Haughton, Percy, 92

Haun, Christine Ross, 207–208

Haun, William George, 207–208

Hayes, Edd, 184; sculpture by, 184 (photo)

Heidi (dog), photo of, 14

Hendrix, Lee, 194

Hensley, Mable, 203

Herefords, 149, 152, 165, 166, 172, 173, 192, 194;
    photo of, 172

Hettinger, Jack, 115

Hettinger, Oppie, 115, 117, 124

Hillis, Art, 117

Hilty, James W.: quote of, 92

Hinn, Harold, 192

Hitchcock, Alfred, 184

Hiwassee College, 221, 222; photo of, 221

Hiwassee Purchase, 220

Hodgen, John, 66

Homestead Act (1862), 36, 38, 126

Homesteaders, 17, 36, 57, 278

Hood, John B., 46

Hope Diamond, 202, 203, 204; photo of, 203

Horse shows, 208, 220, 225–226, 233, 278

Howe, Octavius T.: on migration, 29

Hubbell, Peggy Romick, 91, 95, 103, 105, 107–109,
    130, 134, 136, 138, 139, 140, 142, 144–148, 203;
    illustration by, 105, 137; photo of, 140, 143, 148;
    on Wharton, 116

Hummingbird, photo of, 196

Hurd, Peter, 171; photo of, 171

Huska, Paul, 244

Husted (town), 105, 128, 133, 142, 143, 154, 176;
    Air Force Academy and, 178; photo of, 178;
    story about, 178, 290–291

Husted, Amanda Talbert, 56, 57, 58, 59, 60, 64;
    photo of, 59

Husted, Bert, 60

Husted, Calvin R., 22, 40, 54, 56, 57, 59, 60, 61, 64,
    67, 88, 131, 136, 156, 178, 272, 286, 287, 288,
    289, 291; holdings of, 56 (map); house by, 64
    (photo); lumber and, 62, 66; photo of, 57;
    prospects of, 63; youth of, 55

Husted, Walter E., 59, 60, 64, 291; photo of, 60

Husted House, photo of, 65

Husted Pasture, 122, 152, 156, 205; map of, 123, 153

Husted Ranch, 277

Husted sawmill, 57, 67, 286

Husted station, 60, 66, 138, 178; photo of, 178

Husted Sterling Live Stock Company, 61, 63, 66, 122,
    127, 131; holdings of, 61 (map); map of, 132

Husted Wagon Road, 57, 105, 106, 122, 143, 152, 178;
    map of, 106

Hutton, Betty, 243

Ice house, 88, 139, 268; photo of, 88, 139

Indian paintbrush, 195; photo of, 195

Institute for Creation Research (ICR), 275

Instrument Society of America, 246; photo of, 246

International Stock Show, photo of, 121

Introduction to Non-Linear Optimization (Wismer), 254

Jackson, Francis H., 48

Jackson, Hank, 60

Jefferson, Thomas, 26, 39; illustration of, 26

Jesse, T. J., 287

Jiggs (dog), 104; photo of, 104

Jimmy Reed (horse), photo of, 107

Johnson, Lyndon B., 169, 171, 192, 196, 200; Air
    Force Academy and, 182; Kennedy assassination
    and, 197; photo of, 169, 182, 183, 197

Jones, Courtland: photo of, 119

Jones, Shirley, 204

Kansas-Nebraska Act (1854), 35

Kansas Pacific Railroad, 46, 48, 49

Kansas Tribune, verse from, 31

Kaye, Danny, 243

Kearney, Stephen W., 30; photo of, 30

Kelly, Charlie, 107

Kennedy, John F., 174; assassination of, 123, 197; photo of, 123, 197

Kerosene lanterns, 140; photo of, 140

Key, John, 221

Keyser, George: photo of, 169

Keyser, Mrs. George: photo of, 169

Killearn, Duke of, 119–120

King and I, The (play), 193; poster for, 242 (illus.)

Kinner, Alice, 291

Kinner, J. C., 290, 291

Kinner, Jerome, 291

Kinner, John, 291

Kinner, Mrs. J. C., 290, 291

Kinner Store and Filling Station, photo of, 178

Koch, Nolan, 131

Koch, Susan Elaine Steppler, 128, 130, 131, 199, 200, 201

Korth, Fred, 174, 196; photo of, 174

Krakel, Dean, 185

Krause, George A., 156

Lamborn, Charles B., 40, 48, 49, 59

Leavenworth and Pikes Peak (L&PP) Express Road, 31, 32, 33, 34, 40, 41, 106, 122

Leech, John, 240

Lehigh University, 243, 244, 245, 248; Alumni Building, 243 (photo)

Lewis, Inez Johnson, 142

Lewis Consolidated School, 142, 143; photo of, 142

Libby Lanes (horse), photo of, 224

Lincoln, Abraham, 36; photo of, 36

Lindbergh, Charles A., 175, 176–177, 277; photo of, 175

Linear and Nonlinear Programming (Wismer and Chattergy), 249

Linny (horse), photo of, 271

Lion Oil Company, 165, 166; logo of, 165 (illus.)

Loftus, Kevin, 222, 223, 233, 234; photo of, 223

Log cabin, photo of, 128

Log schoolhouse, 144; photo of, 144

Logging, 49, 51–52, 53, 57

Logging Outfit in the Pinery (Gutshall), 52 (photo)

Long, Margaret, 41, 106

Long, Stephen H., 26

Long Distance (ranch worker), 107; photo of, 107

Los Angeles Memorial Coliseum, 247; photo of, 247

Louis XIV, 203

Louisiana Purchase, 26, 39; map of, 25

Lowry Air Force Base, 176, 179, 180

Mabry, Virgil, 243

MacPherson, Malcolm, 202

Maggie (dog), 104; photo of, 104

Making Waves (horse), 227, 228, 233; photo of, 229

Malone, Terry, 224, 227, 233

Manager's house, 224; photo of, 14, 135, 136, 224

Mann, Jim, 258, 259; photo of, 258

Marcy, Randolph, 23

Marie Antoinette, 203

Marshall, John, 71

Martin, David, 108

Martinez, Ramon, 231

Master's Academy International, 274–275

Master's College and Seminary, 259, 274; logo of, 259 (illus.)

Mayflower, illustration of, 51

McBroom, Clieve, 44

McBroom, Mary J. Peters, 43, 44

McBroom, Paul, 44

McBroom, William (son), 44

McBroom, William Henry, 43, 44

McClellan, George, 46

McCollom, Bob, 154

McCollom, Georgia, 154

McCrea, Frances Marion Dee, 184

McCrea, Jody, 184

McCrea, Joel Albert, 183, 184; photo of, 184

McCullough, Bill, 155, 157, 158

McCullough, Hazel Eva, 157, 159

McCullough, J. Zachariah, 155

McCullough, James Nelson, 152, 154–159, 176, 177, 189; chapel by, 158–159; death of, 159, 161; McLaughlin and, 166–167; photo of, 154; Village Inn and, 155, 156, 160

McCullough, James Nelson, Jr., 157

McGhee, C. S., 158

McGoodwin, Robert Rhodes, 95; photo of, 95

McKean, Elizabeth Wharton, 69, 79, 108, 109

McKean, Henry Pratt, 80, 82, 92

McKean, Thomas, 69, 70, 71, 73, 239;
  illustration of, 71

McLaughlin, Amy Johnson, 168, 187; photo of, 169

McLaughlin, Clarence Thurston, 159, 172, 184, 194,
  200, 201, 202, 205, 234, 237, 239; Air Force
  Academy and, 174, 180, 182, 183; art and,
  170–171; death of, 185, 186, 196, 197; described,
  163; Johnson and, 182; McCullough and,
  166–167; oil business and, 164–166; photo of,
  163, 169, 172, 174, 185; ranch managers of,
  189, 191, 192, 193; uranium mining and, 168

McLaughlin, Cora, 163

McLaughlin, Evelyn (daughter), 164, 186

McLaughlin, Evelyn Claire Littleton, 164, 168, 172,
  173, 237; art and, 170–171; death of, 183;
  photo of, 164, 169, 174

McLaughlin, Jean, 164, 183

McLaughlin, John Mark (father), 163

McLaughlin, John Mark (son), 164–170, 173, 174,
  185, 187, 222; Air Force Academy and, 180;
  on father, 163; foreclosure and, 235–236, 262;
  photo of, 169, 187; Reese and, 237

McLaughlin, Ruth, 164

McLean, Edward Beale, 202

McLean, Edward Beale, Jr., 202

McLean, Evalyn Walsh, 202, 203, 204; photo of, 202

McLean, Michael, 203

McLean, Ned, 202–204; mansion of, 205 (photo)

McLean, Ronald, 203

McLean, Washington, 202

McQuade, Michael, 287

Mears, Otto, 126

Medal of Honor, 46; photo of, 46

Meigs, Merrill C., 176, 177

Melin, Robert E., 168

Merrill Lynch Management Services, *Tradermax*
  and, 254

Midland Terminal Railroad, 63; photo of, 63

Miller, A. J., 235, 236, 262

Miller, Deanna, 193

Miller, Glenn, 241

Miller, Ila Belle, 193, 196, 198

Miller, Linetta, 193

Miller, Willard, 123, 193–196, 224

Miller, Willard "Woody" (son), 193

Mitchell, Billy, 174

Mockingbirds, 198; photo of, 198

Model A Ford, photo of, 138

Model T Ford, photo of, 138

Model T Ford pickup, 105; photo of, 105

Modern Woodmen Tuberculosis Sanatorium, 74;
  photo of, 74

Mola, Jim P., 160

Money, Colorado Springs and, 182

Moneymax, 252–253, 254, 255; brochure for,
  255 (illus.)

Moneymax News, 256 (illus.)

Moore, Donna, 209; photo of, 217

Morast, Ed, 154

Morast, Peggy, 154

Moreland, Ann, 191

Moreland, Francis Wilford "Willie," 189–191, 192

Mount Pocono, photo from, 241

Mountain lion, photo of, 198

Mountain Route, 32; map of, 27

Muffy (dog), photo of, 12, 22

Mulhern, William, 288

Murphy, Chuck, 268

Narragansett pacer, 226

National Cowboy and Western Heritage Museum,
  171, 184

National Ranching Heritage Center, 185, 186

National Security Act (1947), 175

National Western Stock Show, 88, 90, 93, 120, 147,
  223, 227, 228, 231, 234

Nelson, Curtis, 103

New Year's Day stag luncheon, 76; photo of, 76

Newmont Mining Company, *Cashmax* and, 254

Newton, Danny, 235

Nicholson, Edmond, 43

Nixon, Richard M., 242; photo of, 242

Norris, Robert C. "Bob," 183, 201–202, 205;
  photo of, 20–22

North American Air Defense Command (NORAD),
  167, 173, 184

North Ranch, 96, 118, 119, 120, 123, 133, 148, 195;
  photo of, 90, 120

Nuthatch, photo of, 196

O'Donnell, Emmett "Rosie," 116; photo of, 116

Olds, Robin, 173; photo of, 173

"On the Divide" (Tenderfoot), 22, 41, 57, 64, 286–288

*Optimal Control of Distributed Parameter Systems Using
  Multilevel Techniques* (Wismer), 248; back cover of,
  248 (photo)

Optimization Methods for Large-Scale Systems with Applications (Wismer), 248

Oregon Trail, 28, 30, 31, 34; map of, 28

Pace, Frank, 174, 192; photo of, 174

Packard touring car, 104, 116, 138; photo of, 105, 138

Pal, Sujit, 253–254; photo of, 258

Palmer, Dorothy, 46

Palmer, Elsie, 46

Palmer, Marjory, 46

Palmer, Mary Lincoln Mellen "Queen," 46, 47–48; photo of, 46

Palmer, William Jackson, 45, 49, 57, 73, 79, 239, 240, 277; Colorado Pinery Trust and, 51; Colorado Springs and, 46, 47, 48; photo of, 45, 46; statue of, 48 (photo)

Palmer Divide, 18, 19, 23, 33, 42, 48, 278

Parker, I. H., 288

Partridge, Earle E., 173; photo of, 173

Pat (horse), photo of, 223

Payden & Clark, *Tradermax* and, 254

Peacemakers, mediation by, 268

Peale, A. C., 51

Peale, Charles Willson, 109

Pendleton, Alan, 208, 237

Pendleton, Beverly Haun, 207, 208, 220, 223–225, 227, 228, 231–237; photo of, 207, 229, 232

Pendleton, Edmund, 186, 207, 208, 222, 224, 227, 228, 232, 233, 234, 236–237; default by, 235, 262; golf tournaments and, 235; horses and, 209, 223; mediation and, 268; photo of, 207, 224, 232; Reese and, 237, 238; Shannon Rule Sale and, 214; stalls by, 226

Pendleton, Julie, 228, 231, 235

Pendleton, Louis, 208, 220, 223, 227, 228, 231, 235; PENSA and, 237; photo of, 230, 232; riding and, 225

Pendleton equestrian facility, photo of, 208

Pendleton Land and Exploration Company, 208, 235

Penn, William, 239, 240

Pennsylvania farm, photo of, 239

Pennsylvania Railroad, 45, 46, 49

Penrose, Julie, 80, 111

Penrose, Spencer, 80, 111, 147, 240

Pensionmax, 254–255; brochure for, 254 (illus.)

Peters, W. J., 46

Peterson, Guy, 153, 154

Peterson, Harvey S., 44

Peterson, Kathryn, 154

Petroleum Museum, Library, and Hall of Fame, 171

Pfluger, Jim, 186

Phillips, G. W., 287

Phillipsburg, house in, 241 (photo)

Pike, Lieutenant, 287

Pikes Peak, 31, 35, 57, 61, 62, 74, 103, 120, 138; photo of, 103, 139, 234

Pikes Peak Center, 275

Pikes Peak Gold Rush, 31, 32, 33, 35, 40–41, 55; photo of, 33; trails of, 32 (map)

Pikes Peak or Bust Rodeo, 184, 205

Pinery, 22, 38, 48, 49, 51, 57

Pitkin County, uranium mining in, 167

Playhouse, 88; photo of, 88

Pleasant View Hereford Ranch, 150, 151, 152, 153, 154, 269; map of, 153

Pleasure buggy, 237; photo of, 237

Plymouth Harbor, 51; illustration of, 51

Polo ponies, 116, 117; photo of, 117

Ponderosa pines, 19, 49, 50, 228, 274, 277; photo of, 20

Pourtales, Count James, 78, 79, 80, 123; illustration of, 78

Pourtales, Countess Berthe de, 79, 123

Prairie schooners, 29, 30, 31; photo of, 28, 55

Preferred Property, 209, 214; announcement by, 216–217 (illus.)

Profimatics, Inc., Wismer at, 250

Promontory Summit, 36; photo of, 37

ProRodeo Hall of Fame, 184

Psensky, John, 274; photo of, 274

Public Land Survey System (PLSS), 39

Quilt, 145; photo of, 145

Raccoons, 195; photo of, 198

Raines, Ella, 173

Rambouillet sheep, 165; photo of, 165

Ranch house, photo of, 13, 87, 110

Rancher's Daughter (Goodwin), 170

Red Cross, 90; emblem of, 90 (photo)

Reese, Doreene, 198, 238, 269

Reese, Opal Pauline, 220, 234, 237, 238, 269, 270; housekeeping by, 197–201; photo of, 197, 237, 270

Reese, Vivian, 197

Reese, Wanda, 197

Ribbon collection, 227; photo of, 227, 228

Rich, W. H., 43

Riding arena, photo of, 16

Roberts, Dave, 291

Roberts, Dick, 291

Rogers, Samuel, 72

Romick, Coral Meta Lucinda, 103, 134, 135, 140, 144, 145, 146, 147; photo of, 143, 146, 148

Romick, Henry Joseph (Joe), 88, 95, 103, 116, 120, 130, 134–138, 140, 142, 146, 147, 148, 178, 189; photo of, 141, 148

Romick, Joe, Jr. (son), 107, 134, 140, 143

Romick, Margaret "Peggy," 134

Root cellar, 88; photo of, 88

Route 66, 247; map of, 247

Royce Hall (UCLA), photo of, 248

Rusnak, Paul, 259

Russell, William Green, 30, 31, 32

Ruter, Charles, 57

Ryan, Hope Allen, 75, 80, 88, 96, 101–102, 103, 268; photo of, 73, 92, 96, 102

Ryan, James V. Ruthven, 101–102; photo of, 102

Ryan, James V. Ruthven, Jr., 102, 103, 107, 112

Ryan, Kathleen Hope, 102

Sabaka (dog), 237; photo of, 237

Saddle & Bridle, 209, 229, 231, 232; advertisement from, 218–219 (illus.); quote from, 227, 228, 231

Saddle seat–style English saddle, photo of, 226

Sam Stout Ranch, photo of, 53

Santa Fe and Rio Grande Railroad, 158, 178, 290

Santa Fe Trail, 28, 32, 33; map of, 27

Sargent, Mary C., 116

Savings and loan crisis, 236

Savio, Mario, 250; photo of, 249

Scanlon, Tom, 253

School section, 128, 167; map of, 269; photo of, 128, 129

Scott, Thomas A., 45

Scudder, Stevens & Clark, *Tradermax* and, 254

Sennert, Robert, 235

Severance Hall, 245; photo of, 245

Shamrock Estate, brochure for, 263–267 (illus.)

Shamrock Foundation, 275

Shamrock Investments LLC, 262, 268, 269

Shamrock Ranch: article about, 228, 231; false legends of, 204; first house at, 64 (photo); history of, 24; logo of, 270 (photo); map of, 21, 39–40, 42, 123, 132, 152, 157, 166, 168, 269; open house at, 169 (photo); owners of, 43 (map); photo of, 1, 2, 3, 4, 5, 6, 7, 8, 9, 10, 11, 12, 15, 17, 19, 20, 23, 41, 103, 113, 139, 167, 205, 222, 223, 224, 234, 235, 270, 273; satellite view of, 18, 18 (photo)

Shannon Run Sale, 209, 214, 217, 228, 233; advertisement for, 209 (illus.), 218–219 (illus.); photo of, 210, 211, 212, 213, 214, 215, 216, 217, 218, 219; sales record for, 217 (illus.)

Shaw, Robert, 245; photo of, 245

Sheds, 136, 167; photo of, 106, 136, 150, 167

Sherman, Brad, 247

Shober, Sam, 76

Shook, Denton, 58, 59

Shook, Peter, 58, 59

Shorthorns, 100, 118, 119, 120, 121, 135, 147; photo of, 87, 119, 120, 121, 133, 141

Silo, 130; photo of, 130, 150

Silverado Savings and Loan Association, 235, 236

Simonson, Mary, 72

Simonson, Peter, 72

Simpson, D., 291

Sloan Mill, 52, 286

Smith, Jedediah, 30

Smoky Hill Trail, 33, 34, 38

Smoky Hill Trail, The (Long), 41

Snow, 22, 23; photo of, 22

Snow, John Ben, 204–205; photo of, 205

Snyder Area Canyon Reef Operators' Committee (SACROC), 171, 172

Solly, Edwin, 74

South Ranch, 93, 96, 100, 103, 117, 118, 119, 120, 121, 123, 124, 133, 134, 147, 148

Spaatz, Carl Andrew, 175; photo of, 175

Squirrels, 138, 195, 196, 198; photo of, 138, 196

Stagecoaches, 40, 41; photo of, 40

Stalls, 223, 226; photo of, 223

Stanley Steamer, 75; photo of, 75

Star of the East Diamond, 203, 204

State Fair Grounds, 121; photo of, 120

State of Kansas: admission of, 35; boundaries of, 35 (map)

Steppler, Alta Elizabeth Simpson "Betty," 131, 198, 199, 200, 201; photo of, 131, 201

Steppler, Charles, 125, 127, 131; photo of, 127

Steppler, Christian Louis "Lou," 106, 125–131, 145, 146, 200; photo of, 127

Steppler, Irene, 127, 131; photo of, 127

Steppler, Martha Jane Brown "Jennie," 66, 126, 127, 128, 129, 131, 132, 199, 200, 201; photo of, 126, 127

Steppler, Minnie, 125, 126, 131, 200

Steppler, William Albert "Al," 127, 128, 129–131, 198–201; photo of, 127, 129, 130, 131, 199, 201

Steppler, William Allen, 66, 131, 199, 201

Steppler Ranch, 106, 131, 199; photo of, 106

Sterling, W. H., 61

Stevenson, Coke, 169, 170

Stewart, Charles, 103, 104

Stewart, Gloria Hatrick McLean, 202–204; mansion of, 205 (photo); photo of, 203

Stewart, Jimmy, 203, 204; photo of, 203

Stewart, Judy, 203

Stewart, Kelly, 203

Stout, Samuel C., 52, 142, 156, 204, 240, 287; Colorado Pinery Trust and, 51; photo of, 51, 54

Stout, Thomas, 250

Stout School, 142; map of, 106

Stratton, Winfield Scott, 62; photo of, 62

Stubbs, Robert, 58, 59

Stutz Bearcat (horse), 228, 231, 232, 233; photo of, 232

Summer house, photo of, 100

Sunday School, 143, 144; photo of, 144

SunGard Financial Systems, 258, 259, 260, 268; advertisement for, 258 (illus.)

Surrey, photo of, 271

Sweet, Channing, 151, 156

Symphony (horse), photo of, 140

Systems Control, Inc. (SCI), 249, 250, 256, 258

Systems Research Center, Wismer at, 245

Szell, George, 245; photo of, 245

Table Rock, 43, 66, 126

Tail set/tailboards, 226

Talamore at Oak Terrace (Hilty), 92

Talbert, Edward H., 44, 56, 58, 156, 289

Talbert, Joanna, 58, 59

Talbert, Joseph, 58, 286

Talbott, Harold E., 175, 177, 179; photo of, 175

Taylor, Abilgle W., 40, 49

Taylor, Jacob S., 43, 44

Tease, Cameron M., 104, 107, 108, 113

Tease, Esther, 104, 107, 108; photo of, 108

Tease, Sam, 96, 104, 105, 107–108; on Allen Ranch, 106–107; photo of, 104, 107; on Wharton, 116, 117

Teenage Republican Club of Warren County, Wismer and, 242

Tenderfoot, 22, 41; article by, 286–288, 289

Territory of Kansas, 36; map of, 35

Theophilus (dog), photo of, 275

Thomas, F. F., 288

Thomson, John Edgar, 45

Thornton, Dan, 177, 181; photo of, 169

Thornton, Mrs. Dan: photo of, 169

Thunder, Sun and Snow—the History of Colorado's Black Forest (von Ahlefeldt), 21

Time, Pace and, 174, 192

Timothy (dog), photo of, 275

Titleist (horse), 209, 214, 228, 231; photo of, 209, 218

Titus (dog), photo of, 275

Tradermax, 254; brochure for, 255 (illus.)

Trails of the Smoky Hill (Lee and Raynesford), 34

Transcontinental railroad, 36; photo of, 37

Trappers' Trail, 32

Traveller (horse), photo of, 271

Traylor, Leonard, 186

Traylor, Richard, 186

Treaty of Fort Laramie (1851), 30, 37

Treemasters, 274

Trenches, photo of, 91

Trigg, Isabella, 38

Trotting, 225; photo of, 225

Truman, Harry S., 146, 155; photo of, 155

Truman, J. C., 146

Truman, John V., 146

Trumbauer, Horace, 80, 95

TRW, Wismer at, 246–247, 250

Tuberculosis, 74, 75, 76, 78, 88, 96, 107, 146, 181

Tuscarora War (1711), 240

Tutt, Charles L., Jr., 111

Twenty Acres, The, 51, 52

Union Pacific Railroad, 125

United States Air Force Academy, 57, 154, 173, 184, 193, 277, 280, 290, 291; Archives of, 204; building, 152, 174–181, 199; cadets at, 174 (photo); Colorado Springs and, 175, 176, 177, 180; emblem of, 174 (illus.); mascot of, 179 (photo); photo of, 179, 180, 181, 182, 183

United States Army Air Corps, 157

United States Army Air Forces, 170

United States Commissioner of Indian Affairs, 36–37

United States Constitution (1787), 70, 71, 73, 122

United States Department of Agriculture (USDA), 199

United States Department of Housing and Urban
    Development (HUD), 249

United States Equestrian Federation, 225, 226;
    logo of, 225 (illus.)

United States Geological Survey, 51

United States Military Academy, 174

United States Naval Academy, 175

United States Strategic Air Forces, 175

University of California, Los Angeles (UCLA):
    photo of, 248; Wismer at, 247–248, 249, 250

Uranium mining, 167, 168

Vernon, R., 42, 44

Vickers, Jack, III, 262, 268

VICORP Restaurants, Inc., 160

Victrola, 144; photo of, 144

Village Inn, 152, 157, 159, 166; photo of, 156;
    purchase of, 155, 156, 160

von Ahlefeldt, Judy, 21, 23

Walker, Ben, 291

Walker, Doak, 168

Walker, Henry, 291

Walsh, Thomas, 202

Ward, Arthur "Dutch," 172, 194

Ward, Samuel A., 279

Washington, George, 71; painting of, 109

Webb, Gerald, 74, 75, 76

Weekly Gazette, The, 22, 41, 44, 57, 64; article from,
    286–288

Wells, Ray, 252, 255

Wendelken, Ben S., 111, 124

West Hills, 248, 250; house in, 250 (photo)

Wharton, George Mifflin, 69–70

Wharton, Maria Markoe, 70

Wharton School of Finance and Commerce, 124

White, Jake, 234

Wild iris, 195; photo of, 195

Willcox, William J., 78

Williams, Sandy: photo of, 271

Winfrey, Cecil, 189–191, 192, 200

Winfrey, Millie, 189, 190

Wishart, Neil, 133, 134, 135; photo of, 133

Wismer, David Arthur, Jr., 50, 88, 122, 140, 148,
    151, 239, 240, 270, 274; boyhood home of, 241
    (photo); letter to, 260, 261; ownership by, 269;
    photo of, 12, 244, 246, 248, 258, 270, 271, 275;
    present-day ranch and, 24; ranch management by,
    274; service by, 275; youth of, 241–242, 243

Wismer, David Arthur, III, 247, letter from, 260;
    262, 269, 275

Wismer, Jacob, Sr., 240

Wismer, Jacob, 240, 241

Wismer, Jennifer Anne, 151, 259, 269, 270, 275;
    birth of, 250

Wismer, Jill, 262, 279

Wismer, Maria Friedt (Fretz), 240

Wismer, Mary Anne Winkelmann, 88, 151, 239, 240;
    meeting, 244; ownership by, 269; photo of, 12, 270,
    275; present-day ranch and, 24; ranch management
    by, 274; service by, 275

Wismer, Nanny, 240, 241

Wismer, Pearl Celesta Schaffer, 241, 262

Wismer, Susan Elizabeth, 247, 269

Wismer Associates, Inc. (WAI), 253, 254, 255, 256,
    258; offices of, 253 (photo)

Wismer Computer Center, 258

Wismer Enterprises, Inc., 274

Wismer Family History (Fretz), 240

Wismer Investment Systems (WISE) Users Group, 255

Wismer Series 2, 255; advertisement for, 257 (illus.)

Withram, J. T., 44

Womack, Robert "Crazy Bob," 61, 62, 79;
    photo of, 62

Women Auxiliary Service Pilots (WASPs), 170;
    photo of, 170

Wong, Ralph: photo of, 258

Wood, Thomas J., 48

Wooden, John, 247; photo of, 247

Woodmoor Pines Golf and Country Club, 235;
    photo of, 235

Wright, Frank Lloyd, 179

Wyandotte Constitution (1859), 35

Wyeth, N. C., 171

Zeberdee (horse), 227, 228, 231; photo of, 230, 232

Zimmerman, Wade, 234, 272; photo of, 272, 273